EXTREME MOTHERHOOD

EXTREME MOTHERHOOD
THE TRIPLET DIARIES

JACKIE CLUNE

MACMILLAN

First published 2006 by Pan Books
an imprint of Pan Macmillan Ltd
Pan Macmillan, 20 New Wharf Road, London NI 9RR
Basingstoke and Oxford
Associated companies throughout the world
www.panmacmillan.com

ISBN-13: 978-1-4050-8842-8
ISBN-10: 1-4050-8842-7

1 3 5 7 9 8 6 4 2

A CIP catalogue record for this book is available from
the British Library.

Typeset by Intype London Ltd
Printed and bound in Great Britain by
Mackays of Chatham plc, Chatham, Kent

To Saoirse, Thady, Frank and Orla,
in the hope that my writing about you won't cause
too much embarrassment in later life,

and to Richard
— for laughing despite the night feeds and
for being incredibly good at it all

22 December 2004

I'm about to get the biggest shock of my life, which, in turn, is about to change forever.

We're sitting in Whipps Cross Hospital's ultrasound department waiting for my first scan. I'm already fourteen weeks pregnant and should have been seen earlier but various mix-ups between the doctor's surgery and the hospital have meant that we've been delayed. Never mind. It's my second pregnancy in as many years so I know the ropes. There's no rush. I know the weeks will drag on so it's good to spread out the scans a bit – it livens things up. The lady calls us in – me, Richard and our one-year-old daughter, Saoirse. The lady's a bit grumpy. Rich was on his mobile phone and she tells him off. Northern and working class, he reddens, apologizes and slips the phone into his pocket. He hates being told off. We joke around, old hands at this antenatal lark. The lady softens. She realizes we are all right really. I jump up onto the table and pull my trousers down around my hips ready to be smothered in the gluey goo they use to help the probe glide over your belly. As she tucks the rough blue tissue into my waistband I look at Rich and think: 'This is going to be OK. We can cope with another baby. We're good.'

'I can't see the screen,' I complain, before remembering that they always tilt it away from you before switching it on in case they see something they don't like. In this moment I am filled with the terrible, heartbreaking stories of family and friends who have reached this three-month, supposedly 'safe' milestone only to be told, right there on the table, belly exposed and covered in goo, that there is no longer a baby, that there will be no labour, no pink or blue balloons, no need to redecorate the spare room. What an appalling thing to have to go through.

'Just a minute!' says the lady, mock-chiding my impatience. Saoirse is trying to climb onto the table with me. We all want to see this unexpected baby. The lady switches on the screen and places the probe on my tummy, swishing it around and around, looking for the fetus.

Her hand comes to rest and I crane my neck, anxious for the first magical glimpse of my baby. For the briefest of seconds I think I see two prawn-like blobs spooning each other.

No. Can't be. These scans are so hard to decipher. At the best of times the grainy black and white images look like bad footage of the first moon landing.

The lady sharply pulls the screen further out of view. I start to feel a bit dizzy.

'Erm,' starts the lady.

'Is everything all right?' I stutter.

'Is there . . .' *swish swish* 'a history of . . .' *glide swoop* '. . . twins in your family?' she asks with studied casualness.

Why is she asking me this?

'No! Oh God, don't tell me it's twins!'

I look at Richard, appealing to him to restore order. This was not in the plan. He already has wonderful nine-year-old twin girls from a previous relationship. He adores them but he swears he didn't sleep for two years.

Richard has gone grey in the face. He starts pacing the small, hot room. 'Oh Christ,' he manages quietly.

There is a small, gigantic moment. No one breathes. My head wants to burst.

The lady swooshes some more, this time down the right side of my torso.

'No,' she finally says.

'Thank Christ for that!' we chorus. But something is not right. The lady turns the screen towards me now.

'There's three of them,' she says flatly.

I never even particularly wanted children. For twelve years I was a lesbian – not even one of those dykes that mooches around Mothercare waving a turkey baster about. There's nothing wrong with that, but it just never occurred to me. Then at the turn of the century I had a change of heart and decided to go back to men. I know some people claim they were born gay, but for me it was a choice. I'd jumped the fence from straight to gay in the eighties after studying feminist theory at university. We all had dungarees and it just seemed like the logical next step. If men were the problem, why bother with them at all? We'd only end up diminishing ourselves either in their service or by trying to educate them. I'd always got on with women – why not get off with them as well? But a decade later it wasn't so black and white. I'd had very difficult and often painful relationships with women and decided that perhaps the same-sex thing was no longer what I wanted. Perhaps the massive gender differences I had bemoaned all those years ago were exactly what I needed to foster my individuality. I didn't want to look at my lover and see a version of myself reflected back. I wanted that otherness that comes with heterosexual pairing. Paradoxically, I concluded, I had found it more liberating. So I jumped back over the fence and after a string of false starts – I think I dated the entire gamut of twenty-first-century male dysfunction in one year – I fell in love with a rugged and gentle northerner called Richard.

Our first daughter was conceived in a sort of 'I'm 37, let's see if I can get pregnant – whoops! yes I can' kind of a way. Saoirse (an Irish name, pronounced Seer-shah and meaning 'freedom') was born in October 2003. Almost a year later and I'd started thinking about giving her a brother or a sister when whoops! there I was again, fingers covered in wee, staring at a thin blue line. I'd been playing Russian roulette with my ovaries after refusing the pill, literally running away from a clinic where I was due to have a coil fitted and forgetting to buy condoms. After the initial shock we were pleased – at least I would have it all done and dusted by the time I reached the big Four-Oh. I didn't want to be buying maternity bras when I should have been living it up in a Martini-soaked Kim Cattrall 'Life begins at forty' kind of a way.

'I'm sorry, I'm sorry,' she keeps saying to no one in particular as she checks and rechecks the contents of my womb.

I am shaking. I feel angry. The minutes roar past and last a decade. How can this be? I can't have three babies. I can't. I'm not a cat. It's not possible. Three babies. I can't, in this moment, remember the word for three babies. Triplets. It's never featured prominently in my life, why should it spring to mind now? Triplets. I play around with it in my head. It does not compute. An innocent word, nothing to do with me, now full of horror. Triplets. It sounds like a threat.

I keep looking at Richard hoping that he can sort all this out. If it weren't such a cliché I'd be barking 'There's obviously been some mistake!'

'I can get a second opinion if you like,' says the lady.

Of course – she's actually made a mistake. It's going to be all right. It's going to be all right.

'But I am certain there are three babies there.'

'Yes, please. Get someone else.'

It's all I can think of to do. We have to be sure.

The lady leaves the room and Richard and I say nothing, hoping perhaps that if we don't acknowledge what is going on, it will evaporate into the stuffy air. Saoirse points at the screen and lets out a cackle. I can't look. I don't want to see. If I don't see them then they aren't there.

Richard goes out to refill the parking meter. This is going to take some time. I am filled with a sudden fear that I will never see him again. He's probably in a taxi on his way to the airport now.

The door swings open and a second woman comes in. I note with irritation her dangly Christmas parcel earrings. How can she wear earrings like that at a time like this? Never mind, she is going to rescue us from this cruel false alarm.

She takes the probe and begins swooshing.

'One . . . two . . . and . . . yes . . . three,' she counts, like she's in a particularly warped episode of 'Sesame Street'. So she's in on it too.

'Have you had IVF?' she asks.

'No!' I almost shout.

'No fertility treatment at all?' asks the first lady, as if I might have forgotten.

'No! The pregnancy was a complete shock.' I start to cry. Then I laugh. At one point I do that thing people do in bad melodramas – I laugh so much that I start to weep inconsolably. I try to stand up, an instinct to run away from the source of the pain, but they won't let me. Apparently I am very pale. Richard returns and I try to seek solace in his face but he won't look at me.

'Wow. This is only the second time in fifteen years I've scanned triplets. Have a good Christmas – it's the last quiet one you'll ever have,' says the second lady somewhat darkly.

I hate her now too.

'I'm sorry,' says the first lady again. 'I don't know why I keep saying sorry – it's not my fault!'

There is no sense of celebration in the room, just the feeling that a bad thing has happened here. I dry my eyes with some of the rough blue paper. The two women huddle briefly then emerge with a plan. They are as much in shock as I am.

'We're going to send you over to the antenatal clinic to see a midwife. Then you can decide what you want to do,' says the second lady. I have no idea what she is saying.

We stagger along the long hospital corridor. I am crying like a person in a hospital drama, not caring who sees me. I need the loo. I sit there staring at the lino floor. It's pink and speckled, like tinned Spam. What are we going to do? This is a disaster. Instead of the joy, excitement and misty-eyed wonder the first scan normally brings I am actually horrified.

I feel furious with my body for playing this trick on me.

Richard has gone into numbed coping mode. He is busy sorting out the buggy, the parking, Saoirse's nappy – anything but the mess our lives are about to become.

At the antenatal clinic we are ushered into a room where a nice Irish midwife tells us we will have to return to see a consultant in two weeks' time. Because of the delay in the appointment, it is now too late to do the usual nuchal fold test on any of the embryos – I can't yet call them babies – so we will not be able to determine the risk of Down's syndrome. The only other option is an amniocentesis, which, we are assured, is not possible with triplets. The midwife thrusts a help line number for Tamba, the Twins and Multiple Birth Association, into my hand, an appointment is made and we wander out to the car park – no fanfare, no bolts of lightning, just as if everything were normal. Behind us the hospital day grinds on. Patients sneak crafty fags standing shivering at the doorways, their IV drips quivering on their stands. Nurses scurry in and out, pushing sandwiches into their mouths, and visitors pull their coats around them at vandalized bus stops.

Back home, Richard downs the best part of a bottle of vodka, neat. No such luck for me. It is a very cruel irony that now more than ever I need a stiff drink but now more than ever I can't have one. Rich says it seems like as good a time as any to perform his yearly ritual of having a good cry over *It's a Wonderful Life* so he puts the video on and blubs into his empty glass. He says he feels like Jimmy Stewart and *his* life is over –

but for him there will be no saving angels trying to earn their wings. This is real. Too real. We have been together for three years and we will have four children to add to his existing two. He has no money, no job and a head full of dreams of being a successful actor. Until now I have been the breadwinner in the family, taking Saoirse on tour with me and spending weeks away from home in order to keep us afloat. How will I be able to do that with four young children?

But I have no time to let any of this sink in. I have to go to work this afternoon. I'm making a series of documentaries for BBC Radio 4 and I have to be in West London to interview a top Pilates teacher. I get on the train to cross town and stare at the other passengers, some of whom are drunk, all of whom are carrying Christmas presents.

'I'm having triplets,' I want to say. But I don't. I sink back into my seat and wonder how on earth my life turned out the way it did.

'I'm having triplets,' I think again, testing to see if the news has sunk in any deeper. It hasn't. It still sits on top of my consciousness, bobbing about like an empty cider bottle in the canal.

There were a few clues, looking back. From about six weeks into the pregnancy, I felt incredibly sick and dog-tired. My legs would carry me to bed in the middle of the afternoon, where I'd lie moaning and burping. They say, the old wives, that extreme nausea is a sign of multiple pregnancy. The human growth hormone which sustains the pregnancy until the placenta takes over is created in vastly increased quantities, which, combined with the fact that one's body is awash with proges-terone, creates the constant vomiting. I didn't pay any attention to this belief. I know plenty of women who have puked their way through an entire singleton pregnancy, and several mums of twins who sailed through vomit–free. At around ten weeks I had started to show already, and my mum had commented that I looked big and was I sure about my dates? I put it down to the fact that the only thing that stopped the constant nausea (*morning* sickness? Pah! That's for wimps and rank amateurs – I once puked all day, on the hour, every hour, and ended up on a hospital drip) was to eat more or less constantly. It's one of life's great paradoxes – the more sick I felt the more doughnuts I had to cram in. I had chosen to ignore both of these signs – until today. Now there is no denying it.

I call–screen all day. I can't face anyone. Somehow I manage to work, asking questions and nodding and doing microphone sound levels and trying not to peer at my tummy in the many mirrors.

'It's not twins, is it?' my producer Emma, herself the mother of twin boys, asks laughing.

'Ha ha ha,' goes my voice, but I don't recognize it. Later, listening back to the tape, there is a hollow ring to my laughter.

The Pilates lady has taught celebrities such as Liz Hurley during their pregnancies, enabling them to get back into their tiny jeans weeks after giving birth.

'Have a go at this little lot,' I feel like saying.

On the train home I feel full of grief, a knot of it eating away at my stomach. It takes a while to identify the feeling, and when I do I am still unsure why I am feeling this terrible sense of loss, of an ending, not three beginnings. Then I realize what it is I am mourning. It is myself. My life as I have known it is over. I will have to give up huge parts of me – ambition, hedonism, recklessness – in order to bring these three lives into the world and sustain them through to adulthood. These things are how I define myself. I have always been very self-determined. My mum tells a story of how, at the age of six, I was spotted hitch-hiking to the local sweet shop on the first day of a family holiday in rural Ireland. The nearest shop was a mile away and the owners had a large family. As soon as the delivery came in, the chocolate would be devoured by their children, who would leave only the Silvermints, which no one wanted anyway. I knew this from the bitter experience of walking a long country mile only to find the shelves bare. I was determined not to miss out on the Dairy Milk this time. It being rural Ireland, where you can't fart without the next village knowing about it a week in advance, a farmer spotted me and had reported back to my aunty before I even got to the shop. I wasn't punished – just praised for my determination. No harm would come to me there, and I got the chocolate. The story has become how I am defined in my family. Nothing will stop me from pursuing my desires. But how can I carry on with this old, comfortable version of myself with four young babies? And if I can't be myself any more, who will I have to become? One of those lumpen, downtrodden women you see in cheap supermarkets, their hair greasy, their clothes covered in chip fat, hundreds of shaven-headed children hanging off the shopping trolley? It was what life had in store for me until, by sheer force of character, I dragged myself out of my Essex comprehensive and got myself a life. So was all that effort – all the studying, all the classroom jibes about being a swot, all the terrifying nights on lonely comedy stages – a waste of time? Should I have just stayed where I was, resigned to my ultimate fate? You can take the girl out of Essex but . . .

I keep trying to tell myself that it won't be that bad, that we can adapt and include the babies rather than let them take us over, but the reassurances ring as hollow as my laughter. I already feel invaded.

Walking slowly home from the tube my phone rings again. 'Mum and Dad' flashes up on the display screen. It's the third time Mum's called today, unusual for her, so she must be worried. I normally ring her straight away after a hospital visit and it's been eight hours since our appointment. But I can't take the call. I'm a crap liar and I don't want to tell them on the phone. We'll have to go and see them.

In silence we drive to tell my parents. As we come in, Mum is sitting at the table wrapping Christmas presents and quickly hides one. It strikes me as a ridiculous gesture – how can their surprise of socks and scarves compete with the bombshell we are about to drop? Depression has made us narcissistic. It's all about us now.

'Everything all right?'

'Well, yes and no.'

'Is it bad news?' asks Mum, suddenly worried, the present dropping to the floor with a dull thud.

'No, it's . . . interesting news.'

I'm not trying to string it out or play with their feelings, but I just cannot find a way of telling them. I feel as if we are teetering on the edge of two lives. The moment I utter the words will be the moment our future is made concrete. It's the first time I'll say it, and, once said, it will be true.

'It's triplets,' I say simply.

Mum laughs. Dad raises his eyebrows. Within minutes they are cracking open the Jameson's and my dad, a strong silent Irishman not given to outbursts of sentiment, says he thinks this will be the best thing that ever happened to me. I don't believe him yet but I am grateful for their immediate support and lack of hysteria. We sit around the table and they drink the entire bottle until they are declaring it's the best news they've had in years.

'My dad had twin brothers,' says Mum. Now she tells me. Is this the genetic link?

In my bag I have the number for Tamba.

'Call them,' says Dad, once again surprising me with his sensitivity. A very religious man, despite his emotional reticence at home, he has a strong sense of community, especially in a crisis. I remember the many Vietnamese 'boat people' he helped during the eighties.

So I take the phone upstairs and dial the number for the voluntary support group.

A woman with a very kind voice answers and I tell her my news. I think I use the phrase 'diagnosed with triplets', making it sound like a potentially terminal medical condition. She tells me that I am the second woman tonight who has called to say she is having triplets. Instantly I feel a competitive spirit rise up in me.

'Were hers naturally conceived?' I ask briskly. Maybe I'm getting used to the idea.

'No, she had IVF. But you are all very special,' she says. She tells me that triplets are known as supertwins.

'Does that make me a supermum then?' I ask, pleased with the title.

'I suppose it does!' she laughs.

She is lovely and reassuring.

'What a Christmas present you've been given!' she says.

'If I don't like it, can I take it back?' I say, only half joking.

There is a sticky moment when I ask her what the chances are of all three surviving. In my heart, I know I am hoping she'll say 'Unlikely' – but I don't realize this until she says perkily, 'Well, you've got them to fourteen weeks and that's the riskiest bit!' I feel instantly guilty and ashamed. Of course she would assume I want reassurance that they'll all be fine. What am I – some kind of monster? I put those feelings away and resolve to feel a lot better. I have never been a phoner of help lines, a person who needs a lot of support. I can feel a shift happening somewhere around my heart. I am going to have to be more linked to the world. I will have to ask for – and accept – help.

That's the worst of it.

Feeling reassured, I decide that tomorrow we will start to tell people. My phone beeps just as we are going to bed. It's a text from my friend Lou, anxious for news, surprised, no doubt, that I haven't called.

'Did it go well?' she wants to know. I text her back.

'Yes. In fact, it went three times better than expected,' I tease.

The phone leaps into life. It's Lou, of course.

'What do you mean?' she demands. 'You're not having triplets?' she laughs.

'Yes,' I say. 'I'm afraid I am.'

There is a sharp intake of breath.

'I will help you. I will come every day,' says Lou calmly, and I burst into tears for the first time since the scan.

23 December

I awake with that preconscious sense of well-being. Something niggles at the back of my mind, though. What is it? Have I had a row? Have I been dumped by someone? Has someone died?

No. I'm having triplets. Oh God.

I can't be having triplets. That's a *litter*. I'm not a dog, or a cat, or a pig. It's a horrible word. It sounds too much like 'piglets'. I'm having piglets. Besides, *triplets* – it's just so comedy. Phoebe in 'Friends' had triplets. There's a Belgian cartoon called *Les Triplettes de Belleville*. Triplets is comedic hyperbole, not real life. If I wasn't so busy either feeling numb or crying, I'd be laughing myself mental.

I start to tell people when they call. My sister Maggie goes silent for the longest time. I feel like humming 'Greensleeves' in that call centre muzak-while-you-queue style. Finally she realizes it is not an elaborate hoax and offers her concerned congratulations. My brothers, Ray and Adrian, are shocked but delighted. Soon the news spreads and I am mentally ticking off the list of friends and family that need to be informed. It's not just any old baby news, this, to be filtered down second- or third-hand through the grapevine. This is something much bigger than that. People need to be formally told. With every telling the response says a lot about the person hearing the news. I collect a list of my favourite responses.

'Oh my God, your life is over,' says an actress friend.

Yes, thanks for reinforcing that.

'You'll have to retire,' says a stressed working mum.

'You should give one each to all your barren friends,' says the single woman over forty.

Mostly, people respond with jokey doom.

'Rather you than me.'

'Well, it could be worse – it could be cancer.'

'You can get a really chav buggy for four!'

'You'll have to grow another tit.'

And my particular favourite: 'Congratulations or commiserations, I don't know which to say. Well, I suppose like Cadbury's Roses they'll grow on you.'

I think about compiling a top ten of 'Things Not to Say to Someone Who Has Just Told You They are Having Triplets' but I realize that (a) it's a bit Nick Hornby and (b) most people will never need it, triplets being relatively rare.

I decide that instead I will go online and try to find out as much as I can about having triplets. Tentatively, I Google the word 'triplets' and pages and pages of related material come up. This is a bad idea. Outside people are rushing past with shopping bags and gift wrap as I discover jolly things like the average triplet pregnancy is only 33 weeks compared to the normal 40 of a singleton pregnancy, but many are born well before this; 9 per cent of triplets die by the end of the first week of life and the major concerns of extreme prematurity are learning difficulties, blindness, deafness and cerebral palsy. Joy to the World.

I go into town for Christmas drinks with some gay friends well known for their rapier wit and relentless bitching. I decide to tell them, but I preface my announcement: 'Right. I've got something to tell you, and before I do I just want to say that I'm quite wobbly about this, so I can't take any jokes, any teasing or any nasty remarks, OK?'

Then I tell them, and their suddenly concerned expressions frighten me. I long for someone to call me an old slapper, but they don't. Things must be bad.

Then DJ, my dear old beardy queen producer friend, breaks the silence. 'Bloody hell, Clune, I think Richard could get *me* pregnant!'

Christmas Eve

We go to the 5 p.m. Family Mass at our local church. It's full of over-excited children and stressed parents. This is what we have in store for us. I start to sink inwardly. The small amount of optimism and composure I have gathered in the last twenty-four hours evaporates. Then the organ starts up and within the first two bars of 'Away in a Manger' the wobbly, off-key singing of the children has me in tears. Christmas Eve is a great advert for kids. Christmas Day is the antidote.

At the end, as the priest ushers us all out of the church, the organist starts up a spirited version of 'Jingle Bells', the church's one concession to a sectarian Christmas. The children, previously lack-lustre with their vocals, now burst into an enthusi-astic rendition and once again I am in tears.

I can't sleep. Not because I'm on the look-out for Father Christmas, but because I am starting to realize the logistical implications. We will have to buy a new car. A car that will take four baby seats, at least two buggies and a dog. And what about if Richard wants to get all of his six children together? So that's two adults, four babies, two children, a dog and at least two buggies. And where will we find a buggy for four? Saoirse will not be able to walk for long periods by the time the babies are here. Can you get a buggy that will accommodate three babies and a toddler? The EDD – estimated delivery date – is officially 24 June, but we are probably looking at an April or May delivery (that's if I make it that far). The weather will be nice so we will want to go out. Or will we, if we've not had any sleep? Sleep. Where will they all sleep? Do we need three cots straight away or can we pile them all in one, like puppies in a basket? If one wakes, will it wake the others? And how am I going to feed them? After a shaky start I managed to breastfeed Saoirse for almost nine months. How do you breast-feed triplets? The woman at Tamba said she could put me in contact with women who'd done it. But will they be women like me, or hairy hippies happy to sit around all day with their tits lolling on their knees? The key, the lady said, was in organization. You can rotate the babies from one breast to the other and then on to the bottle. This sounds like a logistical headache already. I could scarcely remember which breast I'd fed Saoirse on from one feed to the next, despite the helpful advice in all the baby books about tying a piece of ribbon to your bra strap to remind you. It was a good day if I managed to get both bra straps done up. And our house is too small for triplets. We'll need at least two bedrooms for the kids and one for us. And we'll need an au pair. So that's another bedroom. We've only just moved in to this three-bedroom house in a nice area with good schools. We are that catchment-area cliché. We'll have to get the loft converted. How will we afford that when I'll be too massive to work? I'm now giddy with worry. I poke Rich in the ribs. He's snoring gently.

'What is it, love?'

'We'll have to get an au pair!' I say.

'Great,' says Rich sleepily. 'Can we have a French one? To teach the kids French, of course.'

'No. She'll be twenty stone and from Bratislava.'

'You think that will stop me?'

Christmas Day

6 a.m.

'Rich, are you awake?'

'Yes.'

'We can put the triplets in the blanket box under the bed.'

'OK.'

'Merry Christmas.'

'Merry Christmas, ducky.'

We go to my parents' for Christmas dinner as normal. Probably for the last time – it'll just be too much like hard work taking four young kids. After the riot of toys and games and screaming nephews and nieces all day, we decide that we will be converting to Islam after the triplets are born so that we can avoid the whole bloody thing.

The high point of the day is a visit to my old friend Julia's house. Her mum, Gillian, and stepfather Bill were like second parents to me growing up. Now Bill is very ill. He has had cancer, heart disease and severe breathing problems but has been allowed out of hospital for Christmas Day. When I arrive he is sitting propped up on cushions with a canister of oxygen by his side and a tube up his nose. No one expected him to make it to today.

'I hear all good things come in threes,' he says warmly. The kindness and the optimism in his voice makes me well up and we sit holding hands for a few minutes while I tease him about his new look. I find myself laughing about it.

'You seem very calm about it, Jacks,' says Gillian.

'Well, I have to think it'll be OK or I'd just sit on the floor and cry,' I say, doing my best impression of a brave woman. But somehow, saying the words calms me and I begin to think it might just be all right.

26 December

Richard is off up north to see the twins. I am very emotional as he and Saoirse set off. I have planned to visit my sister and her boyfriend Tim in Brighton. Mum and Dad are going too. We made this plan before the triplet news. Everything will now be known as either before or after the triplets. I am reluctant to go. I want to sit curled up on the sofa but I'm too scared to be on my own with my three fetuses so I go. Mum is worried about me. She hates to see any of us upset. I hope she has the stomach for whatever this pregnancy may bring.

The news is spreading fast and I get lots of calls from friends old and new. Some make me cry ('Your life was meant to be extraordinary', 'If anyone can cope you can – you're hardcore'), some worry me ('Oh no, what are you going to do?') and some make me hoot with laughter (Jenny Eclair: 'Don't worry, people will help you – not me, obviously.'). An old friend called on Christmas Day and asked gently, 'Are you going to have them?' It was the first time anyone had broached the subject of choosing whether or not to continue with the pregnancy and I felt shocked. I realize that I haven't given it a moment's thought.

I relay the story to another friend, Sean, who says, 'Perhaps she thought you said giblets – it *was* Christmas Day.'

27 December

Back home again. On the train to London I feel a fluttering. I am fourteen weeks pregnant. It can't be the 'quickening' can it? The first movements of the babies? They say that you can feel this at around the twenty-week mark, but I've also read you can feel it much earlier second time around. It's a bizarre feeling, and unmistakable. Like a trout turning somersaults in a bag of water. I don't want to feel it yet. I'm not ready to enjoy it. I decide to go online again. I look up 'selective reduction' on the net and read stories about women who have had enormous pressure put on them to terminate at least one of the fetuses. Many of these women have been battling with infertility for years (85 per cent of triplet pregnancies are the result of multiple embryo implantation or fertility drugs) and to be asked to 'reduce' their hard-won potential family before it's even here is horrifying and deeply traumatic. I consider my 'own position. No one at the hospital mentioned selective reduction to us, although Richard says the ultrasound woman made a reference to 'thinking about what you want to do'. Ah yes. Now I remember. I wondered what she had meant but was too shocked at the news to be able to decode it. I'm not a pro-lifer by any stretch of the imagination but having had one child already I'd find it very hard to terminate now. And how would you make the decision which one should go if all three fetuses are healthy? Eeny, meeny, miny, mo? In the end I choose to believe the research that says there is no improvement in the odds of a good outcome by reducing from three to two, and the associated risks of inducing a total miscarriage which come with the reduction procedure outweigh the advantages of reducing. It seems to me that there is research to back up pretty much whatever you want to think.

The Internet is a blessing and a curse. At the click of a button I have found frightening statistics alongside impossibly cute private websites lovingly put together by proud parents of triplets, so I spend the day lurching from tears of joy to spasms of terror. The American websites for multiples are the best – and the worst. Lots of stories of enforced bed rest from eighteen weeks, heart defects, still birth and a mysterious condition called TTTS – twin-to-twin transfusion syndrome. It happens in identical pairs – where the egg has split and two babies share a placenta and in some cases an amniotic sac – and involves one baby taking more than its share of blood, fluid and nutrients to the detriment of the other baby. It is very serious, and can involve the death of at least one of the babies. TTTS is the bogeyman of multiple pregnancies. From what we can remember of the first scan we think we have an identical pair and a fraternal, so we are at risk. All these factors, combined with the strain on the mother and the potential problems associated with delivering multiples, means that triplet pregnancies are deemed very high risk. Perhaps this is why the consultants are so keen to reduce. Or perhaps it's economics. One website estimates the cost of healthcare for multiples requiring aggressive neonatal intervention and prolonged 'special care' at around a million pounds per family. Is it selfish to continue the pregnancy and burden the NHS with that bill, especially if it is a result of IVF, where a multiple outcome is a big possibility and therefore 'chosen'? Lung cancer is very common and very expensive to treat, but no one would deny sufferers the life-saving operations and chemotherapy simply because they have chosen to smoke heavily.

It seems like an age until our next appointment ten days away. I tell myself not to get attached to the babies as in all likelihood at least one of them will not have survived. It just seems so risky. I hope I can hold on to them for thirty-four or thirty-five weeks, but it looks unlikely from what I've read today. I realize that actually I have only really been worrying about practical things and selfish considerations. I have been a complete Pollyanna about the potential outcome. Images of hovering over intensive care incubators flash through my mind. Perhaps I will carry them well, but perhaps they will be sick, and they might not come home all together, if at all. I cry a bit. I feel sick.

Then I find an Israeli website that is very down on IVF because of the instances of multiple birth. Jewish extended families welcome large numbers of children, so fertility clinics routinely place up to five embryos into the womb, resulting in extraordinarily high numbers of triplets – and sometimes more. The pregnancies do not normally go well, and it is very rare for all the babies to survive, the site claims. It also criticizes the large numbers of 'last chance saloon' older women who use IVF, as they face even graver risks. It tells of one woman who had triplets. Two of them had Down's syndrome. I switch off the computer and have some chocolate. Half an hour later I am back online. I need to know more. Knowledge is power. Or, in my case, neurosis. I look for the research that says it will all be fine. Instead I learn that in the UK fertility clinics are now only permitted to implant two eggs. I visit the Tamba website and find two other women who are having triplets. One is seventeen-weeks pregnant, the other about seven weeks. Both report bleak conversations with consultants about selective reduction. Older members of the message board gee them up by telling them how they too were told it was unlikely they would end up with three healthy babies, but that they now have three screaming toddlers. Both triplet mums-to-be seem to be getting a lot more hospital attention. They are going to be scanned every two weeks, to monitor for TTTS. My next scan is not until twenty weeks. Surely this can't be right? I

23

resolve to push for an earlier scan. They might be born at twenty-four weeks. I've read about triplets weighing a pound. That's half a bag of sugar. How do they survive?

28 December

Richard and Saoirse are back. He has told his parents the news. He took his dad, John, to the pub to tell him. John was delighted.

'Twins and now triplets? Bloody 'ell, son, what have you got in there!'

Slowly, slowly, I am starting to become used to the idea. I can't find the scan pictures we were given, and I turn the house upside down looking for them. I need to see them again, to make sure that I have not been hallucinating or having a delusional psychotic episode. I need to see those three little beans in a bag. The Three Little Pigs. The Three Musketeers. The Three Wise Men. Oh God, what if they're all boys? Not only will Saoirse have to tolerate three new siblings all at once, but she'll also have three smelly *brothers* to contend with.

I suddenly feel full of grief for Saoirse – for her lost childhood, for the anxiety such an influx of babies will surely cause, for the lack of attention she will suffer. I picture her, mid-Woody Allen monologue on a therapist's couch thirty years from now: 'My Mum had triplets when I was only a year old and that was basically it for me.'

I scoop her up and sob into her hair, pretending I am laughing. She pushes me off and goes back to 'Balamory', oblivious to the trauma we are all about to go through.

'I hope it's not boys,' says Richard, already the father of three girls.

'Why?'

'Because I don't know what to do with boys,' he says, grimacing.

I keep replaying the day we found out about the triplets in the hope that it will help me come to some kind of understanding. I think this is what people do when someone has been murdered. It's a form of psychological workout, to help you get used to something shocking. A snippet of memory floats up. We are in the scan room and I am sitting on the table shaking. I remember that three months previously I saw a palmist in a booth on Blackpool beach. He advertised himself as a distant relative of Gypsy Rose Lee, but then according to most of the palmists along that stretch she had a very large extended family. I went in for a laugh expecting to find an over-made-up lady in a fringed headscarf. Instead I found Clive, a naff puff in a blazer who had a strange speech impediment.

'You have had a lot of heart-hake in your life,' he intoned solemnly, before doing the generic patter about overcoming obstacles and travelling overseas. He then asked me if there was anything else I wanted to know.

'Yes – will I have another baby?' I giggled. It's what people normally ask.

He peered at my palm.

'I don't see one more baby – I see three,' he said, with all certainty. I guffawed and left to look at the donkeys on the beach.

Sitting on the sonographer's table, his words came back to chide me for my scorn. I remind Richard.

'That man – the one in Blackpool – he told me! He said three more babies!' I gabble.

'He also said you were going to end your days in a bungalow. Let's hope he wasn't right about that,' says Rich, suddenly laughing a bit too hard.

29 December

This Internet habit is getting out of hand, but it's the Christmas holidays and no one at the hospital seems to care, so I have to find my information somewhere. I read a medical case study which asks the question: 'What is the link between maternal age, weight, method of conception and fetal outcome?' I wade through the jargon and try to decipher the results of the various studies. The statistics, I think, are encouraging. Spontaneous triplets in older mothers tend to have a good chance of survival. Then I read that this is mostly because the babies are normally all fraternal and therefore not at risk of TTTS. Also, older women having babies tend to be from 'better' sociological groups and therefore have better health care. So the middle classes have more surviving multiples. As well as better teeth.

Our triplet news has spread worldwide. I check my emails and a very nice rather poetic friend emails me to say: 'Triplets – what a wonderful sense of abundance!'

A rather more prosaic Aussie friend, Simon, is even more expressive: 'Fuck! Jesus! Fuck Fuck Fuck!'

I'm with him.

30 December

It's compelling the way everyone is suddenly a believer in fate and/or God. Time and again over the past few days I've heard the following phrases: 'This was meant to be', 'God only gives you what you can handle' and 'It's amazing what life has thrown at you.'

Isn't it just luck, good or bad? And if it's God who decides who to give multiples to, then why do those people ignore his word when he chooses to make them infertile in the first place? Is IVF defying God's plan? I've read so many posts on American message boards that casually and quite unqueasily refer to 'God's wishes'. They are stories of terrible suffering – of endless rounds of failed IVF attempts followed by multiple pregnancies which end in traumatic and fatal early labour. God is praised as the giver of life and never criticized when he takes it away. I just don't get it. The people who offer hearty congratulations one month when the pregnancy is announced are the same people who offer consolation to the poor bereaved parents and urge them to 'trust in God' the next. Any doubting of God's work is greeted with dewy-eyed patronizing comments along the lines of 'God works in mysterious ways'. Isn't that just another way of saying 'Life's a bitch and then you die'? If it's God's plan to play around with people's hopes and dreams, then God is a very disturbed individual.

Everywhere I look people are talking about babies. There is a news item tonight about premature babies and the high instances of cerebral palsy. Nice. A newspaper article details a new study from the University of Nottingham of mortality rates and disability among 1,289 babies born in 1995. Of babies born at twenty-two weeks gestation, 98 per cent died. At twenty-three weeks, 90 per cent died. Twenty-four weeks and 82 per cent died, and at twenty-five weeks, 65 per cent did not survive. I am shocked. I thought that babies born at over twenty-four weeks stood around a 50 per cent chance of survival. I have taken advances in modern medicine for granted. I read on and discover that in the last ten years neonatal intensive care has moved on a lot and that the statistics are probably much more comforting now. It's amazing how much they can achieve with these tiny scraps of life. I switch on the TV and watch a programme called *Born Too Soon*. Angry red bundles no bigger than a kitten fighting for life, the doctors and nurses daily performing serious operations to keep them alive. It occurs to me that the legal limit for abortion is twenty-four weeks – the cusp of survival for these babies on the telly. What a strange paradox modern medicine has created.

I surf the American website again and find a woman pregnant with triplets who went into labour at eighteen weeks. All three died within minutes. Three months later she adopted newborn premature triplets, one of whom died a month later. I learn this from her sign-off line: 'Mom to 3 precious angels born 18wks 07/01/03 – Mom to adopted triplets born 04/04/03 – precious angel Katie died 05/05/03'. I know I should feel nothing but admiration for this woman's big-heartedness, but I can't help thinking it's all a bit suspect. Would anyone be in a fit state to adopt three babies so soon after losing their own? Is there a kind of addiction to the hyperbole of triplets? Would one baby not have been enough? I contemplate my own feelings about being pregnant with three. If I lost one now, if the next scan revealed that one small heart had stopped beating, I think I would be upset but I think moreover I would feel cheated of a drama. Lots of people have twins – there's nothing that special about them.

Isn't that awful?

It's an uncomfortable realization, but I'm sure it's something that a lot of women feel if they are honest. The initial shock, the special attention, the extra care – for most women a triplet pregnancy is a huge drama in which they are the star. To lose any of the babies must be dreadful. To have that role snatched away from you must be very upsetting on all sorts of levels. Is there an unhealthily attention-seeking aspect to this Internet mom's adoption? I dimly remember a few years ago the woman who got pregnant with eight babies and refused to reduce them, instead hiring Max Clifford, a notorious PR man, to help her publicize them. She lost them all, and, presumably, her lucrative newspaper deals.

It's a very dramatic time. The triplet pregnancies I've read about so far seem to bring about intense bonds between women and their medical practitioners – bonds that are often mourned once the drama of the birth and the first few months are over. I've just read a post on the US message board with the title 'Am I crazy or does anyone else feel like they've just been dumped by their perinatologist?' Several women report that they too feel a sense of heartbreak at not seeing their caring, concerned doctor every week. It's the closest any of them feel to having had an affair. Here is someone who looks out for you, who asks you only about you and who says things like 'Let's see if we can get you as comfortable as possible' while getting intimate with your private parts. It's not sexual, it's just the fact that these men (and oddly it seems to be mostly men in obstetrics) are paid to care for you in a way that most women long for in their personal relationships. The American system is different from our own NHS. Mostly it's private medical insurance, so having a baby in the States must be like a mini spa-break. I resist the urge to post a reply suggesting that those grieving women pay a visit to an antenatal clinic in any inner city hospital in the UK. They'd be skipping out of their sign-off appointment.

New Year's Eve

The last day of the year in which I got pregnant with triplets. 2004BT. Everything will now either be known as BT or AT – Before Triplets or After Triplets. Assuming there is life after triplets. All going well, next year I will have four babies. Somehow the turn of the year, looking through my new 2005 diary, is bringing the reality home hard. I put three exclamation marks in on 24 June, technically my due date, but score a line through April and May – I'd better remind myself that I might be quite busy then. We go out for dinner with some gay friends of mine.

'Richard . . . six children . . . one of them is bound to be gay,' says Chris provocatively. My gay friends like to tease Rich, thinking him to be a little frightened of them. They base this on the fact that when they greet him he doesn't kiss them on both cheeks (as is customary in our luvvy circle), instead preferring to shake them manfully by the hand and avoiding eye contact. That's what you do up north if you meet a man you don't know very well. It's not homophobia, it's politeness.

'Great,' I say. 'I'd like at least one of my sons to be gay. I'll spoil him and fuss over him so that he'll never leave me.'

'And will you make him take you shopping?' sneers Chris.

'Yes, absolutely. I will be that stereotype Mum of a Gay Boy.'

Well, if they can stereotype Rich as a terrified straight bloke breeder then I can play the Gay Men are Mummy's Boys card.

'I'd rather have a lesbian daughter,' Rich suddenly says.

'Really? Why's that?' I ask, looking around the room as if to say 'See? See? He's not homophobic! He's not your stereo-typical geezer!'

'Because then when I'm old and bald and no one's looking at me any more she'll be bringing loads of nice young totty home.'

Well done, Rich. Nice one.

On the way home we stop in at Sean and Anoushka's for a New Year drink. Sean is a stand-up comedian and writer who has the knack of putting an often surreal but strangely upbeat spin on things. He could have had the *Titanic* crew laughing as they went down, so he's a good person to see right now. Anoushka is his long-term partner and now mother to their daughter Daphne. As new parents, they have found themselves stranded indoors on New Year's Eve so they have necked vast quantities of champagne by the time we arrive. They are very merry, and more champagne is opened. I am so tired but determined to have a long evening out. Saoirse is at Mum and Dad's so we can even sleep in.

'I think it's great,' says Sean. 'There's something about

triplets that just says "circus" to me. I can imagine Saoirse just clicking her fingers and the triplets will come tumbling in to do a balancing routine.'

We leave at 5 a.m. and I feel euphoric. It's so important to surround ourselves with positive people. I can't be bothered with the worriers and the nay-sayers. I'll do my worrying now, then put it to rest in a few weeks. After the next scan. Whenever that is . . .

New Year's Day

8 a.m. I am wide awake. Rich has fallen asleep with his cowboy boots on. He really wants to be Clint Eastwood very badly.

It's 2005. I think about my New Year's resolutions. I don't think I have any that I can implement. Normally they are 'Must lose weight, exercise more, join a gym, stay in touch with friends and family, learn Italian' – the usual variations on an age-old self-esteem issue. I won't be able to do any of that. I might even be in bed for half of the year. I'm dreading the consultant putting me on strict bed rest. I am determined to stay active and deliver the babies as late as possible without being hospitalized long in advance. This year my agenda has been cut very short: 'Have triplets.'

I can't imagine it's on many lists around the world this morning.

Wednesday 5 January 2005

I meet with Emma at Broadcasting House to work on the radio documentary series we are doing about fitness trends.

'I need you to fill out this insurance form – it's just a formality,' she says. She knows I am pregnant, but I have yet to tell her the latest. Emma's twins are just over a year old and she is constantly exhausted. I don't want to hear anything bad but I should really tell her.

'Well, I suppose this is the point at which I tell you that I'm having triplets,' I say, as levelly as I can. I don't want to lose this job.

'Triplets!'

'Yep.'

'My goodness! That's amazing. Are you going to get any help? Do the government help you?'

'I don't know. I'm going to find out.' This is something I keep being asked. Perhaps Social Services will provide someone to come over and help us out. I need to look into it once everyone's back from the holidays, and once I gather the strength to jump the inevitable bureaucratic hurdles.

'Right. OK. That's fine. But we must be very careful. I don't think we should go to Luton to meet the joggers tonight. I mean, are you OK? How are you feeling? Are you able to carry on with this?'

'Yes, I'm absolutely fine, honestly. I want to work for as long as I can.'

'But what does your consultant say?'

'I don't know. I haven't got one yet.'

'But how many weeks pregnant are you?'

'Almost sixteen.'

'What? You're sixteen weeks pregnant with triplets and you've not been seen by a consultant? When's your next scan?'

'February,' I say, getting agitated now. Emma knows from her recent twin experience that this is not good enough. And if this really is not good enough then I am going to have to get stroppy with the hospital, which is not the easiest thing in the world to do at the best of times. It's partly a class issue – I've watched how my parents have tugged forelock at the most insulting and negligent health care and I have learned that doctors are like priests – never to be challenged, always to be thanked. It is not our place to demand any more than they want to give. My limited experience of being a hospital patient is that you just put up and shut up and be pathetically grateful if they remember to administer your morphine. Any challenge to the system is met with either inept communication break-downs or undisguised indifference. It takes a strong stomach to run full pelt at the red tape and get anything surplus to the standard requirements.

I suddenly feel nervous and even more tired.

'Which hospital are you at?' asks Emma, in full middle-class 'Not Good Enough' mode.

'Whipps Cross,' I mumble miserably.

'Do they have a fetal medicine unit there? You need to see a specialist. Someone who has delivered triplets before. You'll be having a C-section, I presume, and you'll need much closer monitoring. You should go and see the guy I had at UCH – he's brilliant. Eric Jauniaux. He's Belgian. Very dry. Very good. Call them.'

'Am I allowed to do that? Can you choose which hospital

you go to? UCH is a teaching hospital isn't it?' UCH – University College Hospital – is one of the top NHS hospitals in London.

My head is spinning now. I realize with a start that I've been avoiding the whole issue. Now I'm being urged to face it and I'm scared.

'It's worth just ringing and at least talking to someone. You should be having regular scans. I'm amazed they let you just walk out of the hospital.'

My next appointment at the hospital is on Monday. I am due to see a consultant. I call my friends for back-up. I need to be told what to say when I go in. Normally irritatingly well-informed and articulate in formal situations, I go to pieces when faced with medical professionals. I can't remember what to say when they ask me if I have any concerns, why I've come or even where I live.

'Ask him if he's delivered lots of twins and triplets. Make them give you another scan. Insist that they transfer you if you're not happy with the answers,' says Anoushka.

'Really?' I say, trying to imagine myself insisting in front of a doctor.

'Absolutely.'

I'm not the sort of person who insists on anything much. I suppose if I were pushed, I would insist that someone didn't chop my head off, but even then I expect I'd add, 'If that's OK with you . . .' It's not really that I lack confidence generally. It's my awe of medical authority combined with my easy-going nature. I hate to think anyone is doing something for me against their will. This is going to be hard, but I know it has to be done. I can't risk the babies' lives because I think it's cheeky to demand more. When I see the consultant next week he won't know what's hit him.

Monday 10 January

We go to the hospital and wait for an hour to see the consultant. I am very nervous, partly because I am anticipating a fight ahead about being transferred, and partly because I am gripped by a fear that one of the babies has died. It's been three weeks since I had my scan and it's perfectly possible that they haven't all survived. I don't have a scan booked for another four weeks. My head is spinning, and some of my worries are silly. What if I go around telling everyone it's triplets and then in four weeks' time I find out that one died? Or two? Would people think I was lying? Crying wolf? Why am I worrying about what other people will think in the event of losing a baby! I need to know that everything is OK. I don't want to lose any of these babies now. I sit thinking about all the women who lose children either before or shortly after birth. One woman I read about had twins but one didn't make it. She reported how people had tried to console her by saying, 'You've still got one!' Only a stupid person would say such a thing to a mum.

We are called in and a bored-looking man in his late forties mumbles his name and gets my notes out. I presume this is the consultant and not the cleaner. A midwife tells me to lie on the bed – at least I think that's what she said. She is mumbling too. It's a curtained cubicle, and I can hear the nurses and other midwives chatting loudly through the thin material. The blood is rushing in my ears. Rich perches on the edge of a plastic chair. He is even more mute than me in such situations. There's no chance of him shouting, 'Now look here, she needs special care!' I'm on my own here.

'Triplets,' says the man. 'OK.'

Before he can start examining me, I'm determined to get all of my concerns out of the way. But he is sitting at the desk with his back to me and every time I try to get up the midwife mumbles for me to lie down. It's not anything like the dramatic showdown I imagined.

So I deliver my carefully planned list of questions to the back of his head: 'I've spoken to a few people who say I should be seen every two weeks and I need another scan because I am at risk of TTTS because we think we have an identical pair, but we're not sure, and I want an amniocentesis and that needs to be done sooner rather than later and I just wanted to know do you have a lot of triplets here? Have you got enough neonatal intensive care facilities? Will we be split up? Because if we will, then I want to be transferred to a hospital that can keep us all together. And will I have to go on bed rest? If so when and can I stay at home because we have a daughter who I need to be with and I can't just go to hospital for three months but then I don't want to risk any harm to the babies, so will it make any difference to the outcome if I don't go on bed rest?'

There is a long silence while he scribbles a few notes. Then he turns wearily around and folds his arms.

'Why do you want to be transferred? We have lots of triplets and twins here,' he says, as though talking to a slightly simple child. His tone is a masterful combination of studied boredom and irritation.

'Oh, do you? Fine. And what about the scan?'

'I can scan you now if you like,' he says, pulling over an ancient portable machine. I am filled with relief but also fear. What if something has happened? I don't want to find out about it here, like this, with two uninterested mumblers by my side. He cranks up the machine and I pull my top up, desperate now to get it over with. I am now convinced that at least one of the babies has not made it. The probe glides around on my by now quite swollen belly, and I see two little heads pop onto the screen. He doesn't say anything, so I hold my breath waiting for bad news. Still he doesn't say anything. Is he looking for heartbeats? What has he seen that he doesn't want to say?

Finally, I can stand it no longer. 'What is it? Are they OK?' I ask.

'Er . . . yeah . . . here's one, here's two and I'm just having a look for three—'

'But are they OK? All alive?'

He doesn't say anything for what feels like about an hour.

'Yes, yes, all alive,' he sighs.

'Did you see all the heartbeats? Are you sure?'

'I've seen two fetal heartbeats,' he says.

'What about the third?' I hear my voice in the room but I don't recognize it. Who is this tense woman with the reedy, high-pitched voice?

'I haven't been able to find it, because the fetus is tucked quite high up, but fetal movement was detected so it's alive, yes,' he says dully.

I turn to Rich and there is water in my eyes. He smiles back at me.

I'm happy now I have my good news, despite the off-handedness of the messenger. I take a deep breath and exhale loudly. We are having triplets. Yes, we are. I allow myself a small inward lap of honour. Rich and I have discussed whether or not to find out the sexes. Last time I was pregnant he was adamant that he didn't want to know. I desperately wanted a girl and so felt I should find out just in case it was a boy and the disappointment spoilt the birth. We decided to wait and see, and hearing the paediatrician announce '*She's* fine!' remains the most memorable moment of Saoirse's birth day. This time it feels stupidly romantic not to find out. It's already hard enough relating to them as babies, these things called triplets, so it might help to find out what flavour they are. I decide to ask the consultant. He doesn't seem too open to more questions, but perhaps if I jolly him along he'll have a look and tell us . . .

'So, are you any good at telling what sex they are at this stage?' I smile, hoping he will raise his game to the implied challenge.

'No,' he says flatly, before switching off the machine and pushing it to the side of the room.

'OK, so I'd like to book an earlier scan please,' I say. Now that I know I have definitely got three babies growing inside me I am determined to get them the proper attention.

'You'll have to see the lady outside about that. But come back and see the consultant on Friday and he can discuss your care.' Then he wanders out of the room.

We sit for a few moments until the mumbling midwife ushers us out.

'Is that it?' I whisper to Rich. We have no idea if our consultation is over, and my unanswered questions hang in the air like dog farts. We are laughing now, partly because we cannot believe the indifference with which we have been treated (it's like a particularly depressed service station branch of McDonald's) and partly with relief that, so far, all is well.

We go to the appointments desk and ask for an earlier scan.

'OK, unless you want something in January, in which case forget it!' laughs the lady.

'We do want something in January,' says Rich.

'Oh, no, I can't do that, you need a triple appointment you see, and we've not even got one for the next four weeks.'

'But that's not possible!' I say. 'I've got to be seen before then.'

'I haven't got anything until mid-February. Look,' she says, showing us a screen full of blocked out scan appointments.

'So are you saying you can't help us? Are you turning us away?' says Rich, suddenly finding his tongue. Things must be serious.

'I can't turn you down. I don't have the power to do that,' she says, employing her official voice now to go with the doublespeak.

'So what do we do?' I ask, my head about to implode with the effort of not exploding.

'You'll have to see the consultant,' she says, pointing back the way we came.

We trudge back rolling our eyes at each other. I can't help feeling that something isn't right here. It's like a triplet pregnancy is an everyday occurrence. They are so blasé it makes me panic. Maybe I am making a fuss about nothing. Maybe there is really nothing to worry about and I should just go home and sit things out until my twenty-week scan. No one here seems to be worried.

But I can't. What if something goes wrong? I would never forgive myself.

The mumbling midwife spots us, and we explain what has happened. She goes off to get the consultant's approval to cancel someone and bump us up the scan queue. She comes back brandishing a new appointment.

'Here you are,' she says.

I look at the piece of paper. The new date is two days before the old one. Almost a month away.

'OK?' she says hopefully.

'No. This isn't good enough. I have to be scanned properly *soon*!' I say, getting really agitated now. It is like an anxiety dream where you know everything is wrong but no one else will listen.

'OK,' she sighs, as if she was rather hoping to get away with something.

Off she trots back to the consultant. We are ushered into the room again and after a few minutes he comes in with the air of a truculent headmaster.

'We're very understaffed here, and you need a *triple* appointment.' He places extra emphasis on the word 'triple', like I am some greedy bulimic in an ice-cream parlour. I resent being treated like a troublesome attention-seeker when I am carrying three babies. I am past the point of class-conscious, forelock-tugging now. Seeing the three fetuses again has spurred me on.

'I know that, Mr Whatever-your-name-is, that's why I wanted to be transferred. If you don't even have enough facilities to properly *scan* three babies, how are you going to be able to look after them all once they're here?'

Mr Whatever-your-name-is eyes me with renewed interest. We've got a lively one here.

Suddenly, the curtains pull back and a middle-aged midwife puts her hands on the consultant's shoulders as he sits facing me. It is an odd gesture, intimate and yet domineering. No one touches each other in the NHS, least of all people from different status ranks. What does it mean?

'Are you the lady having triplets?' she smiles. I instantly warm to her soft Irish accent. She's just like my mum – and she is the first person to look at us.

'Yes,' I say, still shaking a little from the confrontation.

'Congratulations,' she says warmly.

'Thanks.'

'But we don't do triplets here. We're going to have to refer you.'

The consultant throws his hands in the air and smiles in a 'nobody tells me anything!' kind of a way.

'She's the boss!' he says, and wanders off again. The midwife is called Bridget (what else?) and apologizes for the confusion.

'I've been away for three months and he's a locum so he wouldn't know the new policy. You should never have been booked in here. Someone's going to get an ear bashing. We just don't have the facilities here, so we decided that all triplets should be referred on to bigger units.'

'But we've been saying all day that we want to be transferred – how long has this policy been in place?'

'About a year,' she says sheepishly.

'Then how come no one knows about it? It's absurd. We could have slipped right through the net, if I'd just accepted the appointments we were given.'

'Well, it doesn't come up very often. Probably about once a year. We don't see lots of people having triplets, so most people here wouldn't know,' she says.

I feel soothed by this, mainly because it appeals to my inner narcissist – we are *so* special, *so* rare that we are a sub-clause in the antenatal care book which needs careful, expert signalling. Either that or the staff just don't know what they're doing.

'Where would you like to go?' asks Bridget.

'UCH. Eric Jauniaux,' I say.

'OK, then that is where you shall go.'

And it is as simple as that. It's time to get us – all six of us – out of here.

Later that night we lie in bed discussing names.

'We can't go for comedy triplet-themed names,' I warn.

'What do you mean?'

'Like Mary, Mungo and Midge, or Peter, Paul and Mary.'

'No, ducky?'

'No – I just read a post on the web by a mother of singletons and she basically said that triplet mums who theme their babies' names – you know, all beginning with the same letter or something – should be sent birth control. OK, so what are your favourite boys' names?'

'I like the old-fashioned names. Walter, Albert, Frank . . .' says Rich.

I start humming the Hovis ad music as he loses himself in a

flat-capped reverie. 'You can't call a young boy Walter! He'll just be called Wally! Wally and Bert!' I laugh.

'Well, they're not having Paddy names. Not all of them,' says Rich, defensively.

'Why not?'

'Because I'm not Irish.'

'You haven't got whippets, but you still want to call your children names like Wally and Bert!'

'We'll see,' he says, knowing already that he's beaten.

'What do you think we're having?' I say.

'Identical boys and a girl,' says Rich without a moment's hesitation.

'So do I.' It just sounds right.

Tuesday 11 January

Bridget calls at 11 a.m.

'You're seeing Eric at 4.30 p.m. today,' she says.

'Today? Great! And when can we get a scan?'

'He'll do it all.'

'And what about an amnio?'

'You won't find anyone in the UK who'll do an amnio on triplets,' she says. 'It's far too risky.'

'Oh,' I sigh. It looks like we are not going to be able to get any tests at all on these three babies. My doctor's dizzy receptionist lost my initial referral to the hospital thus delaying our first scan and it was then too late for a nuchal translucency test for Down's syndrome. Now we are having triplets no one will do anything because of the triple risks involved. I would take refuge in the favourable odds – about 1 in 127 for my age – but if this pregnancy has taught me anything, it is that there is no refuge in statistics.

'Oh, well. Thank you. Thank you so much, Bridget.'

At least we are going to see someone who knows what he's doing, and today! I feel like we have been saved. Saved from hours of inept bungling, of being passed from inexperienced pillar to can't-be-bothered post. I call Rich, who is out with Saoirse, and tell him the news. We are excited now. I need to know in more detail what's going on in my womb. The sonographer at our first scan wasn't totally sure. Were there three fertilized eggs, in which case we'll have three fraternal triplets? Or one egg that split, therefore three identicals? Or two eggs? I start to feel like I'm making an omelette.

We arrive at UCH's fetal medicine unit. Photos of smiling babies adorn the walls and 'Thank You' cards gather dust on the pinboards. Several doctors are flying in and out of the four or five dark rooms surrounding the small waiting room. We play 'guess which one is Eric'. An elderly professor in tweeds walks past and smiles.

'I bet that's him,' I say.

'He doesn't look Belgian!' says Rich.

'What does Belgian look like – Hercule Poirot?'

Then a slim man with Seventies hair and a laconic expression glides past. 'That's him,' we chorus.

We are called in. We go into the darkened ultrasound room and feel like we are in the hands of a real pro. Somewhere in the gloom is Professor Eric Jauniaux. He is indeed the man we just saw outside, and you can sense his casual authority. He is flanked by six medical students who are shadowing his clinic today. They all smile and say 'hello,' keen to see a triplet scan.

'So, you're having triplets?' says Eric. His accent is pleasingly Poirot.

'Yes,' I say shyly.

'Spontaneous?'

'Yep.'

'Your first?'

'No, we have a fifteen-month-old daughter.'

'*Mama mia.* Well, I am happy to do your antenatal scans and keep an eye on things, but you can't deliver here.'

I sink inwardly. I thought we were home and dry.

'Why not?'

'You live too far away.'

'But our local hospital won't have us. They don't do triplets.'

'But it's too risky for you to be booked in here. If you go into premature labour – which is highly probable in a triplet pregnancy – you will have to be rushed in by ambulance and it's too far. You might not make it. And you won't get an ambulance crew to bring you all the way into town if you're in labour. They'll take you to the nearest hospital.'

I'm stumped. Is this the plot of a Kafka play?

'But our nearest hospital won't have us,' I whimper.

'Then the one after that.'

'The Homerton,' I say. It's where I had Saoirse and it doesn't hold many happy memories. All I can recall is being barked at to have a shower the day after my emergency C-section. I hobbled that peculiar C-section shuffle, hunched over and holding my sore belly, all the way to the bathroom to find it flooded and covered in blood. I hobbled back to bed unwashed. I don't particularly want to go back.

'I'll see you every two weeks for a scan, and then if you get to thirty weeks or so you can go to the Homerton – OK?'

'OK,' I say, defeated. I hadn't thought about how far away University College Hospital is. I was quite looking forward to having West End babies. I was already having lovely fantasies about sneaking out for lunch with DJ at the Groucho, post-delivery.

Eric gets down to business. He switches the scan machine on and the room falls silent. The first thing he does is swoop around looking for all three. He finds them expertly one by one, pointing out the small blobs of their hearts pulsing furiously. Everyone relaxes a bit – or is it just me? He lines the cursor up on various limbs and circumferences, calling out measurements to his assistant who sits at a computer across the room. I have no idea what these measurements mean but they seem important. Nobody seems worried by anything. I really want to ask if it is possible to find out the sex of the babies at this stage. Since my rebuttal yesterday, I've learnt that even sonographers find it difficult to determine gender until twenty weeks' gestation, so consultants (who usually don't do as many scans) can be very reluctant to tell you early on in case they get it wrong. They don't want to be held responsible when Martha turns out to be Arthur, who then has a pink bedroom for the first few years of his life. I decide to ask again.

'Can you tell what sex they are? We want to know,' I blurt.

'Yes, of course, it should be possible.' He shrugs, as if I'd just asked him if he would mind shutting the window.

Eric slides the probe around on my slippery belly. I can't believe that we are about to find out if we have boys or girls. How on earth does this work? Something to do with sound waves? It suddenly seems very sci-fi. This shouldn't be possible.

'Now let's see . . . You have . . . an identical pair – here is one placenta . . . They are in one sac but there is a membrane down the middle which is good—'

An identical pair! Two babies who will look exactly alike! How bizarre. We laugh with nervous excitement.

'And number one is . . . a boy . . . Therefore number two is also a boy—'

We giggle. 'Wally and Bert!' I whisper.

'And the third . . . is on its own . . . and—'

'Please let it be a girl!' I think, appalled by the idea of Saoirse being landed with three brothers.

'. . . does not appear to have a willy . . . yes, it is a girl . . . 99 per cent sure.'

Suddenly, it's not just an event any more, a story, an abstract number three. Suddenly, I am carrying two boys and a girl. Three people.

Eric switches off the scan and helps me up.

'Congratulations. However,' he begins solemnly. 'It's not as easy as that.'

He goes into a long list of potential problems but I'm not really listening. I've read so much already, and my natural Pollyannaesque optimism is kicking back in and telling me that none of this applies to me. I'm a big tall woman from Irish stock. Women in my family have loads of kids and never have problems. I was born for this. It'll be like shelling peas.

One thing is bothering me though. As I sit on the hard plastic chair in the semi-gloom I think of the Israeli woman and her Down's syndrome babies. I'm thirty-nine, so statistically I am at higher risk. If I'm having three babies then the chances of one of them having Down's must be higher.

I know I couldn't handle it. At least I think I couldn't. In any case I'd like to be informed so that we are pre-armed.

'Any questions?' asks Eric.

'Yes . . . I'm a bit worried about chromosomal abnormalities . . . but the other hospital told me that I couldn't have an amnio-centesis on triplets as it's too risky.'

Eric snorts. 'Who told you that?'

'A midwife said I wouldn't find anyone in the UK who would do it.'

'This is bullshit, what they are telling you. I can do it for you.'

'Really? When?' I am catapulted into a new decision which I assumed was already out of our hands.

'I can do it now,' says Eric with inspiring confidence. 'It'll take five minutes and you'll have the preliminary results in three days.'

We discuss the risks. The procedure involves inserting a needle through my abdomen into the uterus and extracting 30ml of amniotic fluid. The fluid contains skin cells that reveal the chromosomal make-up of the baby. In my case, *babies*. There is a slight risk – about 1 in 100 – of miscarriage due to rupture and leakage of the amniotic sac. I'm worried that, multiplied by three, the risks are too great, but Eric smiles and says, 'I'll try to do it with just one needle, because I only need two samples. The pair of identicals will share the same profile, therefore I only need one sample from them. Then I will angle the needle and get the sample from the third.'

'And what if there is a problem with one – or more – of the babies?' I say, broaching the subject of termination.

'If you want to selectively reduce because of a chromosomal abnormality?'

'Yes.'

'Well, you need to decide what you want the amnio for. Would you do that if you were to find out there was a problem?'

'I don't know,' I say. 'Maybe. I'd like to know in advance in any case. But if I did want to terminate one, how does that work?'

'We inject the fetus and it is absorbed.'

This is the sort of technical, cold language that drives pro-lifers insane, but I need his clinical approach right now.

'OK,' we agree. It feels like stepping off a cliff, making the decision to find out. No turning back once the results are in.

'I have never lost a baby yet,' Eric reassures us.

A local anaesthetic is applied to my stomach. Eric marks the best point of entry for the needle. It needs to go in as near to the two sacs as possible while avoiding the fetuses. He readies himself with the sample bottles, and a nurse hands him a long thin needle with a syringe attached.

Eric asks if I am ready. I nod my assent and he prepares to insert the needle. For a brief moment I see a blank screen and think that he has not switched it back on. I panic.

'Do you do it from memory of where they are?' I say nervously. Surely not.

He pulls back and looks at me with wry amusement. I notice that the screen is indeed on.

'Oh yes, and I will also be wearing a blindfold,' he deadpans. This makes me laugh so much that he has to sternly tell me to stop – he can't insert the needle while my belly is wobbly with laughter.

'No jokes now,' he says. The atmosphere becomes very serious.

I don't normally mind needles, but I can't look. Instead, I watch the reflection in Richard's eyes. He is focused intently on the screen. I know that he is calm, and it's not paranoia or protectiveness that is prompting his watchful eye. He is just fascinated by the whole thing. Some women might find this disconcerting – how could he be so dispassionate about it? – but I feel massively reassured by his steadfastness. As I watch the black-and-white image reflected in his eyes I feel calmer too. He is calm because he knows everything will be all right. *I* know everything will be all right.

'We can do this. We can do this,' I almost dare to think.

I glance up to see a phial of yellowish fluid being passed over my belly to the nurse. She has carefully labelled the tube and double-checks the details. I am at once reassured and freaked out by the precision. The consequences of a mix-up could be extremely far-reaching. This is grown-up stuff, and here are Rich and me giggling like idiots. A second phial is placed on the external end of the syringe and Eric draws up more yellow gunk.

'Done,' he says. 'No problem.'

I am led into an anteroom to rest for half an hour. The risk of a membrane rupture is slight (a nominal 1 per cent) but it's best to take it easy anyway. I lie there thinking about the two boys and the girl who've just had a close-shave with a needle. They're not even born yet and already they are being poked about. I've read about pioneering in utero surgery. They can separate co-joined twins, divide a placenta with lasers, do all sorts of extraordinary things while the babies are still inside you. This was nothing, this little amnio. With any luck we'll have the preliminary results (the crucial chromosomes which will reveal Down's or cerebal palsy) by Friday and we'll have the whole weekend worry-free.

Wednesday 12 January

I get up early for yet another wee. I sit dazed on the loo, having slept in only twenty minute bursts for the past four hours. As I sit there a strange trickle leaks out of me. I don't think it's urine. It feels different, like it's coming from a different place. I panic. My membranes have ruptured.

Or was it just another wee? How can I not know?

I go downstairs and look up 'membrane rupture' on the web. I discover that you can buy special sanitary pads that can tell if you are leaking amniotic fluid. This is primarily useful in helping women know when their waters have broken, as most hospitals only give you twenty-four hours to deliver from that point. There is a much higher risk of potentially fatal infection if the membranes are ruptured long before delivery. I decide to wait and see what happens. Every time I stand up, I wait to see if I will leak. Nothing happens for the rest of the day but I convince myself I have a slow puncture, and probably by tonight the babies will be in dry, shrivelled sacs. I call the hospital and speak to someone who reassures me that it will be OK, and that if there has been no further leakage I am probably fine. It's possible to have a small rupture that heals over, but I don't think I've even had that, as there has been no further leakage. Nevertheless, I sit tight for the rest of the day, resisting the temptation to enter into a 'What have I done?' guilt trip. All will be well.

Friday 14 January

It's 6 p.m. No call from UCH. Shit. Now it's a weekend of what ifs and maybes. I'm reading the paper when I spot an advert for something called a Home Office – it's a glorified garden shed with electricity and Internet access. I show it to Rich.

'That'll be great for me!' he says. 'Let's get one. We'll need the space.'

'If we get one it's going to be mine, and it will be pad-locked. And the inside will be padded all over.'

If men can seek sanctuary in the garden shed, then why can't I? If anyone is going to need it it's me.

Monday 17 January

I've done my best all weekend to block out the worry. The amnio results should be here at some point today. I know that it is probably going to be fine, and I don't want to be one of those neurotics who seem to almost will themselves into the small likelihood that something is wrong. I keep having visions of the old lottery campaign – a big pointy finger coming down from the heavens and a booming voice saying, 'It could be you!'

10 a.m. The phone rings and I grab it urgently, all pretence of calm now gone.

'Hello?' I shout. There is a pause.

'Hello?' I shout again. I can hear my heart banging in my chest.

'Good morning, Mrs Clune, this is British Gas calling, my name is Julie, would this be a good time to talk about your energy suppliers at all?'

'No,' I say, before slamming the phone down.

Two minutes later it rings again.

'Hello?'

'Oh hello, may I speak with Jacqueline Clune please?'

It's UCH. I feel sick. How does she sound? Neutral. Neutral bad or neutral good? Just neutral.

'Speaking,' I say.

'This is UCH calling. Can I confirm your date of birth and your address please?'

I think I tell her but I'm not sure. All I want to do is say 'Just get to the point – are they OK?' But I think I give her what she wants to know.

'We have the preliminary results of your amnio back.'

'Yes,' I say, sounding impatient now. I could do without the tension pauses. This woman should take over from Chris Tarrant.

'And I can tell you that all three fetuses have tested negative for the main chromosomal abnormalities.'

In the panic of the moment I'm not sure if this is a good or a bad thing. Have they passed or failed?

'So they are all fine?' I venture.

'Yes, all fine,' she laughs.

'Thank you! Thank you so much!' I say.

'You'll get the full report in a couple of weeks.'

I wasn't worried anyway.

Tuesday 18 January

I go to Whipps Cross Hospital to tell them that they have to transfer my notes to the Homerton. Bridget, the midwife, says it seems silly to be scanned at one place and then give birth in another. A consultant comes in to discuss the situation.

'Why don't you just go to the Homerton? It doesn't make any sense, what you are proposing to do. So, you're just going to turn up at the Homerton thirty weeks pregnant with triplets?'

I don't really know what I am doing any more. I'm confused. All I know is that Eric was a very fine port in a very scary storm and we are now on his radar. I don't want to disappear again.

'Wait for your appointment from the Homerton, and see Eric in the meantime,' says Bridget reassuringly. It's a plan. I tell her about the fluid leakage. She's amazed that I got an anmio, but says that as long as the leaking has stopped it should be OK. I should rest.

Hah! How can I rest when the NHS is playing pass-the-partum with me? I am seventeen weeks' pregnant with triplets and I have no hospital to have them in. Maybe, when the time comes, I should just curl up like a cat in an airing cupboard on a nice pile of old towels.

On my way out the receptionist calls me over. What now?

'Are you the triplet lady?' she asks, eyes glowing.

'Yes,' I say. The whole room turns to catch a glimpse of me. I am instantly famous.

I AM THE TRIPLET LADY!

And I always thought I'd be famous for my singing voice . . .

Wednesday 19 January

My second appointment with Eric. Rich can't make it, so Mum comes along to help with Saoirse. I could have left them both at home, but I want her to see the scan. I need someone else, someone from my family, to see the three blobs to make sure that it's not an elaborate hoax. We sit in the waiting room and wait. We wait and wait. I run back out to feed the parking meter which is ten minutes away. I'm too tired all the time for public transport, so we've driven in. I'm sweaty and stressed and Mum is worrying about me, but she doesn't know central London and if I sent her out to do it she'd get lost. Saoirse has grown bored with the few toys left lying around for siblings, and is starting to get cross. Finally we are called in.

'So – what has been happening since I last saw you?' asks Eric.

I tell him about Whipps Cross and the Homerton and he looks irritated.

'I don't understand why Whipps won't have you. But never mind. You can go to the Homerton, it is very good. They have some of the best neonatal intensive care facilities in the UK.'

'Really?' I say. I only had your common or garden full-term birth there, luckily, so was spared the special care unit.

'Yes. They have more premature babies there than anywhere else.'

I've heard this before somewhere. It's to do with the catchment area   a lot of poverty, a lot of poor nutrition and a lot of drug abuse in pregnancy. I lived in Hackney for fifteen years until three months ago, so I know that this is no tabloid generalization.

Eric scans me again and says that all is well. Mum sees the babies on the screen and grins. Eric points out a penis floating among the tangle of limbs and umbilical cords. It looks disproportionately huge.

'Like one of those long balloons!' Mum says laughing.

Two penises growing inside me. That could freak a girl out, so I won't think about it.

It is extraordinary, a triplet scan. How they make any sense of the bits and bobs beggars belief. By the time I deliver, I'll have had so many I'll probably be able to do it myself.

'So you are the grandma?' says Eric, washing his hands.

'Yes, yes, very proud,' says Mum, trying to distract a fidgety Saoirse with an orange.

'You will be able to give her lots of help,' says Eric, making it sound like an instruction.

It really panics me when people say things like this. Every time someone says that they hope I have plenty of support, I don't know what to say. What does it mean exactly? Do I have people who will come and do the night feeds? Or just listen when I moan? I've never been big on 'support'. You just get on with it, don't you?

Eric tells us that Jewish extended families cope very well with multiple births because there are always plenty of pairs of hands willing to help out. I've read this already, so it's interesting to hear it from someone who sees it at first hand. I'm a second generation Irish Catholic by birth, and the Irish diaspora has been a bit more scatter-gun than the Jewish one. Families don't necessarily remain close by. My own family spreads from Ireland through to Essex, Brighton, Hampshire and Australia. My parents are half an hour up the motorway, but they don't drive much any more and are too old and tired to get on a bus. I can't rely on family. Rich's mum is wonderful with babies but she lives two hundred miles away. Let's hope our friends prove true.

On the way out, we chat about statistics and fertility. I'm starting to enjoy this kind of informed sparring with medics.

'Richard already has twins, you know,' I brag.

'He does not hold the record. I have performed IVF for one couple three times. They had triplets, then twins, then triplets again.'

Now it's my turn to say *mama mia*.

Thursday 20 January

On the web again. Someone on the Tamba forum has posted to say that she has just had the selective reduction talk with her consultant. It was particularly upsetting because the doctor in question was insistent that it was the best option, even though there is nothing wrong with the babies. She has been through four rounds of IVF and has finally hit the jackpot with three, but is now being advised to 'get rid of' one. People reply with their advice, most of which is of the 'don't do it' variety. Many of the replies are from mums of triplets who say that it's not as dangerous as they make out. Someone posts some very useful facts about the odds of miscarrying after the reduction procedure versus the risks of a triplet pregnancy. They also quote research that found that the risks associated with a multiple pregnancy are not significantly decreased by reducing from a triplet to a twin pregnancy. They don't tell you these things in the hospital. I suspect it's because, unless you are being cared for by a multiples expert, they don't actually know, and considering there are only about 140 sets of triplets born in the UK each year, how many experts can there be nationwide? It is we expectant multiple mums who have to become our own experts – hence all my net surfing. That's why sites like Tamba and tripletconnection.org are so useful. They have quite literally been lifesavers.

On a lighter note, my research throws up some interesting cultural attitudes to multiple birth. Apparently, Native Americans believe that triplets are salmon in human form. I also discover that both Elvis and Liberace had a twin who died at birth. Wow. Imagine. Two Elvis Presleys. Amazing. Or two Liberaces. Scary.

In bed, we are discussing the car issue. I hate all those yummy mummy urban tractor cars. I don't want a 4x4 or a people carrier. I just want a big old van we can sling them all in.

'I think we should just get a fifteen-seater minibus,' says Rich.

'Why? We don't need fifteen seats, and it will guzzle petrol up and down the motorway to Bolton.'

'But if we want to go on holiday, we can just put all the kids – Alex, Maddy, Saoirse and the triplets – and us, and all our stuff in and shoot off. And if anyone wants to come with us, we'll still have extra room!'

'That sounds lovely, Rich, but we're going to have four children under the age of two. *Nobody* is going to want to come with us.'

'They will!' says Rich, ever the optimist.

'Oh, "Would you like to drive to France with our hyper-active toddler and our newborn triplets and Rich's nine-year-old twin girls in our clapped-out hippy bus?" "Oh yes please, that sounds very relaxing!" Put it this way, I wouldn't want to go away with anyone who'd say yes to that, given a choice.'

'Imagine it, though . . . the kids break up from school, we pick them up at the gates and drive straight to the South of France—' Rich is already at the *boulangerie* picking up a dozen *pain-au-chocolat*.

'Can't it just be you and me, running away half an hour *before* the school bell goes?' I ask.

I don't want to think about summer holidays. There's a long way to go yet.

Friday 22 January

A small parcel arrives. It's a CD from David Benson, a fellow performer. He has heard about the triplets and wants me to hear an old Arthur Schwartz musical number called 'Triplets' from a 1931 film, *The Band Wagon*. The song was performed by Nanette Fabray, Fred Astaire and Jack Buchanan, so I put it on with great eagerness. It's a jaunty comedy song and the lyrics by Howard Dietz make me howl with laughter:

Three little unexpected children
Simultaneously the doctor brought us in
you can see we'll be three forever and
A E I O You wouldn't know how agonizing being triple can be
Each one is individually the victim of the clinical day
E I O Every summer we go away to Baden Baden Baden
Every winter we come back home to Walla Walla Walla

We do everything alike
We look alike
We dress alike
We walk alike
We talk alike
and what is more we hate each other very much
We hate our folks
We're sick of jokes on what an art it is to tell us apart!

If one of us gets the measles
another one gets the measles
then all of us gets the measles
and mumps and grippe

How I wish I had a gun
A 'widdle' gun
It would be fun to shoot the other two and be only one!
Mrs Whifflepoofer loves to talk to Mrs Hildendorfer on the
    fatal natal day she had her silly Willy
Mrs Hasslepoofer loves to talk to Mrs Goldenwasser of her
    major operation when she had her twins
But when Mother comes along she silences the others
She accomplished something that is very rarely mothers

MGM has got a leo but Mama has got a trio
she is proud and says three is a crowd

We do everything alike
We look alike
We dress alike
We walk alike
We talk alike
and what is more we hate each other very much
We hate our folks
We're sick of jokes on what an art it is to tell us apart!

We eat the same kind of vittles
We drink the same kind of bottles
We sit in the same kind of high chair
high chair! high chair!

How I wish I had a gun
A 'widdle' gun
It would be fun to shoot the other two and be only one!

It's funny in that dark way that I love, but it unnerves me slightly too. Do triplets really feel this deep-seated sense of resentment at not getting the one-to-one attention a singleton can take for granted? Or do the benefits of being part of a threesome – the constant companionship, the closeness, the sense of being special – outweigh the negatives? I squirrel the CD away to play to them on their seventh birthday. I'll ask them then.

Monday 24 January

I have decided to get moving on the help front. So many people have told me that I will qualify for lots of special allowances from Social Services and various charities. I make a list of all the suggestions people have made and the organizations I have to call. When I've finished, I bet the whole situation is going to seem a lot more manageable.

1 Redbridge Council.
2 Homestart – a voluntary organization that helps people in need. They can supply volunteers who will come and help you for a few hours a week.
3 CACHE – the training body for nursery nurses. Apparently they can put students on placements with you for a few weeks at a time. Some mums of triplets have sworn by them.
4 Maternity allowance. As a self-employed person I don't get statutory maternity pay, but I can claim maternity allowance for twenty weeks. I knew this last time I was pregnant, but I just couldn't be bothered to wade through

the red tape. This time we will need all the money we can get.

5 Surestart maternity grant. £500 per child! This will be incredibly handy.

6 Tax credit – we will be entitled to more. If we can work out what the hell to put on the forms.

7 Church. So many of the American documentaries on multiple births have shown how the local church has rallied round and got rotas of volunteer helpers in to lend a hand. I feel ambivalent about a gang of zealous do-gooders trouping through our little house, but then I remember that we are Catholics, so they are likely to be lovely Irish old ladies like my mum.

I am buoyed by all this support-in-waiting so I get my special new Triplet notebook and pick up the phone to get the first lot of help on board the triplet bus.

I ring Redbridge Council. I explain to the telephonist that I am expecting triplets and need to speak to someone. She says I need Social Services. She puts me on hold for several minutes then I get cut off. I ring back and she tries again. Eventually someone answers the phone and I tell them our situation. She says we need the children and families department, but I'll have to ring another number. She gives me the number and I dial. No one answers. I try again. After about five minutes a bored-sounding woman picks up the phone. I explain I am having triplets and that I have been told by several people I can expect some help in the form of a part-time childminder or a home help.

'Oh nah,' says the lady. 'Nah. We don't do *them* any more.'

'What, triplets? You don't *do* triplets?' I ask, baffled and tired. It's taken me almost an hour to get to this brick wall.

'Nah. There's too many of them.'

Too many of them? What is she talking about?

'So what do I do? We've got a toddler and triplets on the way. We're going to need help. What should we do?'

'You'll have to pay for it,' she says.

Disgusted, I hang up. We can't afford to 'pay for it'. It's not that we are poor, but there is just not enough money to pay for a nanny. What do people who are living on the breadline do when they have triplets? How do they cope? And what on earth did she mean by 'too many of them'? Has there been a triplet epidemic in E11? Not according to Whipps Cross ultrasound department. I detected a note of disapproval in her voice. Maybe she has an issue with IVF, and she presumed I had undertaken a course of fertility treatment. A lot of people seem to have this attitude – that if you've had IVF you deserve all you get and should not expect help. Plus if you had the money for fertility treatment (around £3,000 a go), then you should be able to afford triplets. Most people assume, quite naturally, that such a huge and extraordinary burden of care would be shared by the state. The next person who tells me that I'll 'get help' from the state will get this stupid woman's telephone number. They can tell her.

The next stop is Homestart. I speak to a nice lady who says that she is very sorry but she has no volunteers in my area, but she will put me on a waiting list. We live in an area where there are lots of elderly people, so perhaps all the volunteers are busy helping them. Oh well. There's always CACHE. I call the

HQ and am given a list of colleges in my area that teach the diploma course in nursery nursing. There are about six quite near us, so I am very optimistic. I can put up with a few nice young women who want to learn about babies in my house. They'd certainly know their way around a nappy and a sterilizing unit by the time they left.

I call the first college and speak to the head of childcare courses. She says that they used to do home placements but they are no longer allowed to because trainees have to be in buildings with public indemnity insurance cover. I have no idea what this is, but I assume we don't qualify. I call the second, third and fourth college and get the same answer. The fifth lady I speak to doesn't mention this and says she will call me in September when the new term starts. She might have some girls who want to do private – as opposed to nursery – placements. This is OK. We can make it through the summer. By September we will be so grateful for the help.

So that's two nos and a maybe (but not yet).

I plough on.

I discover that maternity allowance is paid by the DSS. I log on to their website and download the application form, thinking, 'This will be a complete doddle.' Feeling very smug about being computer literate and thus saving myself a trip to the depressing dole office in Leytonstone, I begin to fill in the form online. By page two my head is spinning. It is classic DSS double Dutch. In order to work out the claim period I have to consult a table that is so impenetrable it makes Sudoku look like noughts and crosses. You would think that it would just be a case of putting down your estimated delivery date and their software doing the rest. But no. I have to find the week I am due within their own (totally arbitrary) calendar and reconcile it with the week numbers they are using, then find the reference for that week and enter it on the form as the start week for my claim. I then have to repeat the process using another chart to find the end date. Now I have a first class degree and an A grade at A level English, but after just two pages of this I am ready to give up. It is mind-bogglingly difficult – heaven only knows how a non-native speaker or a semi-literate woman goes about getting any money out of them. I give up after page three and decide that I'll have to go there instead. Perhaps they'll be able to do it for me. I am not going to be able to work for much longer. I need this money.

Next up is the Surestart maternity grant. I log on and find out that this is payable to families who are either on benefits already or on such a low income that they qualify for more than just the basic child tax credit award. I don't know what we are getting from the tax credit office. Haven't a clue. I call them up and they say that we are on the basic level and therefore not eligible.

'But neither of us will be working soon,' I say.

'Are you on jobseeker's allowance?'

'No, I'm self-employed, but I won't be able to move soon.'

'Is your husband on jobseeker's allowance?'

'No.'

'Then you don't qualify.'

This is mad. Because we're not already in receipt of benefits we're not entitled to any. The only reason Rich doesn't claim dole (I refuse to call it 'jobseeker's allowance' – it's so bloody Thatcherite) is because we are too proud. As an actor, for the past two years he has earned less than his tax threshold, but we would both rather I pay for everything than be put through the humiliation that is the benefits system these days. 'Jobseeker's allowance.' What bloody nonsense. He isn't 'looking for a job' in the traditional sense, and they hound you to go for interviews as office cleaners or abattoir assistants. Bugger that, we'll do without. So now we won't get any maternity grant because we won't claim dole.

Next I dig out our tax credit forms. I stare at them blankly for a couple of minutes. Suddenly I realize that Saoirse has been watching Cbeebies for about four hours now. The programmes are on a loop, and I'm sure I've already seen what the Fimbles found today. I stuff the whole pile of paper into a file and throw it under the stairs.

Refreshed after two Belgian buns, I put a call in to the presbytery of our local Catholic Church. There's an answerphone, so I leave a long garbled message about the triplets and how to ask for help. I'm sure someone will ring back with a whiteboard and a list of eager volunteers. Catholics like a good cause, especially if it involves babies.

My belly is getting bigger every day, matched only by my appetite. I feel hungry all the time. If I am too far away from food I start to panic. It's like a disability. I thought I would enjoy this aspect of pregnancy, but it has already become a drag. I get up at around 7.30 a.m., have some cereal, then some toast, but by 9 a.m. I'm starving again. It's not a neurotic hunger, it's a real physical *need* to eat. I am powerless against it. Give me muffins. I can't help it. I routinely send Richard out to buy me cakes first thing in the morning. I am terrified of how much weight I'm putting on, but I've decided not to weigh myself because even if I wanted to I can't stop eating. I've just been reading some sickening book about pregnancy which gives nutritional advice called 'the best odds diet'. It's full of warnings about saturated fat and empty calories, instead suggesting pregnant women eat fresh fruit smoothies and who-lemeal toast with sugar-free peanut butter. I think I'd barf if I had to drink a smoothie right now. I want fat and sugar, and lots of it. These alternative types always say 'Listen to your body' – well, my body always wants cake.

Monday 31 January

Tonight is the recording of a one-off radio comedy programme that I was commissioned to write back in August last year. It's the first in a series called 'Happy Families', and I was asked to write one of them because I had a baby. Since then things have obviously taken quite a comedy turn, so I have constructed a piece which is primarily about having triplets. It's been thera-peutic to filter this whole process through my stand-up lens. Somehow, publicly joking about things helps me cope. I have called the show *Bad Mutha*, and it is to be recorded in front of a live audience at the Drill Hall Theatre, scene of many triumphs, both professional and personal, back in my lesbian past.

Funny how things turn out, isn't it?

I am looking forward to the show immensely, especially the moment when I tell the live audience that I am expecting triplets, and just in case they think my twenty-week-but-huge bump is one full-term pregnancy, I've written a song with my mate and long-term collaborator Al Collingwood called 'I'm Having Triplets (Oh My God)'.

My favourite bit is:

> I'm only twenty weeks pregnant but I look a lot more
> A group of package tourists tried to board me before
> There's now a pelvic basement where there used to be a floor
> I'm having triplets – Oh My God!'

I've also included a song for Saoirse called 'I'm Sorry' which details all of my failings as a mum.

> I'm sorry, so sorry. I've been a bad mum
> I once put Vicks Vapour Rub all over your bum
> I'm sorry so sorry
> But what can I do?
> When God gave out mummies you were at the back of the
> queue

My producer, Claire, asks me at the last rehearsal to make sure that the audience understand my triplet revelation is not just a comedy set-up. 'I just don't think they will believe you, if you don't tell them twice!' she says. She is right. It takes about two minutes of me saying 'No, really!' to three hundred people before they all gasp and applaud. It is a very strange feeling, saying it out loud to a room full of strangers. I feel as though I'm at a mass AA meeting: 'Hello, my name's Jackie – and I'm having triplets.'

The show goes extremely well, and in the bar afterwards I am high from adrenalin and the extraordinary rush of having made people laugh. There are a few friends here who haven't seen me for a month or so and they are shocked at my size.

'You look about ready to drop!' says Sophie, an old lesbian friend of mine.

'I feel it,' I say. But really I feel wonderful. If I can still do this and have four babies I will be very happy. This evening has shown me that I have not just become a host organism. I am not just the Triplet Lady. I am still me, and I can still perform. For the first time since Christmas I feel the fleeting glow of happiness.

Then a smart young woman taps me on the shoulder.

'Really enjoyed the show,' she says.

'Thanks!' I can feel a 'but' coming.

'But can I just say? I pity you.'

'Oh don't say that!' I cry, appalled. The show even contained a sketch about all the crap and unhelpful things people say to me. I thought I'd educated them!

'No, I do, I pity you. You're doomed,' she said, before turning back to her friends.

I am so shocked I can't speak. Do I hate these comments so much because they are voicing my secret fears?

Saoirse is at Mum and Dad's, so Rich and I take advantage and have a late Indian meal back near home. It's strange to sit opposite him in a restaurant on our own late at night. I feel shy. We'd only been together a year when I fell pregnant and we have now been together three years. I realize that we both forgot our anniversary because we were too busy with Saoirse and absorbing the triplet news.

'Do you know we've been together three years now?' I say.

'Oh yeah . . . When's our anniversary again?' says Rich, more interested in stuffing poppadoms into his mouth.

'The eleventh. We only had a year together before we started breeding.'

'Yeah. Good, innit? Some people try for ages.'

Wednesday 2 February

Still no word from the Homerton. I need my twenty-week anomaly scan. It's the important one, the one where they do all the measurements and check the brain and all the heart chambers. I have seen Eric recently so I know things are OK generally, but it's important that I am at least booked in at the Homerton. I could go into labour at any time. In four weeks the babies will be (technically) viable and I will have nowhere to deliver them. I'm getting very nervous about it now and I keep trying to tell myself that it is all in hand but I am rapidly losing faith.

I call the Homerton antenatal reception.

'Hello, I'm waiting for a booking-in appointment. I'm twenty weeks pregnant with triplets.'

'Twenty weeks? Yeah, we're very busy at the moment. You'll get your appointment through in a few weeks. We're a bit behind.'

'A few weeks? I might have had them by then!'

The girl sighs theatrically. She thinks I'm trying it on.

'What, you think you might go into labour at twenty-three weeks?' she sneers.

'Yes! It's quite likely that these babies will be born very early! I need to be seen.'

'Hang on . . . I'll pass you on to a midwife,' she says. My triplet shocker has failed to move her from her NHS inertia. This is a drama and she sounds like she's reading from the autocue. She clearly does not understand the urgency of the situation.

'Hello, Mrs Clune?' says the midwife. I've been on hold for five minutes.

'Yes.'

'You think you might be in labour?'

'No, no, I just need an appointment. I'm having triplets and Whipps has transferred me to you but I haven't been seen and now I'm twenty weeks pregnant.'

'Oh . . . hang on . . . Yes, we're very busy . . . we can see you in two weeks.'

'No, that's not good enough! I need to see a consultant *now*!' No point waiting for them to play catch-up any more.

'Triplets . . . right . . . Let me see what I can do and I'll call you back.'

'When?' I know what hospitals are like.

'Today, today,' she reassures.

What is it going to take to get someone there to accept that my case is high risk and urgent? I sit and cry for a few minutes before Saoirse comes in. Then I receive a call from a midwife called Sally at UCH who is organizing a clinical trial called VIP. I like the sound of it already. I could certainly do with some VIP treatment right now, but the acronym stands for Vitamins in Pregnancy.

'We're giving vitamins C and K to women with a higher risk of pre-eclampsia, and as you're having triplets you qualify!'

Lucky me.

'So I just have to take vitamins, do I?' I say, thinking that if I could remember to take a pill every day I wouldn't be here in the first place.

'Yes – but it might be a placebo. You won't know until after you've had the babies.'

'OK,' I say. 'That's if I ever find anywhere to have them'.

'What do you mean?' asks Sally, sounding genuinely concerned. I almost start crying again.

I tell her my story and she goes straight into action mode, promising me a result.

Within an hour the phone rings.

'You'll be receiving a call from a Katrina Erskine. She's a consultant obstetrician at Homerton. OK?'

'Thank you, Sally. Thank you so much.'

I pace the floor.

Ten minutes later the phone rings again.

'Hello, this is Katrina Erskine at the Homerton. Congratulations on your triplets. I'm so sorry you've rather slipped through the net a bit. I need to see you. 9 a.m. on Monday morning please, at the fetal medicine unit.'

Hallelujah.

Friday 4 February

I have succumbed to an old addiction. I am watching the Discovery Health channel round the clock. It has wall-to-wall births – 'Portland Babies', 'Home Birth Diaries', 'Mum's the Word', 'Baby's Room'. I love it. I sit weeping as one after another little slimy creatures pop out and women are told they have done very well. After having Saoirse I would watch it for hours on end, and now, almost sofa-bound already, I am at it again. 'Portland Babies' is my favourite because they make it look like it should be – all smiles and 'yes' and lovely rooms. The Portland Hospital is the private place where all the stars pay thousands to have their babies. I'm watching an episode where a woman has been in labour for so long that the midwife calls the consultant in to review her. The consultant is a small stylish woman with an elfin face and extremely coordinated accessories. She smiles kindly at the poor grunting woman in the bad nightie and introduces herself.

'Hello, I'm Katrina Erskine, and you look exhausted.'

Did she just say Katrina Erskine?

A caption flashes up: 'Katrina Erskine – Consultant Obstetrician.'

She did!

I have heard how a lot of consultants flit between private and NHS hospitals. So from having no one to look after me I have now got a woman who might have delivered Posh Spice or Meg Matthews.

For nothing!

Good old NHS.

Saturday 5 February

We are at an old friend's baby's christening. I am just over twenty weeks pregnant now, but I find I can't stand up today without getting strong tightenings in my bump. Several times I am left breathless at the strength of what feel like contractions. I have to pull rank with Rich and drag him in from where he is smoking with the men outside so that he can stop Saoirse from necking all the glasses of wine which are just within her reach. I cannot keep track of her because I can't move fast enough to prevent disaster and I am finding it hard to breath.

On the way home I am worried. It's not exactly painful, but it's uncomfortable. They feel like the Braxton Hicks contractions – what they call 'practice' contractions – I got towards the end of my last pregnancy. Hopefully, it's nothing more sinister than that. I'll just rest up tonight and hopefully they will subside.

While lying on the couch I look up 'Braxton Hicks with triplets' and immediately plunge into panic mode. Several women on various sites report mistaking real premature labour pains for strong Braxton Hicks. Perhaps I should go and get monitored. They do say that if you have any concerns you should go and get checked out. I'll sleep on it.

Sunday 6 February

No more contractions. Panic over. False alarm number one.

Monday 7 February

The Homerton Hospital is an inner city sprawling great modern building set back from Homerton High Street, although the term 'High Street' is rather misleading for the tatty and derelict parade of shops and services on hand. When I lived in Homerton, I used to joke that the only cappuccino you could get locally was in one of those awful packets. The High Street used to be home to the old Hackney Hospital, a Victorian psychiatric unit on the corner of Kenworthy Road. 'The Hackney', as it's known in the area, has long since closed and been turned into flats, but its legacy remains in the number of mentally ill people you can still see wandering up and down, tormented or tormenting. When I left hospital with Saoirse for the first time, feeling vulnerable and institutionalized, I came face to face with a man who was hanging around outside the hospital telling everyone how he liked raping and killing young girls. I've not been back since.

This morning the corridors are relatively quiet. It's early in the hospital day, and the floors still gleam.

Katrina Erskine meets us after my scan in the fetal medicine unit. She is as petite and efficient as she appeared on the television. She has a brisk but friendly manner, and more than anything I like her confidence. She orders blood tests and urine samples and looks at my last bloods.

'Your iron levels are very good. I'm not going to put you on tablets yet – just eat more chocolate.'

How can you not love a doctor who tells you this?

'Chocolate? Really?'

'Yes – and red wine.'

This just keeps getting better.

'Did you see that ridiculous article in the paper the other day?' Katrina asks her attending registrar. He shakes his head.

'Someone's done a study on about twenty women who admitted to drinking during pregnancy and from that small sample they have concluded that even one glass of wine can damage your unborn baby. Ridiculous,' she snorts.

'Why do you think it's not true?' I ask, genuinely interested. Having quaffed my way through my first pregnancy, despite the guilt I felt every time the *Daily Mail* decreed that pregnant women who have so much as a rum 'n' raisin ice-cream might as well abort, I am always keen to hear evidence that moderate drinking is good for you. 'Is it just the fact that it was a small sample group?'

'No, it's more that the women they questioned were heavy drinkers who probably lied about how much they continued to drink during pregnancy, therefore skewing the findings. If they said they had one glass a day and then their babies turned out to have fetal alcohol syndrome, the doctors concluded that one drink can harm your baby.'

I hope she's right.

Katrina is careful with her predictions, but seems sure that everything will be all right. I am anxious to talk about when these babies might be delivered. I've already decided that I want an elective C-section, having read about a woman who tried to give birth to triplets vaginally and ended up being rushed into theatre with the consultant's hand up her uterus trying to drag the third one out. No thanks. Plus I had to have a C-section with Saoirse in the end, so it seems unlikely that I will be able to deliver them myself even if I wanted to. If I am having a C-section then we can choose the date. I'd like to do that today so that I can start to plan things.

'I get all my triplet mums to thirty-four weeks,' she smiles. I like a challenge, and I think she senses that. 'Having said that, they might have other plans, and they could come earlier, so I'd like to give you a steroid shot at twenty-four weeks to help mature the babies' lungs.'

'And if they don't come that early, then do you repeat the steroids?'

'Some do, but I haven't seen any evidence that repeating the shot has any added benefits. So no, I wouldn't repeat.'

'So, thirty-four weeks . . . That will be . . . May . . . the 13th? I can't have them then, it's a Friday!' I say, suddenly superstitious.

'Well, we won't book it now, we'll see how you are at thirty-four weeks and if everything is OK we might go a little bit longer.'

Thirty-four weeks. That's three months away. I'll never make it. I'm exhausted and fit to burst already.

'We'll see you every two weeks to check your blood pressure and scan you – you know about TTTS? Good – but in the meantime, if you have any concerns at any time, then please don't hesitate to come in and be checked out. There's always someone here.'

We leave feeling immensely reassured. We are in safe hands. She's even delivered triplets before – at least two sets from what I could make out. I hope she delivers them. At last it looks like there will be some continuity of care. What I hated about the antenatal visits in my first pregnancy was that every time you went you saw somebody different. There was no sense of being looked after or looked out for.

Back home I decide to measure my bump. I'm already straining at the limits of my maternity clothes. It measures a massive forty-eight inches – with three months to go. How will I ever get any bigger? Where will it all go? I jump online and order something called a Belly Bra. It's a ridiculous lycra vest with a thick band of supportive elastic to hold the bump in place. Even if it doesn't do much in the way of support, it will at least cover the bottom half of my gut, which hangs out from underneath every bit of maternity clothing I can find – even the really big things. No one makes clothes to cover triplet bumps – apart from Milletts, the tent people.

Still, no stretch marks so far. People keep recommending all sorts of weird potions and creams for evading the angry purple stripes a lot of women get as their bump gets bigger – everything from Vitamin E cream to semen.

I dread to think what I weigh. Time for another Belgian bun.

Monday 14 February – Valentine's Day

No candlelit dinner for us tonight. What's the point in going out for a candlelit dinner when you can't drink, eating gives you acid reflux and the only vaguely romantic attire you have left at your disposal is a satin duvet cover? It never usually bothers me, Valentine's Day. I've always rather pitied the poor, embarrassed and monosyllabic couples you see sitting uncomfortably opposite each other in restaurants, and have always suspected that only couples who are not really getting on make the effort to go out in lieu of real intimacy. But tonight I feel a bit sorry for myself. Alex and Maddy are here for half term, and I have a bunch of slightly dead delphiniums which Rich bought me after they nagged him all day, so the atmosphere is quite jolly. But I wish we were away on a mini-break in Rome, or Florence, or even Barcelona. Fat chance.

To cheer myself up, I start my search for the triplet buggy of my dreams. I will not be housebound once these babies are born. I have seen pictures of an inline triplet stroller on an American website. It's called an Inglesina Trio Domino and it looks very smart indeed. It takes children from newborns to around three years of age. Perfect. I'll be able to either put all three in while Rich pushes Saoirse, or, if on my own, have one baby in a sling on my front while Saoirse rides at the front of the triple buggy with the other two behind her. I did briefly consider getting a quad pushchair but abandoned that after working out that it wouldn't go through the front door. I could get all four in it, but we'd only be able to walk around the kitchen.

I look up the buggy online. All of the websites advertising it are either in the USA or Italy, it being an Italian product. I email my details to the Inglesina website requesting details of shipping. I also approach an American firm who quote around $700 for the buggy and a further $400 for shipping and import duties. Then they tell me they have none in stock. They are also advertising another triplet stroller called a Runabout. It is hideous. It's made of white plastic and features hard plastic chairs in bright red or blue. It looks like a customized tandem bike being ridden by some pranksters on a Christian 'Fun Day'. I wouldn't be seen dead with it. You might as well put banners and whistles on and push it around the park shouting 'Look at us, we're not normal!' No, the Trio Domino, with its retro Silver Cross chassis and its Italian elegance is the one for me. But where to find it?

Tuesday 15 February

I check my emails hoping for word from Inglesina. Nothing. I note the phone number and practise my rubbish Italian in case no one there speaks English. I have become obsessed. I will have my Trio Domino.

I dial the number and it rings.

'*Pronto?*' says a brisk-sounding woman.

'*Buon giorno,*' I stutter, not even sure you say this on the phone. '*Parla Inglese?*'

'*No,*' comes the sullen reply. OK.

'*Mi piace un Trio Domino. Ma abito in Londra—*' I trail off here, not knowing where to go and hoping she will fill in the blanks with the number of a supplier in the UK. There is silence on the end of the line.

'*Non e possibile qui?*' I venture.

She takes a deep breath and babbles something, the gist of which seems to be that I should email them.

'*Si, ma no responde,*' I offer, feeling like a character in the Italian version of 'Mind Your Language'.

'*Non e subito,*' I think she replies, meaning 'It won't be straight away.'

I hang up and sulk. They will reply to me when they are good and ready.

Not even the priest has returned my call.

A few buns later, more research reveals that the reason none of the shops I have contacted have one in stock is that the Inglesina does not meet with certain British safety criteria, the details of which are sketchy, so it is not licensed for sale here. What's so wrong with it that we can't get it in the UK? Does it have electric sockets and a water fountain wired into its canopy? Does the shopping well contain a tank of piranhas? Perhaps this is the true meaning of the 'Nanny State'. I'm beginning to think that the triple buggy does not exist. It's like the Loch Ness Monster – everyone talks about it but no one's ever actually seen it . . .

Wednesday 23 February

Our second appointment with Katrina Erskine. We sit in the packed waiting room for over an hour. Wednesday is the diabetes clinic so she is fitting me in as a special patient here, but there is no sign of her. I start to panic. I don't want to have to go through it all again.

Eventually a woman calls us in. She explains that she will be seeing us today if that's OK.

'Not really,' I grumble. I am very disappointed. 'Where is Katrina?' But it's pointless moaning – this isn't the Portland after all.

We go through the routine questions and I am still unhappy. I am surly and unhelpful. The doctor calls in another doctor who says that he is very sorry Katrina is not here but she has had to rush off to keep an appointment for an ongoing problem with her arm and that she will definitely be here next time. I am placated and I waddle off down the corridor again having a quiet little cry. I am a big fat sad duck.

In the car I switch my phone back on and there's a message from Davina, whom I have not been in touch with for some time.

'Oh. My. God,' she says. So she's heard.

'Triplets. That is *incredible*. You are so blessed and that is so amazing! You're going to have three gorgeous babies. And as a present I am going to send you a maternity nanny for a week when you get out of hospital. Ring me straight back – I want to know *everything*!'

I wonder if people who do lovely things like this ever know how much they can turn your day – your *year* – around?

I call her back and her enthusiasm makes me feel so happy. I realize that all the problems of the referral, trying to find out what we are entitled to in terms of help (nothing) and the physical demands of being pregnant with three have meant that I haven't really thought much about the babies at the end of it all. Now I'm crying in the car because it just suddenly feels bloody brilliant.

★

My mood lifted, we head off to Queen Charlotte's Hospital in West London for a talk organized by the Multiple Births Foundation – a charity that aims to help people expecting twins or more. These sessions are run once a month and I booked this weeks ago in the deep dark depths of January when I was still scared witless. I feel quite excited now that we are here. We're late – of course. The journey to West London takes a good hour and a half. I note – not for the first time – that we could have been in Birmingham in the same time. When we arrive everyone is just sitting down and a lady is standing in front of a slide projector. I scan the room to get a good look at my fellow multiple mums. There are about thirty couples sipping tea nervously from plastic cups. What hits me first of all is how old everyone is. At thirty-nine I'm already what the NHS charmingly refer to as a geriatric mother, but I am probably among the youngest here. There is a lot of greying hair and quite a few receding hairlines dotted about the place. Perhaps this is a Saga holiday meeting and we're about to see slides of Madeira in May. Why is everyone so old?

Then I realize that, just like me, these women have left their childbearing until late in life. This decision has a knock-on effect on fertility in one of several ways. Firstly, some of the women will have discovered that their eggs are now past their sell-by date. A woman's egg quality is generally said to deteriorate rapidly after the age of thirty-five. IVF or fertility drugs to promote ovulation are the usual first ports of call in such situations, and with clinics implanting two (and sometimes three) embryos the chances of conceiving twins are higher. Secondly, for those lucky enough not to have fertility or egg-quality issues, multi-ovulation is more common in older women. So basically once you're past your mid-thirties you'll either be almost infertile and need help to conceive or you'll ovulate loads and have several babies all at once. Or something. That's my understanding of what I've read and it's certainly borne out here tonight.

The second thing that strikes me is how white and middle class it is. I ponder for a few minutes on this. Don't black and/ or working class people have multiple births? Of course they do. Then why aren't they here? The answer must lie in the cultural predilection of middle-class people towards support groups. Although open to everyone, perhaps it's only middle-class people who have the time and the information network in place to access the support on offer? Or perhaps the fact that many of these couples will have undergone expensive fertility treatment to get this far means that evenings like this will necessarily be full of quite well-off people? I wish I could do a quick survey.

I start to wriggle in my uncomfortable plastic chair as the lady starts her talk. She is warm and calm, and everyone sits in good-mannered silence as she shows us some lovely slides of triplets, twins, the odd set of quads. I wonder if anyone here is having quads? How exciting. I am *so* uncomfortable now. I get up and squeeze along the row. This room is full of some of the most pregnant women I have ever seen and yet the seats are hard and the rows tightly packed together. I stand at the back of the room trying to stretch my poor aching back. It is crippling me. I can no longer sit or stand still for more than a few minutes at a time. I feel like a cat that is trying to decide which sofa to sit on. How is everyone managing to sit so still, even the really pregnant ones?

I notice a much younger woman in front of me who also looks quite uncomfortable. So it's not just me. Maybe everyone else is in agony but too polite to get up.

At the end of the talk two women and a man are introduced to us as having just had multiples. The women both have twins and the man is the proud dad of two-year-old triplets. I peer at him with huge interest. He is a rare species – a father of triplets. How does he look? Normal. Exhausted? Not really. Mad? Not at all. The three say they will answer as many questions as they can. I bombard the triplet dad.

'We're having triplets and I just wanted to ask you – what gestation were yours born at, and did you put them in a routine and were they in special care at all and where did you get a triple buggy because I've never even seen one and the only ones I can find are in Italy or America and how did you make the feeds up – all at once or one at a time like they advise on the tin?'

The poor guy looks punch-drunk but answers me with much humour and a mine of useful information, all of which I instantly forget. The one nugget I remember is: 'Buy a tea urn. That way you can have hot water on the boil all day for the bottles.' It's not much, but it's something to hang on to. I think I might buy a samovar and pretend I'm in a Chekhov play instead. 'I want to go to bed' can be my refrain.

It's coffee and mingle time so I approach the young woman in front of me. 'When are your babies due?' I ask.

'Well, officially June, but I'm having triplets so—'

'You're having triplets? So am I!' I cry. I am torn between being delighted and slightly ruffled that I'm not the only one here. Maybe there's loads of us, and I'm not so special after all.

'Were yours natural?' I ask, hating myself for the competitiveness and nosiness I am feeling.

'Yes,' she smiles.

Blimey. So I really am not the only one. Not that special after all.

'Clomid,' says the woman's husband. 'She just took one course and bang – triplets.'

'Great,' I smile. Natural? With Clomid, the ovulation stimulation drug? I don't think so. I think you'll find that is assisted conception. Hurrah! I am the winner. But perhaps there are other triplet mums here?

'Ah! I see you've found each other!' says the slide-show woman. 'Our two sets of triplets here tonight.'

Yes! I really am the winner!

Pathetic, I know, but if you can't get a bit of cachet out of being so bloody huge and uncomfortable, what can you get?

Thursday 24 February

The Belly Bra arrives. It doesn't seem to help very much but at least my nethers are now covered. I also receive a second support mechanism – bought in a bidding frenzy on eBay – which consists of a series of hardcore industrial-strength elastic strips that criss-cross over my belly and are attached to a sort of back brace. It probably has its fans among the S & M community, but to me it looks hideous. I stare longingly at my leopard-print thongs as I slip into something more comfortable.

I meet with a documentary maker called Paula, a lovely chirpy Scouser. She is interested in making a film about my pregnancy and the birth. We sit in the plush cocktail bar of the Soho Hotel and I sip water like the good girl I am having to be. I am a bit anxious about sticking my head into the mouth of the reality TV lion, especially when I spot Rebecca Loos in the bar, Paula's next appointment. I don't really relish the prospect of being on the telly because of something random that has happened to me, but I suppose having triplets might be a slightly more savoury reason than having shagged David Beckham.

We talk about the type of programme I would like to make.

'I don't want to be interviewed with Richard sitting on a sofa holding hands,' I say. I use this image as shorthand for the kind of tear-jerking American baby doccos I am addicted to on Discovery Health. I love them, but I don't want to be in one.

'Oh God, no,' says Paula. 'We'll make a fun film.'

Later that day I email her asking about the possibility of getting free things for the babies on the back of a TV deal. I've already asked Anita at my literary agency.

I get an email back.

'Anita says that with a Jew and a Scouser like me on the blag for you, you'll definitely get a load of freebies.'

Maybe it's worth doing after all.

Friday 25 February

An idle search on the Internet throws up a fascinating fact. Apparently, in 1849 a woman in Soho, London, gave birth to triplets. Although rare, this wasn't totally unheard of, but it was quite unusual for a woman of her class to produce three live children all at once and survive it herself. News of the birth somehow reached Queen Victoria, who was so impressed that she set up a royal fund for families who had triplets. Each family was to receive £300 (on receipt of proof that all had been born alive and well) to enable parents 'to meet the sudden expenses thrown upon them' (according to a letter of instruction to palace officials). The fund was called the Queen's Bounty. I wonder if it is still available. I quite like the idea of the Queen buying us a few nappies. She could pay for half of a buggy. However, I read on a bit more and discover that because the value of the Bounty has 'so greatly declined' the Queen has decided to cease the money payment and just send a congratulatory letter instead. Great. Maybe I can wipe the babies' bums with it.

Saturday 5 March

It is the International Women's Day show at the Hackney Empire and I am booked to do a tight fifteen-minute set. I turn the house upside down looking for a tent top I had during my last pregnancy. It is the only half-decent thing I have to wear. The show is being hosted by Jo Brand, and is sold out. Fifteen hundred people in the beautifully refurbished Victorian theatre.

When I first moved to London, a bovver-boot-wearing dyke, I used to tear tickets at the Empire so it holds a very special place in my heart. I want to look like I've made a bit of an effort. Eventually I find the top, and we head out for the night, Saoirse safely tucked up at my parents' house.

In the dressing room there is none of the usual showing off and psyching out of the normal comedy club mixed bill. Tonight all the performers are women, so I sit with Jo and Brenda Gilhooley, chatting about motherhood. We laugh about how, as mothers, we have changed our priorities and no longer stress about work so much.

'How long are you doing?' asks Brenda, slipping into her Page Three Stunna blonde wig.

'Fifteen – but I might only do ten,' I say. It's been a while since I played a crowd this big and I might bomb.

'Yeah, me too,' she says.

'Yeah, let's get home,' says Jo.

There's a brief pause then Jo starts laughing. 'Listen to us! If this was a group of male comics you'd have to drag them all off with a hook! It'd be all "Yeah, I stormed it tonight – I did forty". And we're all "I should get home really . . ."'

She tells a great story about a moderately successful but now out of fashion stand-up who did reasonably well at a gig, but kept going back to do encores despite the audience's growing indifference.

'Fantastic. Four encores,' he boasted, as he came off.

'No, you just went back on four times. That's different,' said Jo.

It's showtime, and I'm booked to close the first half. A couple of newish women are on before me and they do OK, but the audience sounds a bit bored. Fifteen hundred people is a lot, but I've always felt more comfortable with a huge crowd than a small one. Maybe it's the intimacy phobic in me. I hope this goes OK. I'm feeling huge and vulnerable, but I know that audiences smell fear on you, and any whiff of it will result in comedic death.

I walk onto the stage and start my act. I have written something especially for this evening about expecting triplets, and I get a huge hit of adrenalin as I announce my news.

Have you ever heard fifteen hundred people all gasp at once? It's quite something. From the moment I tell them I am having triplets it goes brilliantly, and I leave the stage to thunderous applause. Afterwards I try to work out whether I was actually any good or if it was my shocking and unique triplet calling card that did the job for me. Then I decide that I don't care. It is the last gig I have booked in before the babies come, and I loved it.

Monday 14 March

I've written a piece for the *Daily Express* about expecting triplets. They're not even born yet and they are already quite a cottage industry. Tonight I have to have my photo taken in a studio somewhere in Docklands. I turn up not knowing what the hell they are going to put me in. The photographer is shocked at my size, and the stylist quickly shoves some of the more slinky maternity outfits into the corner. There is no way I will get into anything remotely fitted. We decide on a lovely stretchy outfit in bright green. I look like the missing fifth teletubby, but never mind. I refuse to adopt the usual blissed-out-stroking-my-belly pose that is the staple of any article about pregnancy, preferring instead to straddle a microphone stand and yell punk lyrics. It's not quite what they are expecting, but they seem pleased enough at the end. I feel great during the shoot. It's nice to wear some gorgeous things despite my size. I've not really been bothering with my clothes, hair or make-up recently. When you're the size of a housing estate what's the point? But now I know why very fat women still wear make-up and nice dresses. Just because you're big it doesn't mean you can't feel nice about yourself and make a bit of an effort. Then I catch sight of a discarded Polaroid the photographer has left lying around.

Bloody hell.

I look like a hippo in drag.

Wednesday 16 March

We have bought a horrible great people carrier off eBay. It seats eight people, so even when Alex and Madeleine are here we will all fit in it – six kids, two adults, four travel cots, a single and a triple buggy for that dreamed-about road trip to France. It's beige, with a dirty grey interior. It is not a thing of beauty, but it is massive as it lurches heavily and lumpenly along the road.

I know how it feels.

Monday 21 March

Saoirse and I go to Davina's for lunch. She has got masses of baby stuff to give me, including two bouncy chairs, a beautiful oak cot bed, a high chair, loads of clothes and a baby sling. I am overwhelmed by her generosity and her enthusiasm. We sit on the floor and talk all things baby. She already has two lovely girls but is desperate for more.

'We're going to go again next year, probably. I really want twins. I'd love a big family,' she says, stroking my belly.

'Look, girls,' she says to her young daughters, Holly and Tilly. 'Jackie's got *three* babies in there!'

Holly's eyes are wide with surprise.

I spot three little baby dolls on the floor and we try to place them all on my belly to see how they are all fitting in. We estimate that the babies, now at roughly twenty-six weeks' gestation, are probably about the size of the dollies so it's quite shocking. It must be very crowded in there.

The girls play together while Davina and I wander in the garden. She is attentive and instinctively walks at my pace, holding my elbow when we go down some stairs. I am so slow these days that I often find myself shouting after Rich as he marches ahead of me in the park, so it's nice to feel looked after like this. We all go for a swim in the pool, me lowering myself into the water like a huge steamer on her maiden voyage. The weightlessness I feel makes me want to weep with gratitude. I am finding it so hard to walk, bend or even sit, and here I am bouncing Saoirse up and down, floating and kicking my legs up with no effort whatsoever. Maybe I should get a big tank installed in the garden and live in it until May. I could become a circus sideshow – the Beached Whale Lady – and we could charge a fiver entrance.

It's dark by the time I leave, the car full of donations. As I drive home, I reflect on how this extraordinary event that is taking place inside me is putting me in touch with so much goodness. There are so many people out there who are so willing to help, so keen to respond to the needs of others. Sean and Anoushka want to buy us a dishwasher. My sister Maggie is planning to take a week's holiday to help us out when the babies are here. Al has offered to help us with the loft conversion costs. The women at my parents' church are knitting and saying rosaries for us. I feel full of the milk of human kindness.

Easter Sunday

I am a great big fat Easter egg. At Mum and Dad's, all the assembled children are given egg decorating kits which include green jelly icing pens. I pull up my top and they gleefully set about painting a big face on my belly. At least *they're* having fun. I am finding it increasingly hard to breathe, and I am exhausted from the effort of trying to sleep. In a fit of nesting, I have made Rich move all the beds around again, a job which involves a lot of dismantling, huffing and puffing, and a large dose of cursing thrown in. We are now sleeping in the smallest room, my small double bed squashed into the corner. I have four pillows propping me up because I have started to panic that I can't breathe in the night, and because the flatter I lie the more the bile rises up in my throat. The heartburn is getting really bad now. I spend the night trying to turn over (which takes about five minutes of gasping, heaving and swearing with the pain) so that I can grab the Gaviscon and swig from it. It is aniseed-flavoured and it makes me retch, but it gives me a couple of hours of relief from my stomach acid, which seems to be now positioned somewhere in my chest. I am so tired at night after a day full of pain and general ungainliness, but the minute I get into bed the torture really begins. My heart rate has soared. I place my head on the pillow at night and I can hear it pumping furiously. I take my pulse and it is around the 120 b.p.m. mark – roughly twice its normal sixty. I often feel like I'm going to have a heart attack, and have to take deep breaths to calm down.

'That's normal,' Katrina assured me at my last check-up. 'Your body is carrying so much extra blood that your heart and lungs are having to do a lot of extra work.'

I'll say.

At my fortnightly scans I have to stop myself from screaming at them when they ask me to lie down.

'I can't lie flat,' I explain calmly, 'because I can't breathe.'

'It'll only be for a few minutes,' they'll often say.

'Right, so I'll just die then, in those few minutes, shall I?' I want to say. Instead I try to do as they ask, until they realize just how hard it is for me. It's like having a wet Labrador sitting on your chest. Or so I imagine. I gamely try to lower myself to a prone position but give up half way down and get Rich to pull me back up again. Pillows are fetched from other rooms and they always say 'Gosh, yes, that does look uncomfortable' like I might have been having them on. Far from enjoying the contact with the babies, I have started to dread the frequent scans. It sometimes takes ages because the babies move around a lot, and in order to keep proper tabs on their individual development they have to be sure who is where. One nice young sonographer drew a little diagram of three tadpole-like creatures in a row and labelled them 'Triplet one, two and three' so that we could be sure who was who. The babies, however, have decided not to play ball and often reshuffle between appointments. There follows a game of 'join-the-limbs' while the consultant tries to match legs to torsos, bodies to heads. My womb looks like a family bucket of KFC.

Saturday 2 April

I have been reading too much again. The triplet connection website is full of stories of women going into pre-term labour. One poor girl has been holding on, desperately trying to get her babies to the viable twenty-four-week mark. She was on several different aggressive anti-labour drugs but to no avail. Her mother-in-law has been posting her story, and yesterday, at twenty-two weeks, she gave birth to three boys. They only lived for a couple of minutes each. Tears splash onto the keyboard as I read her story. My own womb has started to feel very weird indeed. It keeps going really hard. I am pretty sure that these are just Braxton Hicks (or Branston Hicks as one confused young woman once said to me) – the so-called practice contractions designed to get the uterus ready for action later on – but they are pretty painful now, and are coming quite early. Last time I didn't get them until the end. I'm only about six months pregnant and already the pain takes my breath away. I start to worry.

'Maybe I should go in to the hospital to get checked out,' I say.

'Come on then. Let's go,' says Rich, packing us all into the car.

I hate making a fuss, but they did say to come in if I had any doubts at all. Even so, I feel like a hysterical woman crying wolf.

Up in the labour ward the midwives are chatting around their desk.

'Hello – I'm expecting triplets and I'm having a lot of painful tightenings. I'm twenty-eight weeks and I'd like someone to monitor me,' I say.

They all gasp, and someone is sent off to find a twin monitor. A nurse puts us in a delivery room and tries to strap a fetal monitor to me. It's almost impossible – the belt won't fit around me and it keeps picking up different heartbeats. In the end it is decided that they will just monitor me for contractions. We watch the squiggly line printing out on the paper roll. There are a few little peaks and troughs, but nothing too dramatic.

'That's just where the babies are moving,' says the midwife. 'Nothing to worry about.'

A young black guy in a trendy tracksuit wanders in pushing a portable scanning machine. I assume he is a hunky porter.

'Hi, I'm the obstetrician on call today. I'd just like to do a quick scan to check they're all OK in there,' he says.

He is absolutely gorgeous and I have to pull my top up and show him my ludicrous belly. He warms his hands before placing them on me.

'Great service,' I twinkle. He smiles mildly and squirts goo onto my bump.

He struggles to find three distinct heartbeats because the machinery is only really designed for one baby, but he sees that all three are fine and showing no signs of distress. We are relieved.

'Sorry to waste your time,' I mutter.

'Not at all. You must come in if you are in any doubt. That's what we're here for,' he smiles.

Back in the car, Rich does a very cruel and very funny impression of me batting my eyelids at the doctor.

'*Ooh, great service, doctor! Sorry for wasting your time, doctor!*' he minces. 'What are you like?'

I laugh, but I'm a bit embarrassed. I keep forgetting that I'm massively pregnant with triplets and can't enter into the normal, harmless sexual banter with attractive men. In my mind's eye, I'm still a foxy nymphette.

I probably frightened him to death. He'll probably never have sex again.

Sunday 10 April

Waist measurement – 51 inches. Puddings and sweets eaten – 2 x apple pie with custard, 1 x Galaxy family bar, 5 x Cadbury's Celebrations

★

Today I am extremely grumpy. I'm sure that even if Gordon Ramsay were to ride up on a Harley offering to cook me dinner alfresco in Sardinia this evening I'd tell him to stick his grilled lobster supper right up his arse. Richard is off on a food hygiene course today because he sometimes cooks for a fantastic charity called The Food Chain which provides meals on wheels for people living with HIV and AIDS. Normally I applaud him. Today it just annoys me because I won't even get any leftover crumble when he gets back, and he is leaving me in sole charge of our eighteen-month-old daughter and two fat dogs. I can still just about get behind the steering wheel, so I go to Mum and Dad's – it's good to get a new audience to moan at from time to time. Mum is always very attentive and sympathetic, offering me hot-water bottles (her cure-all) and insisting on putting Saoirse in and out of the car seat, even though she has no idea how the hideous buckle clips work. Instead of feeling soothed by all this, I find myself even more irritable as I watch her battling with the safety belt, completely clueless. Poor Mum is half blind and seventy-four, and yet I still have to sit on the urge to shout 'Oh just get out of the way and let me do it myself!' I am a complete witch at the moment. Dad's rickety old car broke down yesterday and may be destined for the scrap heap. So it looks as though we will have to take the mountain to Mahomet and pack all four infants into the petrol-guzzling MPV to get help from my parents. That's what you get for having your kids so late in life – elderly grandparents.

I am grumpy and sullen the whole day, huffing and puffing from one uncomfortable position to the next, not even brightening when Mum and I sit down to the task of sorting through the mountain of baby clothes people have given me. I say 'given' – one friend has donated a sack full of clothes only to announce that she'd like them back at a later date. I hate it when people do that – how am I supposed to keep track of who once owned what? I've got piles and piles of identical little vests, milky-smelling sleep suits and London water-hardened towelling all-in-ones and she wants to make sure she gets hers back! The house looks like a disaster-appeal centre. She'll just have to come round in a year's time and rake through the sick-stained pile herself. I'm sure I'll be past caring by then. I wouldn't mind but she's a single parent, thirty-nine and not even seeing anyone so the chances of her needing the bloody baby clothes again are remote.

Feeling too peevish and ungrateful to benefit from the parental bosom, I bundle Saoirse into the car again and come home only to find the house empty. A quick phone call reveals that Richard has decided to 'wait for us' down the pub. Bugger. I resist the urge to moan on the phone, nor do I bid him a breezy goodbye, instead settling for the halfway house of an unimpressed tone and a speedy hang-up.

'Can I get you anything?' he asks sweetly, when he turns up half an hour later smelling of lager.

'A new life!' I bark.

'You'll be getting one of those in four weeks' time, ducky!'

'Yes, an even shittier one,' I grumble.

Most days I try to make the best of it, but some days – like today – I am overwhelmed with a sense of doom and depression. What have we done? I'm half wishing the weeks away so that I can at last sleep on my back, my front, my side and not get exhausted just going from the sofa to the fridge, and half digging my heels into time itself, hoping to put the brakes on the inevitable slide into triplet newborn chaos.

These last weeks are the hardest, apparently. Maybe it's nature's way of making you grateful for the relative luxury of being woken not by searing pain but by the simple newborn cry. One poor woman on an American website is only twenty-four weeks with triplets and already up to her pain threshold. 'Is there anything I can do?' she plaintively asked. 'Toughen up. It gets worse,' came the unanimous reply. It is cold comfort, this triplet mum camaraderie. But at least you get the feeling that these women really know what you're going through. Much as Rich is sympathetic and concerned, I sometimes get the feeling he has started to zone out when I tell him for the hundredth time that I can't breath and my spine is killing me.

'Is it, ducky? Oh dear,' he says, flicking between the golf and some crap black-and-white movie he's found on TCM.

I snap.

'Yes, it is. You know, I wish just for one day you could experience what this is like!'

'So do I, duck. If I could do it for you, I would.'

'You have no idea. Imagine strapping four stone of bones and blubber to your middle and tying it so tightly that it squishes all your internal organs up to the point of failure, then having someone stamp up and down on your spine in hobnail boots for an hour, then being asked to run a marathon in high altitude after no sleep.'

'Right—'

'*That's* what it feels like to be me!'

'Ooh, not nice, ducky.'

They say on the net that relationships are put under enormous pressure after a multiple birth. Many couples split up because it's just too stressful, and in striving to cope with the hard work and exhaustion of it all they forget why they were ever together in the first place. The men just can't cope and leave. One woman posted a desperately sad story last week. After five failed IVF attempts she got pregnant with quads and both she and her husband were shocked but thrilled. Over the next six weeks, however, one by one the embryos died, until by week sixteen of her pregnancy her womb was once again empty. Her husband promptly left her, saying he 'couldn't handle all the death and stuff'. Now I'm normally of the 'Hey, you can never judge other people's relationships' school of thought, but in this instance I just thought, 'Spineless bastard.' Other web posts abound with stories of rock-solid marriages breaking down under the strain of having several small babies all at once. And it's always the men that leave. I've told Richard that he has no more right to leave than I do. We've agreed that if things get really tough we'll race each other to the door.

Wednesday 13 April

Filming has begun. Julie, our director, and Caron, her assistant, have descended with a film crew to follow the 4D scan I have booked at a private clinic in Harley Street. The professor, Stuart Campbell, has pioneered a way of seeing babies in utero in much more detail than the normal 2D ultrasound scans. His four dimensions are made up of a 3D image that moves. I have seen footage of his work and it is amazing just seeing one baby in 4D – three is going to be incredible. Except all I am concerned about when we arrive is that all three babies are still alive. I haven't felt one of them move all day and I have started to get worried, mainly, I think, because we have a crew with us and I don't want to find out something awful in front of them.

I hoist myself up onto the table and Professor Campbell asks me to lie down. I explain that I can't, so I am wedged in a half-sitting position.

'Can you just make sure everything is OK?' I whimper.

'Yes, of course,' he says, his soft Scottish accent instantly reassuring. 'Yes, all fine,' he says, after flicking the probe over my enormous belly.

At this point, the screen is just showing a regular 2D black-and-white image. I see heads, eye sockets, feet, a spine. Then he flicks a switch on the monitor and the screen turns sepia. I see a perfect image of an angelic face pointing towards the camera. This is Baby Number One. He has a curly mouth and his eyes are tightly shut. A small chubby fist is resting on his cheek. The surface of his skin looks like it has recently been moulded with craft clay – almost as if you can still see the thumb prints. The Prof shoots around my womb giving us amazing images of the babies. It's surreal. Now they look like babies. And there's three of them.

'Look – here're the two boys, a great juxtaposition of face against bottom there!' he says.

'Your face, my arse!' I say, inappropriately crude at such an electric moment. I am trying to distance myself from the over-whelming awe of it all.

'And here's the little girl . . . and she looks rather beautiful,' he says.

'I bet you say that to all the girls,' I say.

'No, not at all,' he smiles.

'Really? Do you ever look at a baby and think "This one's a bit of a minger"?'

'Well . . . I suppose so, not that I'd say it!' he laughs.

We get a video to take home. The secretary has written 'Baby Clune' on the label, unused to the need for a plural. I watch it five times over the next two days. I can't believe it. Three little putty babies with perfect cupid's bow mouths and big cherub cheeks. So different from the skeletal blobs you see on an ordinary scan. Has it helped me come to terms with the fact that I am having triplets? Not really. My brain is not allowing me to know that yet. I don't think it will until I am watching them leave home.

Tuesday 19 April

We have so much stuff to get. I am the shopper in the household and I have been either so ill or so huge that I cannot walk more than a hundred yards without the pain or the breathlessness forcing me to sit down. I don't like Internet shopping because I like to have a feel of things before I buy them, so we are woefully underprepared. We have no cots, no buggy, no car seats, no hospital toiletries, no bottles, nothing. I organize a trip to a huge shopping mall with Lou. We leave Harry and Saoirse at home and head off in search of a mobility scooter. As luck would have it, there is a shop where you can hire a sort of old lady's trolley on a motorized base for ten quid.

I snap it up and pretty soon I am whizzing around the mall having a great time. I feel so liberated. I love to shop — I once spent three entire days working my way around a mall in Texas — but it has been impossible since Christmas. I don't care how ridiculous I look, and I don't mind the odd stares I am getting when I park it outside an inaccessible shop and waddle in.

'I think I'm getting some dirty looks,' I say to Lou. 'Like people think I shouldn't be using it if I'm not permanently disabled.'

'I could always fall to my knees and shout "Praise the Lord! It's a miracle!" if you like,' says Lou.

We buy tiny little premature baby vests which look like they should be for dollies. I have to find an outfit for Thursday — Donna Air, one of my best mates since we co-starred in *The Vagina Monologues* then fell pregnant in the same week (that kind of thing makes for a superglue bond among girls), has organized a swanky baby shower party for me at the Soho Hotel and I literally have nothing to wear. I have seriously considered getting a nice duvet cover from John Lewis and cutting a hole out for my head. Lou takes me to a posh maternity shop where I try on about twenty outfits, but even the Extra Large ones look too small. My bump is massive. It defies gravity. Out of habit, I turn to the side to see how I look in profile and keep bursting out laughing. I have avoided full-length mirrors for a few weeks now. It's too shocking. In the end, I settle for a stretchy trouser and swirly dress combo. There is a pregnant mannequin in the shop. I stand next to it and we laugh.

'That's what I look like when I'm *not* pregnant!' I say.

The film crew follow us around and we get freebies from

various shops when they realize my freakish belly is to be on telly. It's a full two hours before I'm tired and want to go home. These days, two hours out of the house is like a three-week holiday. I feel great as I park my disabled chariot and squeeze back into the car.

This is probably my last shopping trip for a while.

Thursday 21 April

The baby shower. I arrive at the Soho Hotel and am ushered up to an amazingly swish apartment. Tiny sandwiches, bottles of champagne and a huge tray of cakes sit awaiting my guests. Donna has done a great job. We have invited about twenty friends and family, mainly as something for the documentary people to film that isn't just me sitting at home moaning.

One by one the ladies arrive.

Davina walks in and falls to her knees in front of my belly. 'You are amazing,' she says.

Jenny Eclair arrives. 'Oh my God. You look like a freak show. I mean, you look amazing but you look like a freak show. You're massive! And why are you sitting in between Donna and Davina, those two skinny birds? Where's Jo Brand when you need her?'

It's a very jolly afternoon, and I am showered with lovely bits and bobs for the babies. Most gifts come in threes – three sets of goatskin bootees from Wen, three knitted hats from Jenny, three soft crib toys from Davina, three sets of pyjamas from Olivia, etc. – and it's still a shock to think I will need them all.

Everyone is amazed that I am still out and about at thirty-weeks pregnant with triplets. I tell them that this is my last planned day out. This day has been a goal for some time. 'If I can just hold on until the baby shower,' I have been telling myself. 'Then it will all be OK.'

Back home I'm in bed by 8 p.m., exhausted and happy. I have made it. My diary is now clear. I am ready for these babies. They can come any time they like now.

Saturday 23 April

I am still shattered from my busy week, and this morning my stomach is tightening a lot. The feeling is quite uncomfortable, and sometimes I think there is cramping too, although it's hard to tell.

'I think I need to go to the hospital,' I say to Rich, who has just sat down to a fry-up and the Saturday papers. He is so used to my panics now that he merely rolls his eyes before getting up to find his car keys.

The labour ward is quiet. It's as if the unborn know it's skeleton staff today. I am ushered into an assessment area and a midwife is sent round to see me.

'Jackie!' she exclaims. It's an ex-girlfriend of a friend of mine from way back in my lesbian past. How weird, for both of us. She flicks through my file and her eyes widen when she reads that I am expecting triplets.

'Triplets! Ooh, you must have been very wicked in a past life, Jackie Clune.'

Thanks a lot. Of all the negative remarks I've had recently

I've never had 'triplets as divine retribution for jumping the sexuality fence'.

A doctor is called in to check me over. She does an internal after monitoring the babies for a while. 'Your cervix is nice and long, no funnelling, and its closed tight so there's no immediate problem,' she says. 'Just try to rest more.'

So these babies aren't coming yet. 'Just hold on to them,' say all the women on the triplet websites. 'A day in the womb is worth a week in an incubator.' It sounds so easy, like 'holding on to them' is a choice you can make. What if my body decides it's had enough? Short of erecting a picket fence around my uterus there'll be no stopping them if things get too tight in there.

Friday 29 April

4 a.m. This is officially hell. I can't sleep, despite falling into bed exhausted. I lie there for ages, heaving myself to and fro trying to stifle the involuntary groans I let out as pain shoots through my body. Eventually, I give up and creep downstairs. I sit in the dark watching the urban foxes rifling through the bins outside. This is a secret time of night. The street is asleep apart from me and the foxes, but instead of enjoying this exclusive club I find myself longing for bedroom lights to flicker on, postmen to come whistling down the road and cars to start up on the school run because then it would signal the morning and I wouldn't have to feel shit about being awake in the middle of the night. I have a glass of milk and a biscuit. The heart burn is awful. My stomach now resides somewhere above

my breastbone, and I can feel any food I eat sitting on my chest. I have developed a major Gaviscon habit, and have taken to swigging it out of the bottle hunched over the sink like a wino. It's foul stuff but it stops my throat from burning. I take my resting heart rate. It's 130 b.p.m., around double what it should be. My internal organs are under a lot of pressure. I feel like my system is breaking down. I don't know how much longer I can go on.

Tuesday 3 May

It's May. At various points during the pregnancy when people have asked me my due date they have met with a rather complicated answer along the lines of 'Well, officially it's June, but they will be early – probably April or May.' But April has been and gone. These will be May babies. I will not be one of the 'twenty-six-weekers' on the web, the unofficial club for women whose babies were born at the margins of viability. I start to relax a bit more. Even if they were to arrive tomorrow, at thirty-two weeks' gestation, the chances are they would be OK.

We go for yet another scan. It's my twentieth so far. At this rate, the babies will be sitting up and waving next time they feel the probe descending. They are the most observed babies in the world. It's like reality TV in there.

'Hop up onto the table,' says today's consultant, Mr Dawson. I give a wry laugh at his use of the term 'hop' and he winces for me as I heave myself up. He tells me that his sister had triplets over thirty years ago and gave birth to them vaginally. Wow.

'I'm having a C-section,' I say.

'Well . . . all three are presenting cephalic today – heads down – so if things stay that way, you could go for a vaginal delivery if you wanted to,' he says. It's tempting, but I know I won't take the risk. I'm too old, too knackered and too sluggish to push three babies out. Best to just unzip me and get them out safe and sound. I couldn't bear it if anything happened to them because I was flattered into trying to be Mother Earth.

'They are measuring very big,' says Mr Dawson. This is a game I have enjoyed so far – guess the weight of the triplets. The computer can estimate the fetal weight by calculating various measurements against gestation. My babies have always been described as 'big'. And he wants me to push three out!

'How much do they weigh today?' asks Rich, who is convinced I'm carrying three ten-pounders.

'Triplets one and two are coming out at around the seven-pound mark . . . and the girl slightly smaller.'

Bloody hell.

'Although these measurements can be about a pound out. It's not an exact science yet.'

We head downstairs to see Katrina, who greets me with jolly hockey sticks enthusiasm. 'You're doing so well!' she says. 'Most women would be on the floor by now'.

I feel proud, but I need her help now if I am to carry on with this pregnancy. 'I need something to help me sleep,' I say. 'I'm exhausted.'

She smiles ruefully at me. 'If this were to go on for a long time I'd say yes, but it's only another couple of weeks. Hang in there!' she says.

I want to stamp on her tiny foot. Two weeks with a huge

bump and a bumptious toddler on no sleep? Waddle a day in my tight shoes before you tell me it's not a long time.

'Well, can we fix a delivery date today then?' I whine. 'It might help me focus.'

'Come and see me on the sixteenth,' she says. 'Then we will decide. You'll be thirty-four weeks plus five days. If everything is OK, we might get you to do another week. I wouldn't let you go beyond thirty-six weeks, but thirty-five plus five would be amazing.'

I'm beginning to feel as though I am a personal challenge for her. Maybe the consultants have a sweepstake going on when my gut will just pop.

'But will I still be able to deliver on the eighteenth, if we don't book it now?' I say, panicking that it's a trick to get me further along.

'Yes, of course, if we think it's the right time. Let's just see how you are,' she twinkles. 'Thirty-four weeks is excellent. You can relax now – you're going to have three babies.'

Sunday 15 May

I sit on the sofa in tears. I can't breathe, eat, sleep, walk, sit down, stand up, stay still, move around. I am in constant pain and I feel drained all the time. I feel as though I have hit a downward curve this weekend. My body is giving up.

'I can't go on,' I cry.

'Don't worry, love,' says Rich, trying to massage my back before I swat him away, unable to even endure touch. 'We'll just tell her tomorrow that it's got to be this Wednesday.'

I'm not convinced. As soon as I walk into her office I know she will fix me with that hockey-mistress challenging stare and before I know it I'll be volunteering for extra practice after school.

To distract me from my suffering – and to give himself a break from my moaning – we go to Meera's for tea and cake. It's a beautiful spring day and Saoirse is oblivious to my suffering, busying herself running around the garden lost in her toddler world of butterflies and apple blossom. She has no idea that her peace is about to be shattered by three screaming interlopers. I could weep for her, but I'm too busy weeping for myself. Forget all that pregnancy bloom stuff – what with the weight gain, the swelling, the wind, the acid heartburn and the constant low-level self-pity, I think I am the least attractive I've ever been.

Monday 16 May

D-day. I try to stride into Katrina's office with a poor imitation of determination.

'How are you?' she asks.

I let her have it, listing all my aches and pains, and my general feeling of unwellness.

'OK,' she says kindly. 'Let's go for this Wednesday, then.'

And it's as simple as that. I was expecting a fight. All of a sudden, I want to backtrack. I want her to persuade me out of it. Maybe this pregnancy's not so bad after all. Maybe I could go another week. Or a month, maybe.

'We'll book you in first thing on Wednesday, but you have

to understand that you might be bumped up if there's an emergency. If not, I'll see you in theatre at around 9.30 a.m. Go home, have a glass of champagne and relax.'

How extraordinary to sit in a calm office and quite casually arrange to have your stomach ripped asunder and be delivered of three babies. Like arranging for a sofa to be dropped off.

We are instructed to come in tomorrow to book a bed and have some last-minute tests done. We get home and I ring around telling people that we are having our babies in less than two days.

I suppose we should buy some cots.

Tuesday 17 May

We take Saoirse to my Mum and Dad's house. They are having her for a couple of days while Rich looks after me in hospital. As soon as we stand up to leave I feel the tears choking me. How do you leave your beloved firstborn knowing that when you return there will be three other little souls in tow?

'Don't worry about her,' says Mum, giving me a hug, although I know that she will be worried sick about *me* until she hears that everything is OK. It's the curse of motherhood. 'Even though you are all grown up and gone, I still lie awake at night praying that you're all safely in your beds,' she's often said.

What have I let myself in for?

We get home. The house is weirdly quiet without Saoirse. Expectant, even. Rich tries to shave me in preparation for the operation tomorrow, but it's not a very successful mission since neither of us can heave the bump up high enough to reach my bikini line (ha ha – when will I ever have a bikini line again?) and I can't lean back for long because it's agony. Plus Rich keeps making me laugh by pretending to find it sexy. As erotic experiences go, it's not high up on my personal *Karma Sutra* top ten.

We go out for a quiet dinner together – possibly our last – and drink a bottle of champagne. It feels surreal, conspiratorial, like the night before a heist. No one in the restaurant knows what we are about to undergo. Or maybe they do, judging by the stares we get as I shuffle out grunting and groaning.

'Night-night, ducky,' I say, as I turn in. I am now sleeping in the bottom bunk, which Rich has had to reinforce with an extra mattress. Even then, there is a large dent in the middle where my bump has rested during the night.

'Night-night, sweetheart. See you in the morning.'

The morning. Jesus. I toss and turn with abandon, happy that whatever happens next this stage is soon to be over. Even if every night from now until Christmas is sleepless and full of tears, I am ready for a new set of problems. Roll on the morning.

Wednesday 18 May

It's today. I wake with butterflies, like it's Christmas. Today I am going to meet three new babies. Today my stomach, then my uterus, are going to be sliced open and three babies are going to be wrestled out of me. It's a strange thought, but I am excited by it. I am ready. I take the second antacid pill and squeeze myself into the shower. I smile as I realize it is the last time I will not be able to wash my own feet. I put on make-up. I want to look my best for the babies, and for the cameras. When the documentary goes out, I don't want to miss the birth because I'm too busy thinking I should have put a bit of powder on.

I eye the bathroom scales. Should I? My waist is 54 inches, so it's difficult to see how big the rest of me is because the bump is so huge it dwarfs everything else. I have avoided knowing how much I weigh so far. Carrying three is hard enough without worrying about the twins that seem to have been growing in each thigh. Morbidly curious, I step onto the scales and gasp.

'Rich! Rich!' I shout. He comes running, obviously thinking I've gone into labour.

'Guess how much I weigh!' I say, part amused and part horrified.

'Fifteen,' he says, nervously. This is a bad game for men.

'Nope,' I say.

'Sixteen?' he almost whispers.

'Nope.' This is bad. Even Rich, so tactful and kind in the face of my stupid weight obsession, looks a bit appalled.

'More than sixteen?' he asks, his eyes wide.

'17 stone 11lb,' I enunciate clearly.

'It'll all come off by tonight,' says Rich calmly. I am mortified. I weigh almost eighteen stone. No wonder the bed has a huge dip in it. No wonder I've had to sleep on a double mattress. I am massive. But what's a girl to do when she's got the Triplet Hunger?

We gather my stuff together and drive to the hospital. It's weird leaving the house knowing that I will return a mother of four.

It's a beautifully sunny day, and the traffic is much lighter than usual. Is it me or are people pulling over to let us pass? I imagine a police escort, or a royal cavalcade alongside us. We arrive early and Rich finds a wheelchair for me. There is no way I can walk the long corridors today.

Up in the ward, I am pushed into a gloriously quiet side room by a lovely midwife called Maggie. She inspects me.

'Right, you need to take your jewellery off, and I'll get you some make-up remover too.'

'Why?' I say, alarmed. If the public are going to have to look at my uterus then I at least owe them some mascara.

'No make-up in theatre,' she smiles.

Maggie sets about prepping me for theatre. She is my dresser, but I don't much care for the costume. A backless hospital robe is slipped on, followed by a sort of hairnet/baker's hat thing and finally a pair of incredibly unflattering white surgical thigh-length stockings. They make my legs look like two overstuffed white puddings. She inspects my pubic region and decides to shave me a little lower, which delights Rich as he gets to stand behind her leering suggestively. At least he makes me laugh.

Julie and Caron arrive, giddy at the prospect of dressing up in surgical gowns and witnessing their first birth. Katrina's allowed them to film because they are small and won't get in the way. Rich and pass a few minutes taking funny photos of each other, me in my attractive get-up and him in his blue theatre wear. We've been told to be ready to go at 9.30 a.m., but if there is an emergency we will be bumped up the queue. I feel like a plane on the runway, waiting to take off. A further two midwives come in and introduce themselves – Michael, a good-looking young man, and Denise, a very friendly Scot. Then an extremely glamorous black woman walks in. I notice how exquisitely coordinated she is, her yellow and cream sling backs matching her lovely handbag. She is dripping in gold. Who is she? She looks like the editor of *Harpers and Queen*.

'Hello, my name is Sade,' she smiles coolly.

Sade. Like the eighties singer.

'Hello, Sade,' I say, just to try it out.

'I'm your anaesthetist today.'

I resist the urge to tell her to not bother with the drugs and just to sing me a few lines of 'Your Love is King'.

She talks me through the spinal block I am to have, and tells me that if there is any problem locating the space between the vertebrae they might have to put me under a general anaesthetic.

Crikey. Better make that 'Smooth Operator' as well. I wasn't ready for that. I don't want to go under. I want to see it all.

I'm sure it won't come to that.

Katrina pops in to say that she's on her way to theatre and not to worry. 'I've booked you in to a delivery suite post-op and you'll have one-to-one midwife care for the first twenty-four hours. There are even two beds in the room so Richard can stay and help with the babies!' she says.

This is fantastic news. Every time I've tried to imagine my first night on the ward post-caesarean trying to cope with three newborns I have come out in a sweat and blocked it out. Katrina has thought of everything. One of the midwives comes back to say that they are almost ready for me. So far no hold-ups. I send Caron and Julie out of the room. Like a diva preparing herself for a gala performance, I need my space now. Rich and I sit chatting in the room, talking about anything but the babies. Text messages from friends and family flood in wishing us luck and sending love. I try to store the memory of these last few minutes so that, in the hard times no doubt to come, I can remember what it was like to sit opposite each other before they were born and feel excited.

The door opens and a tiny hospital porter appears.

'Ready to go,' he says.

'What? No emergencies?' I say. I can't believe it. It really is time.

'No emergencies, off we go.'

How on earth is this little man going to wheel an eighteen-stone woman on a heavy hospital bed round three corridors to the operating theatre? But he is wiry, and pretty soon we are flying along. I want to tell the babies to prepare themselves for a shock, that it's showtime. I feel a small sense of regret that I have not gone into labour. I was so passionate about not being induced with Saoirse. She was twelve days overdue and I fought hard to not be induced. Babies should come when they're ready. These days they want to whip them out at the slightest hint that something might be wrong.

'Maybe I've been a bit hasty with this whole elective caesarean thing,' I want to say. But I don't. It's too late now.

The bed crashes through the first set of theatre doors and I am in the wings. I realize that Maggie has not come at me with the make-up remover, so my entrance at least will be glamorous.

There is a slight delay. Inside the theatre around twenty people are preparing for my arrival. I hear chatter, laughter, the hum of activity. Finally, I am wheeled in.

'Good morning!' I boom, determined to storm this gig.

'Good morning!' laugh the team. I am a pro. No showtime nerves from me.

My smile quickly fades when they try to transfer me from the bed to the extremely narrow operating table. It's like a plank on stilts. Surely I will roll off? It takes four people to roll and drag me from the bed to the table, and it is terrifying. They'd better not drop me, I'll never be able to get up again. I yelp that they mustn't leave me lying flat or there will be no need for the spinal block as I will be dead and senseless. It really feels as though lying on my back will kill me. This has been my biggest fear. How on earth are they going to get these babies out of me when I can't lie down? I am rolled onto my side and Sade performs the spinal block. It is much quicker than an epidural.

Within seconds, my body feels like it is being dunked in crushed ice. My hips then my legs go numb. Sade is concentrating very hard and keeps saying things like 'Kill the alarm on that resus would you?' She knows what she's doing. A large screen is erected over my chest partly for hygiene but mostly to obscure the gory bits from view. Tubes and cannulas and catheters are poked and jabbed into every available extremity. I am piped up and ready for action.

Rich is given a stool and sits by my head rhythmically stroking my hair. I'm not sure if it's me or him who is supposed to feel comforted by this, but I find it very relaxing. Katrina arrives, gowned up and ready to go. She stands next to me and smiles her reassurance. Then she frowns.

What's wrong? I start to panic.

'As a vertically challenged person, could someone please fetch me a box to stand on?' she says.

My belly must be three feet high, and she can't reach.

I am issuing instructions now.

'You've remembered that I want to see them being born? Can you make sure they lower the screen as you pull them out?' I say.

'Yes, of course. In fact, if you look straight up at the theatre lamp you will be able to see quite a lot in the reflection,' she says.

Thanks, but I don't want to see my own guts. Just the babies will be fine.

I want to sit up and watch the preparation. It's fascinating. Behind me three resuscitation tables are set up, labelled 'Triplet 1', 'Triplet 2' and 'Triplet 3'. It is very exciting.

'You're going to see your babies soon,' says Katrina. 'I'm just about to go in.'

'I've changed my mind!' I yell, and everyone laughs.

'Too late – I'm in!' she replies.

There is a slight tugging sensation in my belly. Someone once described having a C-section as feeling like someone is doing the washing-up in your stomach. I don't often do the washing-up so I'm no expert, but it doesn't feel quite like that. It's more distant, more vague.

'Are we ready for these babies?' shouts Katrina.

Someone lowers the screen onto my chest just in time for me to see a pair of legs being pulled out at a right angle to my body.

'Wow!' I say. It is an amazing moment. It is the closest I will get to enjoying a natural delivery. I look at Rich and he is watching closely. Katrina wrestles with the slippery feet of baby number one, finally freeing his head. He starts mewing immediately, and pees all over her hand. Michael the midwife grabs the baby and wraps him in a towel. As he rushes past on the way to the table where the paediatricians are waiting he gives us a quick glimpse. The baby is thin and indignant, mouth wide open and roaring his disapproval at being 'untimely ripped' from his comfortable chamber. He is covered in gunk and blood. I don't cry. It's too odd. I don't know what I thought I had in there all this time but seeing the first baby is profoundly shocking.

'Let's go fishing for another baby,' says Katrina, rummaging around again.

Baby number two also comes out feet first. Good job I wasn't swayed by all those stories of triplet vaginal deliveries. Two breech births would be very tough.

This baby screams too, and there is a sense of relief in the room. Modern technology has advanced so far that scans reveal a huge number of disorders and abnormalities, but so many things can go undetected, or go wrong at the very last minute. It is only at the moment of birth that one can really be sure the baby is alive and well. Baby number two gets whisked past and I don't even get to see his face.

'Two down, one to go,' says someone behind me. They

probably haven't had to say that very often in these circumstances.

This time I really feel it. At the very top of my chest I swear I can feel a fist – and it's not the baby's.

'Ow! Ow, ow, ow!' I moan.

'Are you OK?' asks Sade.

'I've got a terrible shooting pain in my chest – ow!'

'Sorry,' shouts Katrina from the bottom end. 'The third one is tucked right up under your ribs.'

'It's probably your diaphragm – do you need some pain relief?' asks Sade, her concerned face hovering inches above mine.

'Yes, yes,' I gasp. I feel winded.

Within moments she is injecting something into my IV line. Ten seconds later, I am floating above the room.

'Wow – what was that?' I drawl.

'Morphine. Better?' asks Sade, smiling.

'Oh, yes,' I say. 'I feel like I've had ten gin and tonics.'

The saxophone line from 'Smooth Operator' is going boozily through my head. Baby number three is finally tugged out of me. I am oblivious now. Heads and voices float above me. There is a moment when I hear three newborn babies screeching far off in the distance. Everyone is buzzing around doing things. Rich leaves my side briefly to take pictures of the babies.

'Well done,' says Katrina. 'You did extremely well.'

'Thank you,' I say, only sorry that I can't get up and take a bow. 'So did you.'

Things become a little blurry now. As Katrina sews me up, I become aware of some quiet conversations behind me.

Minutes pass. The babies have stopped crying. Rich is still next to me stroking my head. I feel dizzy, and manage to communicate it to Sade who puts an oxygen mask over my mouth.

Eventually, a paediatrician comes over.

'The boys are grunting a little bit, so we're just going to take them down to the NICU to check them out and give them a bit of oxygen. It should only take a couple of hours,' he says.

Oh.

'And the girl?' I ask, instantly going into coping mode.

'She's fine. She's going with you.'

Baby number two is thrust under my nose for the briefest of seconds. I see hair, a screwed-up face. Then, wrapped in a foil blanket, he is taken off on the resus table.

'I don't even know how much they weigh,' I say.

'Baby number one is 2.85 kilograms.'

'In old money please!' says Rich.

'Oh, sorry – 5lb 13oz. Number two is 5lb 8oz and number three is 5lb 4oz. Very good sizes!' says one of the nurses.

Bloody hell. Despite my drugged-up state I work out that I have been carrying almost eighteen pounds of baby. Amazing.

I am wheeled out on the bed with baby number three – the girl – following in a cot. We are taken to the recovery room and Rich rushes off to the neonatal intensive care unit to check on the boys and to take Polaroids. Maggie and Denise the midwives are still with me, and they ask me if I want to try feeding the girl. I am still lying prone – it will be some hours before I can be lifted to a sitting position – but they hand her to me and hover by my side. I get a long look at her. She is tiny. Her fingers are long and bony, and her eyes are wide open. She stares at me. She looks like ET. She has a small bruise on one cheek where Katrina had to hook her out, one finger in the roof of her mouth, the others gripping her face like a bowling ball. A caesarean delivery is not necessarily just a case of popping them out easily. Gingerly, I place her on my left breast. It feels so bizarre, even though it is less than a year since I last breastfed Saoirse. How will such a tiny thing, born almost six weeks early, know what to do with a great big nipple shoved in her face? The sucking reflex may not even have kicked in yet. But miraculously she starts to suck. I drift into a doze. I wonder what the boys are doing. I can't wait to see them all together. I feel cheated of the moment they all emerged. I wanted to see them side by side, kicking and screaming their way into the world together. There is a sense of anticlimax. Oh well. I'll see them in a couple of hours.

We are taken along the corridors to the special room they have set aside for me, no doubt expecting me to have three babies by my side. Denise and Maggie settle me in and Rich arrives with pictures of the boys.

'They're OK,' he starts, but I feel a 'but' coming on. A paediatrician follows him in.

'They're doing well, but we've had to intubate them for a while. They were having a bit of trouble breathing – it's pretty common, nothing to worry about. They should be off the ventilators soon.'

Rich hands me two pictures. Both show a small baby, face down on a white sheet wearing nothing but a nappy and a white hat, a large grey tube stuck down the throat and IV drips coming from both hands.

These are my boys.

I can't think straight. This wasn't in the plan, I'm sure. At thirty-four, almost thirty-five weeks they should be fine. There should be no need for all these tubes and plastic boxes. What's gone wrong?

I am filled with guilt. Perhaps I should have struggled on. Perhaps I could have gone another week, and we would all be together now. I stare at the pictures but still feel alienated from myself.

Rich goes home to pick up the post, a totally unnecessary trip but he needs a breather. The NICU was quite overwhelming – hot, busy and confusing. He can't really give me any information. It's hardly surprising – he can barely remember our telephone number let alone the minutiae of medical procedure.

Katrina comes in and kisses me on the cheek.

'Well done,' she says.

'The boys aren't breathing properly so they're on ventilators,' I say, eager to get her medical opinion. 'I feel really bad now.'

'I've just had a look at the placentas and they were starting to calcify a bit. It's a good thing that we got them out today,' she says firmly.

I am stunned. I *knew*! Somehow I just knew it was time to get the babies out. It's an immensely gratifying and humbling moment. I've never been into all that 'listen to your body' yogic kind of stuff, but I had an overwhelming impulse, not just based on my own personal discomfort, that it was time to end the pregnancy.

Once the placenta starts to malfunction, things can go downhill very fast. The results can be disastrous. I can't even think about it in this moment. I am just deeply grateful that my body told me it was time, and equally grateful that Katrina listened, and didn't make me go that extra week.

Rich returns with the post. There is a card from Alan, my old mate from college. I open it and a piece of paper flutters onto my sheet. It's a cheque. For £5,000. I read the card, confused. The card is to wish me luck today, and the cheque is 'to help look after the babies'. Now I am even more stunned. Flowers arrive – already – and we sit in the room staring at each other. I can't believe our good fortune. For the moment – whether it's the drugs, the glow of loyal and kind friendship, the fact that at least the little girl is OK – I don't feel worried about the boys. All will be well. How can it not be? We are here in this room together, not squeezed onto a busy, hot ward.

Another paediatrician comes and examines the girl again. I watch her as she watches the baby, fascinated by the procedure. She places the baby on the heated resus table, leans on her elbows and just watches, occasionally turning her head from side to side. She looks like a new mum, fascinated with her firstborn. But she is clinically observing in order to make sure she is not missing anything.

'I'm just going to take her down to the NICU for a minute. Nothing to worry about – she's just grunting a tiny bit and I want to make sure she's OK,' she says, wheeling the baby out of the room.

And then there were none.

Where are these babies that have caused such a fuss? My instinct is trying to fight its way to the surface. I should be with them. How is it you have three babies one minute and then none the next? I doze for a while. Suddenly it's three o'clock, and Denise says that maybe I could try getting into a wheelchair so that I can be wheeled round to see the babies. I am excited. She tries to heave me into the chair, but as soon as I am sitting up I feel very dizzy. My blood pressure is still low after the operation, and with all the will in the world I cannot get up, let alone face the transition from bed to chair.

'We'll try again at six,' she says kindly.

Maybe the babies will be out by then anyway.

The afternoon passes quietly as I slip in and out of sleep. The girl is brought back and declared fit as a fiddle. Relief. At five o'clock there is a shift change and a new midwife arrives. As she is checking my temperature the door flies open and a consultant walks in flanked by several junior doctors. Perhaps they've come to see the triplet freak show.

'Hello, how are you feeling?' he says. He is wearing a bow tie, and I marvel at his lack of inhibition at being such a stereotype.

'Fine,' I say.

'Got a bit of a problem. We are very busy today and I'm afraid we need this room.'

Oh shit.

'You don't look very happy about that,' he says.

'Well, I'm not,' I say. 'I don't want to go on the ward. I'm exhausted, and I've got three babies to look after.'

'They'll put you in a room,' he says.

So I have to move. They gather my things together and I am wheeled around to the room. At least I will have some privacy and there will be enough space for three cots in here, even if it means Rich can't stay the night.

The ward sister comes in.

'I'm sorry, but you can't be in here,' she says.

'But this is my room!' I squawk.

'You need to be on the ward for observation. You've had major surgery and you have to be closely monitored in the first twenty-four hours.'

'Can't you just monitor me in here?' I am desperate now. The ward is full, hot and incredibly noisy. I will not sleep. I have not slept for months. I need to sleep. And where will my babies go?

'No, we can't, I'm afraid. We only have two on duty at night and we have such a lot of ladies today,' she says 'I promise you will come in here tomorrow morning'

So that's the end of the special treatment for now. I am wheeled into a space right by the nurses' station so that not only can I be woken by everyone on the ward but also get to listen to the phone ringing and loud chatting all night. I am very depressed. The only reason I have been able to keep it together is because I have had some solitude and quiet.

I am settled in, the baby girl in a plastic cot beside me and Rich on my other side. The baby is quiet, but I try to feed her now and again to get my milk supply going. The colostrum produced in these early days is really important in helping the babies' immune system. These babies will need it, being six weeks early. I am amazed that the girl is so small and yet is absolutely fine. We still don't know what is happening with the boys. I keep asking to be taken around to see them but the evening shift is on and they are very busy. At 9 p.m. I am in tears, telling one of the two midwives that the consultant said I could go and see the babies as soon as I felt able. Like a kind torturer she quietly explains, as if to a small child, that they are too busy to take me and that it would be better for me to rest and see them in the morning. I feel like I am in one of those nightmares where you know what you are saying is right but no one seems to be listening.

At 10 p.m. a different paediatrician comes in to see us. She pulls the curtains around my bed. This looks ominous.

'The boys are basically fine, but they are suffering from RDS – respiratory distress syndrome. It's just a way of saying that the lungs are not working properly yet. They will be OK, but they need help breathing at the moment so they have been intubated.'

Why is she saying in*tu*bated? Surely it's in*cu*bated? In time, I will learn that 'intubated' is the process by which babies are placed on ventilators, but right now I keep thinking she's saying it wrong and I'm irritated. She's looking after my boys and she can't even speak properly. She tells me that they have been given something called 'surfactant' – at least I think that's what she says – to stop their lungs sticking together. It's normally present in newborns, but sometimes premature babies need a synthetic boost of it.

'When will they be with me?' I ask.

'It won't be tonight, obviously,' she says. So at least I won't have three babies to look after on the ward. Small mercy, I suppose.

'Possibly tomorrow,' she says.

'When can I see them? They're saying I can't go round because they're too busy, but I haven't even laid eyes on them yet,' I say, my bottom lip trembling. It feels like the first hour in a deeply foreign land. I don't speak the lingo, I don't know the customs and I have no idea what the next twenty-four hours have in store for any of us.

She goes off and I hear a slightly heated exchange at the desk. A few minutes later, a massive shaven-headed nurse appears and heaves me into a wheelchair. She looks fed up and harassed, all seven feet of her, and I try to thank her for her trouble but she grunts. Never mind – we are going to see the boys!

The NICU wards are just across a quadrangle from the ward, and my bed is close to a door marked SCBU (special care baby unit), the adjoining unit to the NICU (neonatal intensive care unit), but to get to the boys we have to go all the way around the square to the proper entrance, where visitors must be buzzed in and must wash their hands and apply an alcohol solution to prevent the transmission of infection. It is the longest journey. When we arrive in the NICU corridor there are three or four small rooms off to the right, each of which is housing six babies in incubators. Each baby has its own dedicated nurse, and all the nurses are busy recording data on clipboards, feeding or changing nappies. The atmosphere is quite relaxed, and I notice the large bowl of sweets on the reception desk.

'In here,' says Rich, guiding our nurse into the last room. She wheels me up to the first incubator, and there is a moment when I am not sure if this is one of my babies or not. How should I feel? Sorry for this little unfortunate stranger's child? Or moved to tears by the plight of my own flesh and blood? A blue tag hangs from one corner.

'Triplet 1' it reads.

The tiny boy is flat out, a huge pipe taped in place over his mouth. His hand is bruised where the drip has been forced into his little veins. His chest is heaving up and down, inflating and deflating with great effort, like an old pair of bellows.

I burst into tears. I thought I had prepared myself for the possibility of this vision, but how can you?

'Don't cry!' says the big nurse, clomping a huge fist on my shoulder. 'I didn't bring you all the way round here to cry.'

She doesn't mean it unkindly, but it irks me. If you're not allowed to cry when you've just had triplets and the first time you see two of them they are attached to loads of monitors and drips and they need help just to keep breathing, then when can you?

Triplet 2 is across from his brother. I take a peek at him too, and his chest is rising and falling with equal difficulty.

'It's the ventilator,' says a NICU nurse. 'But don't worry – they're the biggest triplets we've ever had in here. They'll be out in no time.'

My boys.

During the night, the ward is chaos. A woman is wheeled into the bed next to mine at midnight. She is in labour, but this is the post-natal ward.

'They're queuing up in the corridors to give birth,' I hear someone say. The poor woman is in agony. Finally, she is wheeled away to theatre for an emergency C-section. I doze for a while, our baby girl fast asleep next to me.

Two hours later, the woman is back, the baby screaming heartily. But all is not well. The woman's friend calls the nurses repeatedly. The woman is bleeding a lot. A doctor is called. I hear feet clattering down corridors. He examines her and says she is haemorrhaging badly and needs to go back to theatre. She is rushed off once more.

I sit up in bed eating fun-sized Mars bars. There's no point trying to sleep. And they tell you to stay in as long as you can 'for the rest'! The ward is so hot I can barely breathe.

I call a nurse and ask her for a sleeping pill as I can't sleep.

'Can't sleep?' she laughs. 'You've been snoring for the last two hours.'

Oh.

Friday 20 May

As promised, first thing I am moved to a blissful side room where I have a shower and a loo all to myself. It is slightly shabby, but it feels like five-star luxury. There is a pay-per-view TV above me and *windows* to the outside world that will allow me to get some air. I am ecstatic.

A woman in surgical gear comes in.

'Hello – just come to collect Triplet 3 for her brain scan,' she announces cheerily.

'Brain scan?' I say, alarmed.

'Oh – has no one told you? Oh. The boys have already had theirs this morning,' she says.

'Have they?' I splutter. No one has told me anything. Already the babies feel like hospital property.

The baby girl is wheeled off for the first of many tests. When she returns, she has a cannula inserted into the back of her hand. The boys have been placed on antibiotics to ward off any infections, so the girl must have them too. Once a threesome, always a threesome.

Rich arrives and wheels me round to the NICU to see the boys again. I gaze at them with a mixture of fear and love. They are hairy. Not big dark male hairy, but peachy, a blond down covering their faces. Their chests are still heaving disturbingly.

'Typical boys!' says one of the nurses. 'Now that they know there is a machine to breathe for them, they can't be bothered to do it by themselves.'

It appears that the boys' lungs have stopped working independently of the ventilators. A doctor walks in and explains that this is a slight setback, meaning their stay in the NICU will be longer than the day or two they anticipated.

'How long?' I ask.

'It's difficult to say. The care will depend on what they decide to do. We are not feeding them milk because they are too weak. They are on IV fluids. We will keep trying them, but we're looking at least a week. We usually say that you should bank on having them home around their due date.'

I'm in shock. That's almost six weeks away. How will we manage?

I canvas opinion among the nurses.

'It won't be that long,' they say. 'These babies are not sick. They are just lazy! They should be ashamed of themselves! But they'll get there.'

It's an odd thing to hear a nurse say, but it is exactly what I want to hear. It's curiously heartening to hear my little struggling boys described as 'just lazy'.

But everyone I ask gives me a different opinion. I ask the nurse looking after Triplet 1 when they are likely to start feeding. 'Well, his aspirations aren't good,' she says.

What does that mean – he's not aiming for Oxbridge? I need a phrasebook. She shows me a syringe full of murky yellow liquid she has just extracted from his stomach. There is some gunk that shouldn't be there, which shows his digestive system is struggling. Milk is a few days away at least, and even when they start to feed it will take a long time to get them up to even an ounce of milk in one go.

We go back to the ward shell-shocked. This was so not in the plan. I thought we would be home in a week with three new babies. Now it looks as though we will be here for some time, juggling one at home and two in hospital.

I need to get my milk supply going. Triplet 3 is sucking away, but I'm not sure there is anything coming out, plus I need to start stockpiling some for the boys.

'The colostrum is like moon dust,' says one midwife. 'It's so precious. Even if you just get a tiny bit to the boys it will really help their immune systems.' I sit with the hospital breast pump attached to one boob and switch it on to a gentle cycle. It groans and wheezes into life. Nothing happens. I stare at our baby girl, hoping this will encourage the let-down process. Nothing. I turn the pump action up to medium. Still nothing. After five minutes I get fed up and turn the dial up to maximum. My whole boob is now being sucked in and out of the plastic funnel. After what seems like an uncomfortable hour the tiniest trickle of yellow syrupy liquid makes its way down the funnel and into the waiting bottle. It is a minute amount, but I feel like I have struck gold. Every little helps. I consult friends via text message and get lots of advice on how to stimulate milk production. I have to do this every three hours and drink fennel tea. OK.

As I sit and pump out my thimbleful of goo we discuss names. The babies are two days old and we don't know what to call them. In the NICU they like to put a poster up in each baby's incubator that reads 'Hi, my name is—' so that all the different doctors and nurses who work there can relate to the babies as people. Our babies are still 'Triplet 1' and 'Triplet 2'.

I draw up a shortlist.

'I still like Walter and Albert,' says Rich.

'No way,' I say. 'I am not having children called Wally and Bert.'

'Why not?' says Rich, looking genuinely disappointed.

'It's too comedy. We might as well just call them Stan and Ollie, Eric and Ernie.'

'That's a good idea—'

'No. I like Lorcan and Aidan for the boys. Or Thady.'

'I'm not having all my children with Paddy names,' says Rich hotly.

'Oi!'

'I'm not being funny, but I'm not Irish. Saoirse was bad enough.'

'OK. Well, what then? Is the girl going to be Maeve?'

'I don't know. She doesn't look like a Maeve.'

'I know. She's more of an Orla.'

'Yes, Orla suits her.'

'Let's call her that then!' I say, excited to have agreed on at least one of them. Naming a child is hard. So much of who you are and how you are perceived in the world depends on your moniker. Orla means golden in Gaelic, and since the slight jaundice is giving her a sort of all-over St Tropez tan, it seems to fit.

'Well, my next favourite boy's name is Frank,' says Rich.

'As in Francis?'

'Yes.'

'OK. One of them can be Francis, known as Frank. That's nice. That'll be Triplet 2.'

'And since you chose Saoirse and Orla, I should choose the boys. I like Reuben.'

'No – much as I sometimes have Jew envy, we are Catholic and Reuben is just too Old Testament.'

'All right. What then?' Rich hates this naming game. He has refused to talk about it until now, but we must make a decision soon.

'I still like Thady,' I say. It's the abbreviated form of the name Thaddeus, pronounced with a hard 'T' as in 'Thomas'. I first heard it in Ireland years ago, but I don't tell Rich that. I'm going to sneak another Paddy name under the wire.

'Thady . . . Thady,' says Rich, trying it out. 'Thady Bear . . . Won't he just get called Thady Bear?'

'What's wrong with that? I like it.'

'OK. Thady, Frank and Orla,' says Rich finally.

We smile, and head round to the NICU to get the boys' names up on the boards. It's a very moving christening, standing by their incubators with a marker pen and a piece of paper at the ready. We spell out the names. No going back now.

The nurses have no problem with Frank, but for the first few hours Thady is known as Tabby due to a mishearing. As soon as the boys' names go up we giggle, like we've just told a big lie. We've just created a Frank and a Thady. Who will they be and will their names affect them?

My stomach, although much smaller, is still massive.

'Are you sure you haven't got another one in there?' the nurses laugh. Thanks for that. Just what I needed. In fairness, I look like I'm about eight months gone with just one on the way. Tentatively, I step onto the scales in the ward. Sixteen stone. Two stone lighter than Wednesday.

IS THAT ALL?

I had managed to kid myself quite successfully that I would lose at least four stone after giving birth. Bugger. That means I am clinically obese. I have been eating for ten and now I will pay the price.

How am I going to lose the other five stone? It's too depressing to think about. I stuff my face with truffles and have a good cry.

Friday 20 May

Bedlam should have been a maternity hospital. The Victorians would have been royally entertained by the shuffling C-section mad-eyed ladies, the leaky zombified wild-haired women trying to tame their squealing, screeching newborns. The nights are extraordinary. The variety and volume of the cries beggars belief. There is no such thing as *a* newborn baby cry. Yes, there is the conventional 'A-wah! A-wah!' (ad nauseaum), but others bray like donkeys, some whimper, some yelp like puppies being trodden on, some shout insistently and some sound like they are trying to emulate a ghost train. I am woken constantly by blood-curdling screams and odd squawks. Every night there is a high turnover of fresh meat on the ward, but there is always one screamer. So far, it's not in my room. Orla is, however, feeding every two hours through the night. Hmm. Times that by three and that makes . . . very little sleep indeed.

I don't even know what the boys look like – we creep around the incubators pulling at corners of the bundles inside like they are Christmas presents we are not allowed to open yet. They both look like they have really bad eighties highlights. They are a mini Wham! tribute act.

It's only my third day in hospital and already I feel institution-alized. Staying here is like being on an ultra-long, long haul flight – the food on plastic trays, the stifling heat, the intimate proximity to strangers, the big white socks I'm forced to wear to stop me getting DVT (deep vein thrombosis – although I have assured them my veins, like the rest of me, are resolutely shallow). Although it is awful, I feel nervous about leaving. How can they let me go home with three babies? It's not right. Even registered childminders aren't allowed to have more than three children under the age of five, and they are usually trained.

Mum, Dad, Maggie and Rich visit. Round to the NICU – we can only go two at a time – and Dad is very moved by the sight of his two grandsons hooked up to all those machines.

'Hi, my name is Frank,' he quotes, having seen their name sheets. He bursts into tears.

'He shouldn't be in there. Someone called "Frank" shouldn't be in an incubator,' says Rich. It's true. A lot of the tiny, very sick babies are called things like 'Hope', 'Blessing' and 'Precious', in an attempt, no doubt, to will them into good health. The Franks of this world don't belong in here – they should be propping up the bar, scoring a try, rolling a ciggy in a greasy-spoon cafe.

Saturday 21 May

Lou is smuggled in before visiting hours and brings me a pizza and some cake. I have mostly been eating chocolate because the food is not only foul but unrecognizable. Yesterday they delivered a pink thing with some grey stuff. I'm starving. The pregnancy got me used to about four thousand calories a day, and my belly thinks my throat has been cut.

Very tearful. Is this the baby blues? Very tired. I shuffle round to the NICU. I can't understand one of the nurses at all – a combination of her very strong accent and her use of jargon. I feel as though everyone is too busy to give me an update on the boys, who seem to have settled into a groove well enough without their mum. They look like they belong here, which I hate. There is some movement though. Thady is off CPAP (the continuous positive airway pressure machine) – I get a lovely shock and see his whole face and head for the first time. He has indeed got a full head of brownish blond hair, the blond bits streaked through from roots to ends. I ask if I can get him out, but he has just been fiddled about with and his nurse wants him to settle. I am told to come back at 2 p.m. for a long-awaited first cuddle.

2 p.m. Thady is back on CPAP. Bugger.

'He did OK for a while, but then he started to struggle so he's back on CPAP again. Not to worry – he'll be off it again soon. We'll keep trying him,' says the nurse.

Saoirse and Rich visit for an hour. It's about as much as she can manage without getting really bored. We take her around to see her brothers again. She looks serious but obviously doesn't understand.

'Bye-bye Thady, bye-bye Frank,' she says very solemnly.

Then it's 'Bye-bye Mama' and off she trots, not a care in the world. She is heartbreakingly OK to leave me in here. Toddlers can be very cruel. I feel like we have switched roles and she is the cool mother waltzing off and leaving me at nursery for the first time without so much as a backward glance. I really want to go home now but I have no idea how we will manage visiting times. I've been told that we shouldn't really take Orla round to the NICU – although she is healthy, she is premature too and may either bring in infections or pick one up herself. I won't be able to manage Saoirse and Orla when visiting the boys, but I really want to bring expressed breast milk (EBM) for them. It will mean that Rich will have to stay at home with the girls while I go to hospital, but even then the visits will have to be fleeting because Orla will need feeding at home. I wish I could take the boys home now. I can't rest here.

Jules, my oldest friend from home, calls and I burst into tears on the phone. 'I don't know what's going on. The boys have been in the world four days and they still haven't had a cuddle.'

Jules is kind and philosophical, which makes me cry even more. It's a relief. She tells me to go round again and ask someone how the boys are doing. I dry my eyes, eat a few chocolates and hobble around to the NICU for the fourth time, determined to get the low-down from someone in the know.

But the atmosphere is tense. A thin Indian doctor is talking to a group of nurses and the parents of Daisy, the baby next to Frank. They are looking at some X-rays and the mother is crying. I walk past trying not to get in the way. The parents walk off and the doctor seems agitated.

'This baby is very sick!' he says, as if admonishing the nurses. They scurry off and there is a lot of silent activity around Daisy's cot.

I can't ask them anything now. I open Thady's porthole and stroke his hairy arm. I realize that I am crying again so I wander out to the corridor for a bit.

'I'll go back,' I think. 'Orla might be crying. I should get some sleep.'

So I walk up the corridor again. Then I realize in all the quiet chaos I forgot to see Frank, so I turn around and go back. But he is hemmed in by all the nurses, who are uncharacteristically serious as they crowd around Daisy's incubator. So I slope off up the corridor again, crying openly now. A nurse shoots out of a door and stops dead when she sees me.

'What's the matter? Why are you crying?' she says.

I blub my story. 'The babies are four days old and I haven't held them yet, and everyone is so busy all the time and I don't know what's happening or how long they will be here and I just want to go home but I can't leave them here.'

'You can have a cuddle – I'll get them out for you,' she says.

'Can you?' I ask. 'They've got all those tubes in and everything.'

'I can get them out for you. Come with me.'

And she takes me to Thady, pulls a nursing chair up behind me and lifts the lid off his incubator.

'You'll have to sit nice and close because the tubes don't stretch that far,' she says.

I am as nervous as a first-date teenager. Slowly, expertly, she arranges his wires and tubes and passes him onto my lap. I sit and cuddle him while hot tears plop down onto his blanket. I feel very happy. I could never have imagined feeling this happy holding a baby who is in an intensive care unit, but none of the paraphernalia matters. He is my son. My first son.

There is more commotion near Frank's incubator, so I decide to put off holding him until tomorrow as I must get back to check on Orla. The nurse places Thady back in his box like he is a very expensive diamond necklace that I can't afford yet.

Back in the room, Orla is awake but silent. It has grown dark outside and there are no lights on, but I can see her large eyes glinting as I open the door. Do these triplets know that they can't all demand me at once? I half expect her to sit up and say, 'How are the boys, Mum?' I feel a massive wave of guilt wash over me. I feel guilty that the boys are in the NICU, that I didn't pick up Frank, that I came back to find Orla quiet and neglected.

It is only Day Four and already I feel pulled in all directions.

Sunday 22 May

5 a.m. I wake to a terrible keening. Not one of the babies in the ward, surely? No, the sound is coming from a woman. It sounds like the noise that drunks make when they fall into self-pity. The noise dies down and then resumes again a few minutes later. Muffled female voices offer reassurances. The noise is coming from the NICU corridor across the way. My window is open. For some reason I have a terrible feeling in the pit of my stomach.

'Daisy's dead,' I think. I go back to sleep.

9 a.m. I take EBM round for the boys – 2 ounces this morning. Daisy's cot has been replaced by a shiny new incubator. It's empty, still in its plastic sanitary wrap. I feel sick.

I hobble back to the ward, my scar still hurting and preventing me from standing fully upright.

I am very well looked after here. Everyone wants to see the Triplet Mum. Heads pop round the door offering tea/water/ 'observations'. It's very sweet.

11 a.m. After feeding Orla, I go round to see the boys again. A nurse hovers.

'The little girl who was sick last night . . . is she—' I ask.

I know it's nosy but you can't help but get involved in this place as your own babies lie struggling for breath.

The nurse looks at me levelly.

'We're not allowed to discuss clinical issues with anyone but the parents,' she says quietly, before adding, 'but yes . . . she didn't make it.'

Poor Daisy.

I look at the little boy next to Thady. He is big. He looks about a year old – an incongruous sight in this ward. I peep at his label. 'Nathaniel D.O.B 25/12/04. Weight 540g.'

Bloody hell. Born on Christmas day weighing less than a twentieth of the average British turkey, and yet here he is. It is incredible. The nurses tell me that they treat more boys than girls, and the boys tend to take longer to move out of the NICU. The strongest babies are the African girls. Evolution has made them tough – they have to be. White boys are the slowest and the weakest. Well, there's a surprise. I look at my two boys struggling to breathe. It seems like we might be here for some time yet. By chance, the doctor is doing his rounds and allows me to sit in and listen to the latest on my boys. Thady and Frank are a little jaundiced and a doctor tells me they might be put on something called a Billy Blanket. It's a light pad that they lie on in the incubator. Sounds quite nice. They have started giving the boys milk. A nurse proudly announces that Frank has taken 7ml of formula in an hour via a feeding tube. That's about a thimbleful. They have to breathe by themselves and be taking 125ml every four hours before they will be allowed home. That looks depressingly far off right now. The doctor says I should bank on between two to four weeks.

★

I head back to my room to attach myself to the milking machine again. Those boys need whatever dribble I can give them. Orla will have to have formula. They supply you with tiny bottles and throwaway teats in hospital, but you have to go and ask for them one at a time. Sometimes there are three or four women waiting in line until a nurse is free to rummage in the cupboard. I hate it. It does nothing for my sense of working-class shame to feel like I am begging for milk. It takes me back to the ignominy of milk tokens and free school dinners. I ask for two bottles and I am given a look that says 'Don't think you can stockpile here, freeloader' until I explain that I have three babies. This, coupled with the guilt I feel for not being able to breast-feed all three exclusively, makes the whole experience rather uncomfortable. In my mum's day breastfeeding was seen as a bit common. It was what poor women did because they couldn't afford formula milk. The new orthodoxy – the militant breast-feeders who declare that 'Breast is Best' – makes me feel like every time I give a baby some formula milk I might as well be injecting heroin into their eyeballs.

Monday 23 May

Thady and Frank are in cots. Both are breathing for themselves and things suddenly look a lot brighter. Rich gets a good look at both of his sons for the first time.

'What do you think?' I ask nervously. Quite against my largely feminist principles, I feel stupidly proud of having provided him with sons, even though he is more than happy with his four girls.

'They're a bit—' he starts.

'What?' I say. I want him to fall in love with them.

'A bit . . . chinless and snouty,' he says.

It's true, their little noses are turned up and their mouths are forced open by the feeding tubes which have now become a temporary fixture down their throats, giving them a slightly, shall we say, aristocratic appearance. I'm sure it's just the tubes. If not, we can always rename them Lord Chinless and Sir Snouty.

I have decided to go home tomorrow. I have been hanging on indefinitely in the vain hope that the boys will pick up rapidly and we can all go home together, but looking at the pathetic amount they are taking down their feeding tubes it is clear that their homecoming is some way off. We have Dona, the maternity nurse, on hold until we know when all three will be at home. No point blowing that little luxury on just one baby. Despite my constant badgering, no one can tell me when the boys will be allowed home, mainly because nobody knows. It's up to Thady and Frank. We have a couple of weeks at least of running backwards and forwards between home and hospital as I ferry EBM to the boys and keep Orla happy at home. Dona is worried that my milk will dry up with all the stress. She doesn't seem to think breastfeeding is a viable option with three.

'I've seen it with my twin mums. I wouldn't even try it,' she says. My reaction, as ever, is to vow to prove her wrong. I have decided I'll give it my best shot, and my instinct is that it will be OK.

'It causes a lot of rows between couples too,' she says. Rich and I will be OK. It's been oddly romantic here. Every evening, while my mum babysits Saoirse, we walk hand in hand round to the NICU, me swinging a freshly expressed bottle of milk from the other hand. The evening sunshine pours in through the corridor windows and I feel in love all over again. They say that romance flourishes or flounders in times of crisis, and we seem to be doing well. Romance is not candlelit dinners and red roses – it's the two of us washing our hands together and rubbing alcohol solution in to stop infection at the NICU door. It's Rich being kind enough to make suggestive and lewd comments about my clearly hideous surgical stockings. The nurses have noticed how present he is. He comes in early and leaves late. We will come out of this smiling.

There's a programme on TV about a woman with a fourteen-stone tumour in her tummy. I know how she feels. I stare down at my own bloated frontage. It looks like a cluster of balloons three weeks after a toddler's party – sort of deflated and wrinkly. Now that the babies are out, I can see that I did indeed get stretch marks. I couldn't see them before because the skin was stretched so tight the whole surface was red. But now I can see angry purple stripes on the underside of my belly. The skin is puckered and tired looking. I switch channels to try and cheer myself up. 'Celebrity Love Island' is on. I watch ridiculous pseudo-mating rituals being acted out for the cameras by anorexic girls in bikinis who think they look fat. The men ogle them nonetheless. How I'd love to be para-chuted in wearing a fetching skimpy two-piece to replace Rebecca Loos and really piss the boys off. I turn off the TV in disgust and flick through a magazine. Apparently you can 'Get a Bikini Body in 10 Days!!!'. What's a bikini body? I've got a bikini body. A really horrible one. I flick on and discover that Anna Friel, eight months pregnant with her first child, has already agreed to do a nude scene three months after giving birth. Apparently, she has been determined not to let herself go, and has not given in to any cravings. 'It's better to just not have it,' she says. I can't work out if she's talking about ice-cream or the baby.

I'm just jealous because I'm a big fat greedy pig and I had the perfect excuse to be.

Tuesday 24 May

Awake at 6 a.m. dripping with sweat, shivering. My breasts are leaking milk, making great dark patches on my delicate pastel PJs. I think my milk has 'come in', and I have what they call milk fever. They don't tell you about this in the books. Some women get a short fever when the milk finally arrives after a few days. But my bladder hurts too. Oh no. Don't let this be a complication from the C-section. One woman on the ward is still here after ten days because they damaged her bladder during the operation. I waddle round to the ward desk and it takes the nurse two minutes to look up from her paper work. I am so institutionalized now I don't even think to get her attention earlier.

'I'm in pain,' I manage. 'I'm shivering.' I can't stop my teeth from chattering.

She says someone will come and see me. I go back to bed and cover myself in tiny baby blankets to stop the shivering. Forty minutes pass. No one comes. I find some paracetamol in my handbag and take them. I know we inmates are not supposed to self-medicate, but if I had morphine in my purse I'd take that as well. Thank God Orla is asleep. I couldn't feed her right now – I'd drop her. I go back to the desk and a different nurse tells me off when I say I've taken pills already. I snap and tell her I was desperate because no one came. I will not be told off for taking fucking paracetamol after having triplets. Finally, at 10 a.m., a doctor comes and diagnoses a urine infection. Lovely. So I'm going home with a bag full of antibiotics and horse-strength painkillers.

Going home. I feel so bad leaving the boys here, but I can't stay in hospital for however many weeks it takes for them to get out. Orla needs to get out of here. She is far more at risk from infections and viruses than she would be at home – a fact which amuses me greatly given the sorry state of our domestic hygiene.

Rich arrives to collect me and we head round to the NICU. Frank is face down on a glowing green light pad, naked except for a nappy and a rather fetching pair of goggles. He looks like he's having a smashing chav holiday in Benidorm.

'They're moving!' says a nice nurse. 'They're both going round to the transitional care unit next to the SCBU.' This is great news. We will be leaving them side by side, and it looks like it won't be long before we have them all home. I am part thrilled and part terrified. Actually, mostly terrified, but I act as though I am just relieved. I don't know how we will manage their hospital stay when I get home.

'Do parents with just the one baby to worry about spend all day here?' I ask. I have no idea what the protocol is, or how many hours a day I will be able to manage.

'It depends,' she says, nursing a small baby opposite Frank's cot. 'Some have other health problems, some have to go back to work, some just don't bother to visit until they are discharged, some never come back.'

'What do you mean?' I say.

'They don't want them.'

'They abandon them here!' I say, incredulous.

'Yep. Sometimes. I saw a mum the other day in the corridor out there and I said, "Oh, are you in to see your baby?" and she said, "No, I'm visiting a friend". She hadn't been in here for over a month.'

Bloody hell. Fat tears plop down my cheeks. I whisper into Frank's glowing ear. 'I won't leave you here. I'll come back for you.'

The film crew arrive. We had hoped that this day would be full of shots of us all leaving together, but instead they get some footage of me blubbing as we walk out with just one baby. I kiss the boys goodbye in the transitional care unit, which is much more user-friendly with cheerful green sofas and pull-out beds for mums, and we melt into the melange of other parents leaving with just one baby.

It's great to be home. Lou pops in and we open champagne. Orla lies in the corner asleep while we wet her head. The house is full of flowers and I want to cry with happiness. I am home. And I can walk up stairs! I have to declare a moratorium on bad news. I feel mental with hormones and cannot be allowed to see anything more upsetting than a traffic jam for the next month. Rich gives me my first edible meal in a week and heads back to the hospital to deliver some EBM. I have produced three ounces. It feels like buckets. Orla sleeps in the room with me, and despite the fact that I wake to feed her at 2 a.m., I get the best night's sleep I've had in months. I cannot get over the novelty of being able to turn over in bed, lie on my back, and, look at me, almost lie on my stomach! I feel like Ronnie Biggs newly escaped from gaol.

Wednesday 25 May

A bit of a shock when we visit today.

'Thady is ready to go home,' says a paediatrician.

I find myself trying to stall, suggesting that we wait until Frank is ready too. The doctor says that they normally discharge babies as soon as they are ready because of the risk of infection. Crikey. I feel like we are being asked to adopt. We've already got a new baby at home! We can't take another one, sorry . . . we'd like to help and everything but . . .

'And you know about the brain scan?' she asks.

'Well, I know they had one,' I say, worried now.

'Yes, well, his left ventricle is larger than the right one. We don't think it's of any clinical significance. He looks well. But we'll scan him again at some point just to check.'

I love they way they just drop this stuff in casually. I only found all of this out because I asked how they were doing.

'Frank is not ready. He has already lost 9 per cent of his body weight and he is very tired. We need to work on his feeding. Maybe next week.'

I try to calm down. I had prepared myself for at least two weeks of just Orla at home. I had convinced myself that having their homecoming staggered like this would be useful. Now it feels like they are going to let an avalanche of babies rain down on us. I know a lot of first-time mums feel so scared of the responsibility that they feel like saying, 'What are you doing letting me take this baby home? I'm only twelve years old!' I feel like that. Three times over. How can they possibly expect us to take all three home?

We are told to come back tomorrow and expect to be taking Thady home with us. As we leave, a couple with twins are being discharged.

'So we'll see you back next year with triplets, will we?' says a nurse.

'Ha ha ha!' laugh the couple, a bit too heartily, like that would be the worst thing ever.

I pop into the chemist on the way back. An old lady peers at my still massive belly and laughs. 'You wanna stop eating all them Christmas puddings! Ha ha ha!'

She clearly thinks I am pregnant and this is a great joke. I don't disabuse her, and also manage to resist the urge to paraphrase Winston Churchill by saying, 'Yes, I may look pregnant, but in six months' time I will be lithe and slim again, whereas you, Madam, will still be a toothless old hag.'

Thursday 26 May

Thady's homecoming. We go to the hospital with another car seat.

'We've been calling you,' says a nurse anxiously. 'The consultant wants to see you before twelve.'

We sit and wait. And wait. An hour goes past.

'He knows you're here – he'll be with you shortly.'

We are a bit worried. It sounds serious.

Another hour passes. Saoirse is tired and cranky. The unit is so hot and stuffy that we both feel sleepy. I watch the little boy who is always in a baby swing because he screams unless he is in perpetual motion. Backwards and forwards he goes, at what looks like about seventy miles an hour, his eyes drooping now and then.

It's 1 p.m. and still we wait. Thady has one gunky eye. Frank still has a feeding tube up his nose.

Rich gets cross and asks someone to call the consultant again.

'Ten minutes,' says the ward sister. She is a very quietly spoken but very scarily efficient woman and she looks cross that we have been kept waiting.

Finally the consultant arrives in a flurry of notes and apologies.

'Can you come into this office, please – I want to speak with you privately.'

Oh God. What is he going to tell us? Is Thady's brain weird? What have they discovered?

We sit down and he begins flicking through the notes.

'Yes, Thady has an eye infection but can go home today. His weight is OK—'

'Oh! I thought it was bad news,' I say, a bit cross at his serious demeanour.

'No,' says the sister calmly. 'He has lost 11 per cent body weight.'

'It says here 9 per cent,' says the consultant.

'I weighed him this morning. It's 11 per cent.'

'Oh well, you should have told me,' he says, flustered now.

The sister looks even more cross but keeps quiet.

'Well, in that case, no, I'm not prepared to discharge him yet.'

I feel both disappointed and guiltily relieved. I'm confused by all the different information. I'm tired, hot, fed up.

Saoirse falls off the stool she has been sitting on. She bangs her head and howls. I burst into tears too.

'She's OK, don't worry!' says the consultant kindly.

'She's not crying because she's worried, she's crying because she's fucked off!' says Rich. His honesty and bad language ring round the room like a church bell on a winter morning.

We get reassurances that we will be properly informed in the future. The nurse checks my details and we discover that they have the wrong number for us. No wonder they couldn't get through. I have two newborn sons in hospital and they didn't have our number. My confidence in these people is wavering. I go to kiss the boys goodbye. Thady has been sick and Frank is crying. I have to leave. Saoirse is howling the place down. We weep our way back home.

Friday 27 May

Rich's birthday. He tried to make me wait to deliver the babies until today, but there was no way I could hang on a minute longer. We go to a pub near the hospital. Saoirse is with Lou and Harry – we couldn't make her sit through another hospital visit – and I just have Orla strapped to me.

As we walk into the beer garden, I notice a group of young women staring at me. They look from Orla to my belly and back up again. They clearly cannot decide how I have managed to get pregnant again so quickly as my baby is still tiny. They are not thick – I really do look heavily pregnant. My waist measures a massive forty-seven inches, only seven inches smaller than just before I delivered. They gossip not very subtly about us while we neck some champagne. Drinking too! Tut tut. I lip read one comment, 'Well, if that's what being pregnant does to you—' She doesn't have to finish the sentence. They all laugh.

Saturday 28 May

I go to the hospital with Orla. Maybe it's the fact that Saoirse gets bored so quickly, but Rich is worryingly OK about letting me go alone. He doesn't seem very keen on visiting the boys. Or maybe my sensitivity levels are set irrationally high. Frank is still not feeding well from a bottle. I try to breastfeed him, but he really can't get the hang of it. A few half-hearted sucks and he falls asleep. Cherry, one of the nurses, takes him from me and manages to get a couple of ounces down him. The nurses here are jolly and take great pride in 'their' babies' little achievements. They talk to them all the time, and try to do as much as they can to make it feel like a loving environment.

I get the bus home with Orla and the ten-minute journey takes an hour. Orla is hungry and crying, and I have a pounding headache. I fall through the door to find Rich sunbathing. The fact that he doesn't jump up when I come in has me in floods of tears, but he simply did not hear me. He fetches pills, takes Orla, strokes my head. I am being too sensitive. I just feel so alone with all this. Rich seems to have got so used to dealing with Saoirse on his own during my incapacity that it feels as though they are the couple here and I am the child. Time and again he says 'Saoirse, I love you!' before tickling her belly, biting her neck, throwing her onto the bed. Is it normal to feel supplanted by your baby daughter? These days I find myself shouting 'Rich? Rich?' all over the house. He disappears. Saoirse has taken to copying me, and in my sensitive state it feels like a cruel parody of a nagging wife. 'Rich? Rich!' she screams up the stairs, delighted with herself. He always answers when she calls.

Dona, the donated maternity nurse, and Deanna, her niece and our soon-to-be short-term nanny, come to visit and meet the babies. They decide to set up baby boot camp downstairs in the back room where it is cooler. We have a cot set up for when all three get home, and a pull-out bed for whoever is doing the night feeds. The plan is that the nannies will have sole responsibility for the babies from 11 p.m. to 6 a.m. If we can get seven hours sleep for a few weeks then we should be set up for the months it will take to get them sleeping through. That's our plan, anyway. Dona and Deanna seem unsure. The prospect of juggling three screaming babies all night entirely alone would be enough to daunt the most hardened Mary Poppins, but if there is any benefit in having a stranger in your house when it is already overrun with nippers it has to be that we get some sleep.

Sunday 29 May

I go to the hospital while Rich looks after Saoirse. The family are descending today, so I arrive early with some EBM for the boys. While I am here I like to try and breastfeed them so that they get a bit of body contact. Frank tries and manages a few minutes on my left breast. Thady feeds quite well for about ten minutes and I am really pleased. I put him back in his plastic bassinet and go to pick up Frank to change him. When I turn back a nurse is hovering over Thady with an oxygen mask in her hand. I freeze.

'What's wrong?' I say.

'Can you go and get help?' she says calmly.

I shout but someone has already seen and is coming.

'He's gone blue,' says the nurse. I can't speak.

The ward sister hurries over and instructs them to take Thady to the resus table next door.

I follow mutely, not sure how I am putting one foot in front of the other. They lie his tiny little body down and try to rouse him. He is floppy and blue and I think he might be dead. How can this be? 'I've got people coming for lunch,' I think stupidly. 'How can I tell them one of the babies has died?' I just fed him. He was fine. I notice his tiny feet are purple. The oxygen mask fills his entire face.

'He's coming round now. He's fighting back,' says the ward sister quietly.

Thady starts to wriggle and cry. Everyone relaxes. Except me. I am crying uncontrollably now, hovering behind the four or five nurses who have assembled.

'Is he OK?' I ask.

'The doctor will tell you,' the ward sister says.

I have been worried that I have not bonded with the boys properly. It is hard to have such a part-time relationship with your new babies. You need whole days and nights to examine every crevice of their little bodies, to learn their likes and dislikes. Two or three hours a day split between two babies is not enough, but it is all I have been able to manage. But looking at Thady surrounded by people in uniforms, his little feet the colour of ink, I know I would give my own life for him right now. It is a completely involuntary and surprising feeling.

A doctor appears.

'It might be reflux,' he says, looking at Thady's chart. Apparently, it happened at 7 a.m. too, but somehow during the shift change nobody told me.

'And you know about the heart murmur?'

'No!' I say, shaken anew.

'Oh, sorry. Yes, he's got a slight murmur. It's quite common in premature babies, where the chambers haven't fully closed. It will probably close up on its own.'

Again, it's just casually dropped in mid-conversation, and only then when I have managed to corner a doctor for two minutes.

'I think we should put him back into the NICU for closer observation,' says the doctor.

So Thady is to go back to intensive care, and will be taken off milk feeds. And to think he was almost home on Thursday. I start to panic. What if he had come home and this had happened and I hadn't noticed? It was only the vigilance of the nurse that saved him. If she hadn't noticed his colour change, I don't know what might have happened.

'You would have noticed,' says Irish Helen, the mum with the baby in the cubicle next to Frank.

'Would I?' I ask, not at all sure.

'You would. You're a sharp cookie.'

'But I'm not usually a worrier – I tend to be less observant.'

'But you're not an idiot.'

I cuddle Frank and cry some more. This is terrible. No one should have to see their baby go blue.

The ward sister has a heated argument with a very stern doctor who wants to swap Thady with a baby in the NICU.

'We don't have space, so you will have to take baby James in Thady's place,' he says.

'You can't do that. Thady and Frank are brothers, they are sharing a space,' says the ward sister.

'Well, you'll have to do it,' says the doctor.

'No I won't,' she says quietly. 'I don't care what you say, I'm not going to do it. You can't put another family in one space.'

The doctor goes off grumbling and I feel very grateful that she was so protective of my boys.

'I don't think Thady needs to go next door anyway,' she says. 'The nurse looking after him is intensive trained.' I see this a lot – the nurses at grassroots level with their own ideas about how things should happen, while the doctors float around dishing out unworkable orders. It's hard to know who to trust in this status minefield because the nurses can't really give clinical diagnoses and the doctors are always busy somewhere else. I'm still no clearer as to why he stopped breathing. Thady is prepped for the NICU, and they have to send me away while they try to get the IV line in because I am crying so hard and because he stops breathing a couple more times. They are going to attach a monitor to his heel in order to gauge the level of oxygen in his blood, and he is to be put on antibiotics in case he has some sort of infection.

I call Rich and cry down the phone.

'Is he OK now though?' asks Rich.

'Well, no – it keeps happening. Something to do with his saturation levels, but I don't know what that means.'

I cancel my brother Ray's visit without realizing that he is with my mum when I call. I didn't want her to know about Thady because I always try to protect her. Now she will worry, and I hate that. I know what a burden she finds the terrible empathy that comes with motherhood. Now I understand it only to well, having jumped on board the prem-baby roller coaster today.

Back home, I try to set my mind at rest by posting on the Triplet Connection website, hoping that someone has had a similar experience to the one I had this morning. I post a worried message and await replies. Someone has posted to say that they have heard of a family expecting their second set of quadruplets, and they want to know if this is a record. Apparently not, by quite a long way. The replies list a string of incredible statistics collected over the past two hundred years or so. In Casalini, Italy, a woman gave birth to two sets of quads, one set of triplets, one set of twins and nineteen singleton babies. Most did not survive, however, this being long before the neonatal intensive care era. Another family in Ohio had, by 1913, two sets of quads, three sets of triplets and *five* sets of twins. You would think that would be the all-time record, but no, for in Vassiliev,

Russia, between 1725 and 1765, one woman gave birth to *four* sets of quads, *seven* sets of triplets and *sixteen* sets of twins. Only two of the children did not survive, and the father went on to spawn eighteen more children with his second wife! If ever an afternoon in front of the laptop could put something in perspective this is surely it. We have nothing to worry about, and Rich, with his solitary singleton, his meagre set of twins and his paltry pack of triplets, is a lightweight.

Monday 30 May

'Thady examined really well today – there's nothing wrong with him. He's a fraud. He should be home with you,' says a doctor. I still haven't received any answers about what happened yesterday. I am terrified they are going to release him without me knowing what's wrong. I am determined to get to the bottom of it. In the meantime, he is attached to a desaturation monitor via a very low-tech plaster on his foot. If his oxygen levels dip below 85 per cent, or his heart beat goes above 170 b.p.m., it lets off a disturbing alarm. It goes off ten times in the hour I sit by his cot, sending me leaping to my feet to prod him. I don't want him home with any beeping bits and bobs. I've read about babies sent home on oxygen or with alarms, and it must be terrifying. Apnoea, where babies 'forget' to breathe, and bradycardia, where the heartbeat is abnormally slow, are so common among premature infants that they are referred to simply as As and Bs. I hope Thady hasn't got As and Bs. Not until they are marks for homework.

★

On the way home I pop in to a clothes shop in search of an outfit I can wear for a wedding we are madly hoping to go to on Saturday.

Top tip: if you are ten days post-partum after carrying big triplets and gaining five stone in weight along the way, don't go clothes shopping. I try on six skirts, and each one makes me look like I have a space hopper shoved down my knickers.

Back at home Rich is doing a weird hybrid new man/cave man routine. He has holed himself up in the kitchen and is baking bread. He's always either cooking, ironing or hoovering. He's obsessed with hoovering. This morning I caught him hoovering the hoover. 'You have to hoover Henry,' he said sheepishly. 'He gets dusty.' I don't really care about dust at the moment, and I don't need fresh bread, but I would like a chat and some emotional support.

Why do some men do this? Retreating into the world of the fixable, the practical, as a way of body swerving the enormity of their new responsibilities? A lot of women could cheerfully throttle their partners in those first few weeks after giving birth. I remember one of the new dads at the first post-partum NCT (National Childbirth Trust) reunion we went to. We had all agreed to bring food to share, so we took some frozen pizzas, and other people brought bagels and crisps and so on, but this one guy turned up proudly brandishing a platter of fresh figs wrapped in Parma ham, drizzled in olive oil and delicate Parmesan shavings. 'Wow, they must really be coping well,' we all thought, suddenly ashamed of our shop-bought offerings. Months later, his wife confided that she had been livid with him about it. He'd spent two hours faffing around in the kitchen while she struggled with a colic-ridden newborn.

Meera arrives with a home-made quiche and a huge bag of nuts. 'They're a traditional gift for new mothers in Indian culture,' she says. 'They provide warmth and they're good for milk production.' It's lovely to get home-cooked food as a gift – not least because it means Rich will have no excuse to spend all night in the kitchen.

Mum calls and tells me that an Irish dyslexic friend of hers keeps asking after the Twiglets. You couldn't make it up.

Tuesday 31 May

Thady is back with Frank. The nurse swears she saw Frank wave when his brother came back in. I'm glad they are back together, even though they are probably too little to notice each other. I wish they were in the same crib. It would be easier to leave them if they were cuddled up together.

A fetal medicine professor is in the unit today and she does her rounds, spending a long time watching me feed Thady. She examines his notes carefully. 'I think he has been pushed too hard, too fast, because he looks too big to be in the NICU. Plus he only got one dose of surfactant at birth, whereas Frank got two because he was worse at first. He'll produce his own in time. His stomach can't cope with being full. We may have to give him some Gaviscon in his feeds.'

How do I do that with breastfeeding? Although the amount of Gaviscon I swigged has probably made my breast milk at least 5 per cent Gaviscon.

'He needs time. He is having problems coordinating his breathing, sucking and swallowing when he feeds. He'll learn.'

This makes sense. Thady's immature system can't cope with doing all three things at once. Is it true what they say, that men can't multitask?

Poor Thady has an oxygen tube shoved up his nose as a gentle reminder.

'Frank could probably go home,' says the Professor casually, before moving on to the next cot.

I panic. Today? What do we do, just scoop him up and walk out with him?

'Not today,' says a nurse, spotting my panic. 'Maybe tomorrow.'

I am stalling them. I want to make sure they are both absolutely fine before we bring them home, and I want them home together. Thady and Frank are playing chicken with us. Which one will run first? I look back as I leave. They look very weak, their eyes lifeless and their wispy hair giving them the appearance of two old men in a care home waiting to die. I shudder and shake off the image.

I switch on the TV at home and get absorbed in 'Big Brother'. It is full of absolute arseholes, and will be great late-night breastfeeding entertainment for me. I can enjoy my three babies growing and evolving while I watch ten idiots degenerate and regress. That's if their self-obsessed narcissism doesn't turn my milk sour.

Wednesday 1 June

Awake at 5 a.m. shivering. I crawl into bed with Rich and make him fetch me paracetamol and more blankets. I drift into sleep and wake an hour later bathed in sweat. Great. Another infection. I manage to beg an appointment at the doctor's surgery and stagger round there for 9 a.m. The receptionist is a large 'fun' lady whose desk is bang in the middle of the waiting room. I don't like her, mainly because I find her loud – and I have an irrational dislike of white people who corn-row their hair.

'Hello,' she shouts. 'Haven't you had them yet?' She points at my belly.

I'm not sure if she's genuinely confused or if this is her idea of an amusing remark.

'Yes,' I say, shocked at her rudeness.

'Oh.' She's flustered now.

I come to. 'What do you mean "Haven't you had them yet?"'

She doesn't answer me, and scurries back behind her desk mumbling something.

'Take this and do a wee for me,' she says, thrusting a plastic drinking cup at me.

'In that?' I say.

'Yeah, well it's easier, isn't it? Otherwise you pee all over your hands!' She lets out one of her foghorn nervous laughs.

Minutes later she comes back carrying the yellow cup aloft, having presumably tested my urine herself.

'Yeah, there's an infection there,' she says. 'You'll have to get some antibiotics.'

★

Mum, Dad, my brother Adrian, his partner Silvie and their son James turn up to visit and Rich busies himself entertaining them with pasta and wine while I am quizzed by Eva, our new health visitor. It's a weird sensation becoming someone's 'case' – I feel like we've been placed on an ASBO, or under a social worker. Fortunately, Eva is lovely – very homely and supportive. Within minutes of meeting her she is calling me 'Jack' and has said she will come round every week to weigh the babies to save us the trouble of getting all three to the clinic. This is a big help. Weighing them will be important because they are premature and I am partially breastfeeding, so I will want to make sure that they are getting enough and thriving. Eva can't believe that there is no statutory help available for families with triplets, and says she will look into it.

'I can't promise anything,' she says. I won't hold my breath, but I like the fact that she is at least going to try.

From the back room I can hear laughter and merry-making. I feel left out sitting here. Why is it that when people come to visit when you've had a baby they end up consuming everything and leaving the place in more chaos than they found it? I should write a visitors' guide for people planning to call on women with new babies.

1 Don't turn up expecting to be fed and watered. Bring food, and wash up after yourselves.
2 In your enthusiasm to wet the baby's head, don't get plastered and stay too long being boring and generally grating on the poor new mum's brittle nerves.
3 Don't think that just sitting holding the baby is 'helping'. Coo over the baby and then do the ironing, make the bed, cook a meal and put it in the fridge for later.

4 Generally, act like you're not there and tiptoe around the new mum as if you are walking in a minefield and might be blasted at any minute. Remember – those Mothercare shots of ladies gazing wistfully at their new baby are a load of nonsense. In reality, we are vile hormonal ingrates – weepy, leaking, self-pitying malcontents who must be handled very carefully for at least six months.

I lighten up a bit and go to join them. There's no pasta left. Bastards.

DJ and John come over. They take one look at my miserable face and steal me away to a local tapas bar for an hour. It's lovely to be out, even though I can't stop talking about baby stuff. I tell them about the little boy in the NICU who was born on Christmas Day.

'Blimey,' says DJ. 'Five hundred grams. That's a lot of cocaine, but not very much baby.'

Friday 3 June

Saoirse is awake at 5 a.m. crying. I fob her off until 6.30, when I get up to feed Orla, who only nibbles a bit while my milk drips onto the bed, soaking the sheets. I have to sit with an empty bottle under the other breast so as not to set us afloat. I change into my Victorian antique nightdress, bought in a moment of 'what shall I wear in hospital?' madness, but within minutes it is soaking.

Tip. When buying maternity nightdresses, don't be tempted by the image of a floaty new mum in virginal white cotton and lace. By the time you've given birth, it will look like you've

murdered someone in it. Opt for something more practical –
like a butcher's apron, or a sou'wester.

Either Saoirse has undergone a horrible personality change
or she's not well. She refuses her milk and moans for a story,
but every book I pick out is rejected. I express four ounces of
milk for the boys then try to force Saoirse to eat her Weetabix.
She screams and flings it across the floor, spraying me with it.
I change for the second time today and it's only 7.30. She must
be ill. I make another appointment with the doctor. Rich is
wandering about in his pants trying to decide what to wear for
a pasta commercial casting he is going up for this morning. He
hasn't bothered to find out what the character is.

'Wear your new linen suit,' I say.

'Hmmmm . . . I'm not really in a suit mood,' he says.

'It doesn't matter what sort of mood you're in – they don't
care.'

'But the suit's too new – I'm a bit shy of it.' Rich will leave
new clothes in the cupboard for at least three months before
daring to wear them outside. Even plain white T-shirts.

'Look, do you want the job or not? Because if you can't be
bothered to dress the part, then don't bother going. You can
stay here and look after Orla while I take Saoirse to the doctor.'

He caves in and puts on the suit. Even in my foul mood I
appreciate how fantastically handsome he looks in it. I suppose
that's the point of having a good-looking partner – you can
cheer yourself up on a rotten day just by looking at them. Like
finding a Christmas tree bauble under the bed on a wet
February morning.

Rich leaves, late and flustered, but two minutes later he's
back.

'I should have checked my messages. My agent rang. They want jeans and rugged.'

He throws his suit on the floor and changes.

Round to the doctor's again at 9 a.m. The receptionist cowers when she sees me coming, Orla strapped to my chest, like my family is about to wipe out the entire global supply of antibiotics. Saoirse perks up a bit in the waiting room and plays with some toys. A lady coos over Orla.

'Isn't she tiny? How old is she?'

'She's two weeks. She's a triplet – the other two are in hospital.'

'Triplets? Ooh!' she says, turning to the receptionist and gurning stupidly in a 'God how awful' sort of a way. The receptionist gurns back, eager to take part in anything gossipy.

'You're going to need help!'

No shit Sherlock. Why do people always feel the need to tell me how hard it's going to be? No one ever offers help – they just like to tell me I'm going to need it. If they'd just heard I was suffering from a terminal illness, would they feel obliged to say, 'Ooh cancer! That's going to really hurt. You'll probably die!'? Some people are so thick and insensitive I wouldn't put it past them.

Saoirse keeps running into the hallway and trying to get upstairs. I drag her back in, Orla swinging from the sling on my chest, and she does her floppy leg routine. I grab her by the hand and pull. There is a sickening clicking sound and for a horrible moment I think I've dislocated her shoulder. But she runs off unconcerned and I chase her again. Her shoe comes off and in my struggle to put it back on she bangs her head on the wall and howls. This wakes Orla up, who screams too. I realize she needs feeding, as she didn't eat this morning. I can't do it now – how can I chase around after Saoirse with one boob hanging out? So I give up and sit down on the stairs for a good cry, my tears plopping onto Orla's head. Finally, we're called in and Saoirse is diagnosed with a raging ear infection. Yet more antibiotics. On the way to the chemist I cry some more, guilty that I have been cross with Saoirse when she has been in pain. I buy her a gingerbread man and myself a Belgian bun – for old time's sake. Sod the diet.

Saturday 4 June

We make it to Meera and Sanjeev's wedding celebration. This has been a goal for the past few months. Even though we have only one triplet with us, it feels great to be here. All week I've been dodging the issue of the boys' homecoming because I don't think they are ready, and the upside is that we are able to be here today. 'Don't make eye contact with the doctors,' I said to Rich when we visited the boys today. 'They might make us take them home.'

Getting ready has been a nightmare. All my good clothes have been banished to the loft because I can't get into anything and they were taunting me. I take a look at myself naked in the full-length mirror. Bad move. Comparatively, I am whippet thin – my 54-inch waist feels like a distant memory – but the mirror tells a different story. My arms don't quite lie flush with my body because the bingo wings have inflated, my short legs are bloated and doughy, but it is my belly which takes – nay, devours – the biscuit. It is both taut and saggy. The top section has shrunk down a lot, the middle bit still looks six-months pregnant – tight and round and baby-looking. Then there's this hanging, saggy, stretch-marked sort of flab apron that flops down dejectedly over the C-section scar. It's huge, ugly and defeated-looking. I can pick it up in both hands and waggle it. If I turn one way, it decides to go another. It has its own mind, its own will and probably its own eco-system. How on earth will I get rid of the overhang? *Picnic at Hanging Rock* keeps going through my mind. Small children could shelter under its precipice.

In vain, I search for a forgiving maternity outfit which is not frayed or sick-stained. This is going to be a glamorous party with lots of gorgeous Indian women in saris. I ask Rich to iron the least offensive items I possess and jump in the shower. Two minutes later I hear the hoover.

'What are you doing?' I ask, dripping wet.

'Hoovering.'

'Why? We have to leave in ten minutes and you're meant to be ironing my clothes!'

'Sorry, love.'

Two minutes later I hear the hoover again.

'Rich! What *are you doing now*?' I shout.

'*Waiting for the iron to heat up!*'

Poor Rich. He must be the only man in the world right now being bollocked for hoovering while the iron heats up.

I needn't have worried about my outfit not passing muster here tonight. I've got something much more alluring than a jewel-encrusted sari – I've got a baby. Men, women and children stream up to us to coo and give us their congratulations, and the best thing is that when we tell them Orla is one of a set of three *not one person says*, 'You've got your hands full!' Lots of fellow mums stare at me in astonishment when I tell them Orla is just two weeks old. 'And you're here! I didn't go out for three months after I had mine,' they say. 'You're very brave.'

I find this a bit disconcerting. Am I mad to be here? It never occurs to me not to do something that I feel like doing. Is it 'brave'? I couldn't stand staying indoors looking after babies for three months. It's not so all-consuming that a night out is out of the question. Plus it can get very boring. Why not throw on a tent dress, chuck on a bit of lippy and head out for a drink? Even if you can't get a babysitter, newborns are very portable. We notice the cloakroom ladies eyeing Orla, so we check her in and leave her with them for a couple of hours. She stays fast asleep despite the noise, her shutdown reflex kicking in.

Towards the end of the evening, when the music gets a little loud, the women start staring at us disapprovingly as if to say 'Come on, you should take her home now' and we probably should, but this may well be the last time we get out in a while. Taking *three* babies out is another proposition entirely. Instead, we dance together. Rich loves to dance – he often goes out on his own and ends up dancing in the corner of the pub. But it occurs to me that we have never danced together. Our relationship moved quickly on from what Rich charmingly calls the 'courting' stage to procreation, completely bypassing the going-out-dancing window. I feel awkward, sober, unable to let go. Rich grins at me, half drunk.

'Ducky, it's weird dancing with you,' he says.

He looks shy. I feel shy. The record ends suddenly and the

DJ plays a tune that empties the dance floor. Maybe that was our first and last dance.

On the way home we negotiate sleeping arrangements for the night.

'So are you sleeping in our bed tonight?' asks Rich. We have taken to sleeping in separate rooms – no point in us both being woken up by the baby.

'Yes, if I'm having Orla.'

'OK, I'll sleep in the spare room,' says Rich.

'Run this by me again – we go to *my* friends' wedding, you get to drink and I get to drive you home, then because you've had a drink, I get to have the baby all night?'

'Yeah.'

'Why's that then?'

'Because when you've had a drink it's not nice to be woken up by a crying baby.'

'Ah. I see. Silly me.'

Monday 6 June

We are discussing the future. The boys aren't even home yet and already I'm worried about how we will bring them up.

'You do realize that there will be an awful lot of fighting in this house, don't you?' I say.

'No there won't. They will all share nicely,' says Rich.

'They won't. They'll fight and bite each other.'

'They won't. They'll do string quartet recitals for us and read poetry in Italian and bring us tea in bed.'

So that's the plan then. Glad that's sorted.

The house is a mess. We try to get everything ready for the boys' homecoming, which seems imminent. Dirty nappies litter the floor, crusty breast pads lie discarded everywhere. This place is a health-and-safety time bomb. We shouldn't be allowed to have one child here, let alone four.

We go to the hospital. A paediatrician approaches.

'Hi, I'm here to do the boys' discharge examination,' she says.

'Discharge? When?'

'Today if you like. Today's good.'

'*Today?*' I panic. In the back of my mind, I think I've been in denial that these babies are actually mine. They feel so much a part of the hospital institution.

'Or tomorrow,' she allows, seeing our stress.

'OK, tomorrow,' I say quickly.

I spend the evening on the verge of tears. We're going to have three babies in the house tomorrow. So far Orla has just slotted in, easily absorbed into the family. One extra baby is no problem. Three. Wow. Dona, the maternity nurse, is stuck in Norfolk with a broken-down car and can't make it to us until Wednesday, so we will have a whole night on our own with all three of them.

'Worst case scenario is you don't sleep for twenty-four hours – but you'll sleep when I get there,' she says.

I'm very scared. I realize with a start that I can't even run away because my passport is out of date.

We go shopping in preparation for hunkering down and I try to stock up on contact lenses. The optician is insisting I have a check-up before I get any more throwaways.

'But you don't understand! I don't have time for check–ups! I've just had triplets.'

He is unmoved by my triplet trump card.

I bath Saoirse for the last time on her own. She splashes around and doesn't need me at all. I console myself with the fact that they are only very dependent for a short time. Only a year really. That's nothing. It'll be OK. Then the words of Emma, my radio producer and mum of twins, float into my mind. 'Ah, but a year is 365 days long, and each of those days is twenty-four hours.'

Quite. Time for some wine. A bottle. And a straw.

Tuesday 7 June

The phone rings. I know instinctively that it's the hospital.

'Not to worry, but Frank's had a bit of an episode and went a bit blue so we have to keep him in for another twenty-four hours,' says a nurse.

It seems Frank doesn't want to be left out of the drama.

'You can pick them both up tomorrow, if you'd rather they came home together.'

'Fine,' I say, worried but also, if I'm honest, slightly relieved. What's happening with these boys and their 'blue period'? Maybe Frank is also struggling with coordinating his breathing with the feeding.

I get a call from my elderly drag-queen friend Bette Bourne.

'How are those darling babies?' he drawls.

I fill him in on the latest. 'The doctor thinks they have got a problem with coordinating their sucking, swallowing and breathing. I reckon it's a boy thing. They just can't multitask.'

'Darling, I'm a boy and I can suck, swallow and breathe all night long, no problem!'

I laugh out loud for the first time in days.

Wednesday 8 June

The boys are home. Leaving the hospital with three car seats is our first taste of being triplet celebrities.

'Look – triplets!' whisper passers-by to their companions. In the short walk from the ward to the car park we get used to the triplet double-take as people spot one, then two, then three babies. In the car I feel a sense of foreboding.

'I feel like I'm being driven from the courthouse to the gaol,' I say doomily.

'You are, love – but it's an open prison. You'll get passes out for good behaviour and parole is only eighteen years away.'

We put all three babies side by side in one cot and then run into the living room laughing maniacally. It's the most bizarre and wonderful sight, even though the room now resembles a Romanian orphanage. Three babies lined up in a cot, all staring blankly ahead as if to say, 'Where the hell are we now?'

At least the delay in their homecoming has meant that Dona is able to be here for their first night. She arrives and is very tender with the babies, especially Frank who she is keeping a close eye on. It's very reassuring. We have put the babies on a tight four hourly feeding and changing schedule. From what

I have been told it is the only way to survive. If we were to stagger the feeds, we would be feeding all day. They are to be breast- or bottle-fed at six, ten and two round the clock. Dona is taking the 2 a.m. feed on her own, and has brought some Podee feeding system bottles to experiment with. They have a long tube attached to the teat, and the idea is you can rest the bottles next to the babies and they can suck on it like a straw, leaving your hands free. Rich and I go to bed feeling very naughty. How can we have three babies in the house and be going to bed at 11 p.m. for a full night's sleep? What an absolutely brilliant present. I can't help feeling very guilty.

Thursday 9 June

The triplets' first outing. Rich gets the triplet buggy out and puts it all together. It is the most absurd thing I have ever seen. It's five-feet long and we can't stop laughing as we stand at the handlebars and imagine pushing it down the street. It's like a bendy bus without the bendy bit. It looks like a really naff stretch limo. It should have drunk teenagers hanging out of it.

'I'm not going out with it,' says Rich.

'Not even with me?' I say.

'I'll walk ten paces behind.'

Lou comes to help feed the babies and Rich decides that he can't resist the novelty factor. He loads the babies carefully into the buggy and sets off for the High Street. The babies look like a dwarf bob-sleigh team in training.

I put Saoirse down for a nap and go to bed myself with a

packet of biscuits and knowing that the washing is on the line. Triplets. How hard can it be?

An hour later he's back.

'How did you get on? Did you get mobbed?'

'No. I just kept my head down and scowled at people.'

'What – no one said anything?' I ask, slightly disappointed. I've read so much about how you have to plan at least an extra hour for all the questions and comments on a simple trip to the shops. One woman had even taken to putting a sign on her buggy saying 'Donations welcome' to deter people.

'Well, I walked past a woman in the park and she didn't say anything to me, but as I went by she whispered, "Jesus Christ."'

Friday 10 June

I'm not sleeping well, even though Dona is still doing the night feeds single-handed. The Podee system didn't work, so she is having to feed them one by one, which takes about an hour and a half, and then prop them up to avoid reflux. Frank in particular is quite sicky after a feed. We can't lie him down or he possets everywhere. I can't relax with Dona here because I am so unused to 'help', and I know that when she leaves here at 7 a.m. she is going back to her own four children and a childminding job. I don't know how she does it. I keep hoping that she gets a good night's sleep, rather than enjoying the luxury of it myself. Some maternity nurses, I'm informed, are expected to do laundry, clean and cook between night feeds.

They don't expect to sleep. OK, I suppose, if you are able to go home to bed, but not for Dona.

I am feeling anxious a lot of the time. A sort of low-level, non-specific fear. Could this be the dreaded post-natal depression? Losing my mind has always been my personal bogeyman, and here I am with a toddler, newborn triplets, no financial support, no regular income, a total lifestyle change, huge weight gain and an even bigger mortgage – surely a recipe for disaster.

In an attempt to feel calm I write out a large feeding/ changing chart which details who has had what and done what hour by hour. You'd think it would be easy enough to remember which baby was on which breast from feed to feed but it's impossible. Sometimes I forget who I'm carrying from one room to the next. 'Come on Thady – erm, Frank – erm, baby,' I'll say.

I take the triplets out for my first road test of the buggy. A group of mums in the park literally reposition themselves to have a better stare. I stare back and they smile. I look away, scowling. Why am I such a grouch? I should be proud. I think I feel so defensive because in my vulnerable state I know I couldn't cope with any negative comments at the moment. I feel totally alienated already. In one sense, I am the biggest mamma of them all – an ubermum – but in another I am having an experience that is totally removed from theirs. Another group of mums with a single baby each in a sling stop as I walk past. One whispers to the others, 'God! Can you *imagine*!' I turn back and glare at them. They smile, expecting me to join in their mirth at my 'dreadful' life. I don't. Instead, I try to perfect a jaunty 'I'm *so* coping' swagger – no mean feat when you're pushing a tonne weight, you haven't washed your hair in a week and your only clean top has just been covered in vomit.

I am stirring up triplet fever just by going about my business. In the local supermarket, all the Asian cashiers actually get up from their tills to come and see the babies, leaving a queue of customers to wait as the shop comes to a standstill. No one seems to mind. Some even discard their shopping and join in the goggling. Outside, a woman pulls back the babies' sunshades without asking, just so that she can get a proper look. As I walk back through the park, an elderly woman blocks my path, even though I am on the phone, so that she can see the babies.

'Aren't you lucky! What fun you're going to have!' she says, and I'm touched. I don't mind stopping if people are going to be nice, but I really have to get home now as the babies are due a feed.

Dona notices that the two babies that get breastfed are not settling as well as the third formula-fed baby.

'Don't get me wrong, I think breastfeeding is great, but formula makes them sleep better. I know maternity nurses who have dumped expressed breast milk and fed the baby formula without telling the mum.'

I'm shocked. Is this the price you pay for having someone else look after your baby? I thought people chose to be nannies because they love babies, and would therefore want what was best for the child and not what would help them get a better night's sleep. I'm so naive.

Saturday 11 June

We head out en famille with Linda, our lovely supermum neighbour, and her kids, Nansai and Finn, to what sounds like an oxymoron – a 'family fun day' at the local cricket club. Not wanting to draw attention to ourselves, we park the triple buggy behind the bouncy castle and relax. But then the castle is deflated and descends, revealing our triplets. We are mobbed. Most people are lovely, but a few comments sting.

A man with twins comes over to have a look. 'We had triplets, but we lost one early on. They spotted a third sac, but by then it was empty, just hanging there like a plastic shopping bag. To tell you the truth, I was relieved.'

'I know what you mean,' I start, not sure what is going to come out next because my brain is still processing what he's just said. 'It was shocking enough to hear it was twins, but then she spotted the third and that's our Orla – and how could I wish her away now?' Tears well up in my eyes.

Another man approaches. He's a big guy with lots of tattoos. 'Triplets?' he says, incredulous. 'I don't envy you!'

'That's—' I stop myself from carrying on with 'not very nice'. Instead, I mutter something about it being not too bad.

What I want to say is: 'And I don't envy you either, you big fat cretin.'

Already I am noticing the animosity people seem to feel about children. The way people talk to me about our situation is bizarre for a supposedly child-friendly nation. Parents are the worst. 'Are they *all* yours?' they gasp, horrified. It makes me wonder if they hate their own children as much as they seem to be appalled by ours. Or is it a way of drawing attention to the self-sacrifice we all feel as parents? 'I'm having such a terrible time, poor me, please tell me you're suffering too.'

Later, in the park, two women approach me. The younger, carrying an older baby, stares at the buggy as if the triplets have '666' tattooed on each forehead.

'Do you get *any* sleep?' she asks.

'Well, yes, because we have a maternity nurse doing nights for a week,' I say, almost apologizing.

'I haven't slept for nine months,' she says, shaking her head and looking down at her daughter with such defeated love that I feel sorry for her. She is exhausted.

Some parents are tortured by their infants. Sleep deprivation is the most common complaint, and yet I always assume they must be doing something wrong because we've never had any serious trouble. I hope the triplets don't prove me wrong. We walk on and stop for a coffee at a pavement cafe, parking the buggy alongside the tables and chairs. A middle-aged waitress spots it and screams.

'Triplets? Oh my god! The poor mum! Who's the mum?'

I duck my head and she gets distracted. A pregnant lady nearby catches my eye and smiles. 'What did you have?' she says.

'Two girls and – no, hang on, that's not right,' I say. I can't remember the word 'boy'.

'One girl and two of the other flavour,' I say eventually.

This is happening more and more. I can't remember the babies' names, let alone who I've just fed. I say things like 'That one with the stripes on – I think he was on my left tit.' I used to think that 'baby brain' was a misogynist myth. Now I'm not so sure.

Wednesday 15 June

Dona's time with us is over. We are flying solo and we are scared. It will be three weeks before another temporary nanny, Deanna, can join us. Luckily, Dona got the babies into a great routine and we hope we can stick to it. I breast-feed two at once in what they call the 'rugby hold', one baby under each arm, while Rich bottle feeds the third. The only problem I have with feeding two is when they need wind-ing, although Thady has perfected the art of only partially unlatching before burping himself, and sometimes even treat-ing himself to a little vomit on my nipple. What a charmer. Let's hope I'm the only woman he ever does that to. After each feed we change them. We did try changing them before the feeds to wake them up – they still sleep for most of the day – but they kept pooing mid-feed and we'd have to change them all over again. When you're already doing eighteen nappies a day, that's not a situation you want to encourage. Their poo is changing from the green sludge of the early days to the chunky wholegrain mustard variety. Nice. When the babies have been fed and changed we tidy up, do the wash-ing, sterilize bottles and keep Saoirse entertained. God bless PlayDoh. Then, as the babies wake up again, we jiggle them until the next feeding time. We've taken to going up to bed for a lunchtime nap. We leave the babies in the cot downstairs and shut the doors. We can hear them if they scream, but not if they are just crying. I know I should feel guilty about this but I don't. I should be one of those very dedicated co-sleeper mummies who jump up at the slightest whimper and bring their babies into bed with them, but we have an extreme situation here, and it calls for extreme measures if we are to survive.

Rich is philosophical about it: 'If we can't hear them, they're not crying.'

The surprise is that this routine is quite pleasant. I've always rebelled against structure and repetition, but I am finding it curiously comforting to know exactly what I will be doing from one hour to the next. No time for existential angst, just mouths to be fed and bottoms to wipe.

Thursday 16 June

Rich has taken on the night feeds for now. He's not even complaining about it. I head for the supermarket, but halfway through my shopping I remember that we have a triple appointment at the Town Hall to register the triplets' birth. I call Rich.

'Get them in the car – we have to be in Hackney in twenty minutes!'

'Why don't you go and I'll stay here with them?' he says, exhausted. He got about three hours' sleep.

'Because you have to come if you want to be registered as their father, because we're not married.'

How chav.

Even though the babies start off cranky because it's their feed time, it turns into a jolly occasion. We leave with three birth certificates. The triplets officially exist, even if they aren't meant to be here for another eight days. And if the triplets officially exist, then we officially have triplets. Gulp.

I am still massively fat despite not having had any chocolate or a single Belgian bun this week. In fact, I have put on two pounds. How can you breastfeed triplets and put on weight? That's just bloody cruel. I am now two stone heavier than I was in 1993 when I first joined Weight Watchers. And to think I used to call them 'my fat years'. But as sure as I am not losing my blubber the triplets are piling it on. Eva weighed them today and they are doing really well. Thady is now 6lb 10oz, and Orla and Frank are both 6lb 13oz. I feel so proud I could cry.

Friday 17 June

The house is in chaos even though we are both constantly doing something. The hours fly by and there's very little to show for it. The clean nappy pile seems to shrivel before our eyes. It's like time-lapse photography – one minute I see a neat, tall pile of Pampers, the next they're all gone and I'm being weed on by a baby while I grope around in vain for a nappy with my spare hand.

Rich did the night feed again last night, and I am so grateful, but when I came down this morning he had Orla and Thady in bed with him. I am dead against this, not just for safety reasons but, more selfishly, I don't want to get them into the habit of sleeping with us. Cute now, but three one-year-olds in your bed every night would be no fun. Things are already starting to slip since Dona left. I feel like our mum's gone and left us teenagers in charge. Orla had her 6 a.m. feed at 8.30 this morning, and Thady has started fussing around on the breast screaming. I'm losing it. I jump into the shower, then dash upstairs to get dressed. I can hear screams from downstairs, but when I open my underwear drawer peace is restored. All my pants, from distant memory foxy thongs to big grey floral bin bags are folded and ironed, placed neatly in size order. Rich has been fiddling while Rome burns, ironing pants while the house is covered in jam, but right now I don't care. I may have leaky tits, awful hair and acne, but at least I've got smooth pants to put on. They can't take that away from me.

Saturday 18 June

Rich has got cabin fever. He has been asked to audition for a profit-share play and even though it would mean personal chaos back home we decide he should go for it. It's important that his dreams don't get buried under a pile of shitty nappies. It would mean I would have to cope on my own for a month. He heads off for his 'workshop audition' and I go to my parents with all four children. We spend the day being visited by a succession of elderly Irish ladies, all of whom said a rosary for me the day we had the babies. I am enjoying these early baby days so much more than the first time – the lovely snuffly noises, the little dreamy moans while feeding, the beautiful tai chi of their hands and legs moving contentedly after a feed. Magical. Maybe I needed a triple dose to really get it. It's always taken a lot to intoxicate me.

Monday 20 June

Rich didn't get the part. I have to stop myself from saying 'Phew!' out loud. It is stiflingly hot, and the babies sleep most of the day. I feel like a character in a Tennessee Williams play – except fatter. Rich is shattered after a bumpy night with the babies, so I pack him off to bed for a siesta. After the feed I join him, only having had about five hours sleep myself. I even remember to unplug the phone and switch off my mobile. I stretch out, luxuriating in the knowledge that all three babies and Saoirse are fast asleep too. If we're lucky we'll get an hour. Within minutes I am in a coma. Suddenly, there is a furious rapping at the door. Bloody hell, what's happened? Have I left the babies in the car? Is the pram in the road? Rich jumps up and runs downstairs. A minute later he returns.

'It was some cheeky bastard delivering leaflets,' he says crossly.

So that's it for sleep, then. Because of some devious marketing strategy whereby leafleters are required to draw attention to the junk they are posting through our door by actually knocking on it, I am now wide awake and fuming. If it's a takeaway pizza menu I'll chase him down the street and ram it down his throat. We get about ten pizza menus a week, and I can't help taking it as a personal comment on my huge belly – how many pizzas do they think we eat?

I go downstairs and discover it's not for pizza – it's worse. It's for a local estate agent: 'Are you thinking of selling or buying? All we ask for is the opportunity to help!'

I consider ringing them up and asking them if their offer stretches to a bit of ironing, but I'm so hot and tired I can't find the energy to plug the phone back in. Instead, I go and stare at the babies. Thady has been sick on the one bit of sheet not covered with a muslin, but apart from that they are peaceful, their faces flickering in a windy smile relay. I love the way they smile in their sleep – like they are suddenly remembering a private joke. Lucky bastards.

Tuesday 21 June

The longest day. They're all pretty long at the moment. Milk trouble. I have defied all the nay-sayers and attempted to at least partially breastfeed all three babies, but things have started to go wrong. The triplets seem to be suffering from what's called 'nipple/teat confusion'. Because they get both, they are never sure at each feed how hard to suck – there is a slightly different technique required for each. On top of that, I have discovered that the combined output of both breasts is about four ounces – one feed – and I have been feeding two at a time. By my calculations they are probably only getting two ounces each per feed. No wonder they have started to fuss around and get cranky between feeds. They are probably hungry. Now, I know what to do to increase my supply; somewhat perversely, you should feed more often, express between feeds, eat more, rest more (yeah right). Breast milk works on a supply and demand basis – the more you ask of your body, the more it will try to create. This advice is probably fine for a mum of one baby, but it seems practically impossible for me. A feed/change cycle already takes two hours. If I were to feed more often, I would never be able to do anything else. The one hour I currently have between feeds/winding/settling the babies is when I go to the loo/eat/shower/attend to Saoirse/go to the shop/chase up work calls. I can't give it up.

I post on both the British and the US triplet websites to ask for advice. The American women are incredibly helpful and supportive, if a little tub-thumping. 'Stay in bed and pump every two hours, day and night.' Crikey. Not likely. The British women are much more circumspect: 'Don't kill yourself over it! Bugger all that!'

It's very tempting to give in, especially as everyone – apart from Rich – seems to think I'm being really stubborn and weird even attempting to breastfeed triplets. Most people seem to hate the idea for some reason, but I really enjoy it once it's going well. I find it strangely rewarding, feeding a baby. Even filling a 125ml bottle fills me with the sort of pride I'd normally get from a much more public and supposedly significant achievement. I've been in *EastEnders*, I've hosted several evenings and sung at the Albert Hall, I've released two singles and starred in six solo shows and none of these things has given me the same sense of achievement.

Bugger it. I never thought I'd turn into the sort of woman who would say such a wet thing. I've become one of those milch cows mooing on about breastfeeding because they don't have a life of their own or are financially supported by a goatee-wearing bloke so can afford to spend all day lolling around lactating.

Another American mom posts a message in response to my request for advice: 'I pumped for my triplets for 9 months every two hours round the clock and I'm a single Mom.' Bloody hell. I hope she fed them as well. When did she get time to do that?

Saoirse has been playing round at Lou's house. Lou has been a star, taking her off regularly for some quality toddler time with Harry. Saoirse comes back and asks for 'supper'. That's the trouble with letting middle-class people look after your kids – they come home asking for 'supper'. Everyone knows it's 'tea'. She'll be asking for a pony next.

We sit in the garden while the babies snooze inside. Then one wakes up and starts crying.

'Who's moaning now?' says Rich, tired and irritable. 'Shall I feed him or give him a dummy to shut him up?'

'"Shut him up"? How about rephrasing that – "meet his needs"?' I say, aware of what a ponce I sound.

'They're just doing it to wind me up. They know I'm tired, they know I'll get up for them in the night, and still they goad me by making all these stupid noises,' says Rich only half-joking.

I suppose it's easier for me to be sympathetic to the babies' every whim – I'm not the one on call twenty-four hours a day. I don't know quite how I've swung it, but I'm not going to question the status quo. The surface reason is because tiredness will affect my milk-production. Maybe I should stick at the breastfeeding for a while longer, if only to protect my six hours' sleep . . .

Wednesday 22 June

Eva puts my fears about not producing enough milk to rest. She weighs the babies and they are doing really well – Thady is 7lb, Frank 7lb 4oz and Orla a massive 7lb 8oz. Normal baby sizes. Their official due date is two days away, so this feels very good indeed. I tell her about the advice I have been given by one of the American moms who basically said it was selfish and unrealistic of me to expect to do anything else apart from feed the babies. Eva rolls her eyes and says that I am doing the best I can, given that I also have a toddler to take care of. Thank God for British pragmatism. I am buoyed by the babies' weight gain and resolve to carry on for a while longer. Apparently, how much you can express with a pump is not the same as how much a baby will be able to get out of you – they are more efficient than a bit of plastic, and your let-down will be stronger when your baby, and not the pump, is drawing on you. I'll feed two at a time and then express straight afterwards just to make sure they have emptied both breasts.

Rich's ironing fetish continues apace. Today he has spent an hour ironing and beautifully folding about twenty muslin cloths before placing them in a neat pile above the babies' cot. These cloths will only be sicked on and used to mop up the wee the boys insist on doing just when you think you're safe at the end of a change, but Rich says it gives him a feeling of calm that at least there is one corner of the house that is a model of organization. When the babies vomit, it will be on smooth, fresh muslin.

★

When I'm out for a walk with the triplets, a woman in the baker's shop looks at the babies.

'I'm not being personal, but did you have HIV treatment?'

I assume she means IVF. And yes, that is quite personal.

Walking back through the park, an elderly lady in a wheelchair stops to have a peep.

'And as I'm on your tummy level, I can see that you're doing it all over again!' she says gaily.

'Erm, no, actually. My stomach just hasn't gone down yet fully,' I say, turning pink and stuffing the bakery wrapper deep into my pocket.

'Oh, I'm so sorry. I didn't mean to be personal,' she says, flustered. Accusing someone of being pregnant is deeply personal. I walk home smarting. It's all the fault of those celebrity mums who 'snap back into shape' moments after giving birth. They give the rest of us a bad name.

'THIS IS WHAT A WOMAN LOOKS LIKE FIVE WEEKS AFTER HAVING TRIPLETS!' I want to shout.

'Doing it all over again' indeed. You should never ask a woman if she's pregnant unless you can actually see the baby coming out of her.

Thursday 23 June

Rich is taking a nap with the babies on the pull-out bed. He has propped them all up on a single pillow and they are lying on their sides all facing the same direction.

'Choo choo train!' says Saoirse.

I think they look more like the albino Three Degrees.

Friday 24 June

The babies have an appointment for a hearing test. This was precipitated by an inconclusive test Orla had soon after she was born because of the possible side-effects of the antibiotics she had been given. She only had antibiotics because the boys had had them, and they were only given them because they were intubated and may have been more vulnerable to infection.

So we have to lug the whole family to some hospital or other with a specialist baby audiology department because of a series of maybes and possible outcomes. We know none of them are deaf. They have that fantastic startle reflex – their arms and legs shoot up then float back down again like someone juggling with silk scarves. But we have to take them anyway – a letter from the local health authority arrived ordering their attendance and one does not defy the LHA. The only problem is I have mislaid the letter somewhere, but I'm pretty sure it said we should attend St George's Hospital, Ilford. We pass Saoirse on to my parents for the day and load all the babies into the car.

'The health visitor said St George's is about seven miles away,' I say.

'But where is it?' asks Rich, irritated by the unnecessary journey. It's a hot day and the car is already stuffy. He's very hardy but cannot stand to be hot in a confined space. He routinely downs everything in the middle of a shop and announces that he has to get some fresh air or he'll explode.

'Oh, it's in Ilford somewhere,' I mumble, equally cross.

An hour later and we're pulling up outside St George's,

which, it turns out, is not in Ilford seven miles away but on the outskirts of Hornchurch in Essex. It also transpires that it has no infant audiology department. Largely because it is a geriatric hospital. My error dawns slowly but surely.

'Or maybe it was *King* George's?' I stutter.

'What?' shouts a flustered Rich. We're already ten minutes late for a triple appointment.

'But this must be the same one! There can't be two hospitals called George so close to each other!' But I know I'm beaten. I've remembered the name incorrectly and sent us all hurtling down the wrong dual carriageway for an hour on the hottest day of the year.

Without speaking, Rich does a dramatic U-turn and we speed off in the direction of *King* George's. I anticipate the silent hostility one would normally associate with such a cock-up, but it takes only two minutes for good humour to return.

'Never mind, ducky,' says Rich. 'It's nice to get out of the house, isn't it?'

We turn on Radio 2 and have a little sing-song. I revel in the ease of our relationship and realize what people mean when they tell us that if anyone can cope with triplets we can. It used to baffle me; I'm so disorganized and undomesticated, and Rich is so undisciplined and so laid back he's practically horizontal, so I thought it would be a lethal combination, and the babies would be dirty and hungry most of the time. But in fact we have exactly what it takes – we have the long view, the 'what does it matter if we haven't washed in a week?' take on life. Our low standards are exactly what is required here.

Finally, we arrive at King George's half an hour late with

three sweaty babies. We make a short tour of the entire hospital, courtesy of the confusing site map, before being ushered into a tiny cupboard where the hearing test will take place.

I expect a hairy-nosed prof to creep up behind the babies and burst crisp packets to see if they jump – or whisper 'There's sweets under your chair' in order to test their hearing. But things have moved on a bit since my day and a nice lady in a short skirt plugs each baby up to a laptop and places pads and wires all over them to monitor the reception of sound waves.

As predicted, all three babies are fine and pass the tests with flying colours. I have that familiar sense of weird disappointment. At school as a child, tests like these were for failing, for being marked out as someone special who needed things other kids didn't. I wanted the attention of having to have glasses or a hearing aid. I suppose it was classic middle-child syndrome – 'Notice me! Notice me!' – but I always felt let down by my utter normality. I wanted to be different, even if it meant slightly disabled. A part of me still feels this way, and look at me now – mother of triplets.

Be careful what you wish for.

Saturday 25 June

Ben and Charlie's wedding. Ben is another friend from the comedy circuit and his wedding to long-term girlfriend Charlie has been in the diary since just before our triplet shocker. We have decided to go largely thanks to Lou, Tom and Harry, who have heroically offered to babysit. I leave four bottles of EBM in the fridge and instead of a bijou little handbag I take a huge insulated cooler and two breast pumps. We are hoping to stay out all day. Hurray!

The service is very moving and I blub all the way through. Rich is philosophical, having been married himself. 'Your wedding day is weird. Nothing changes on the surface, and yet everything changes. When you have kids, there is something tangible to show for it – the change is there, in front of you – but when you get married, an invisible dark cloud descends.'

So I guess that's *our* wedding out of the window then. I don't even particularly want to get married, but it just feels so, well, *common* to have four kids and not be spliced. Maybe we'll do it when we're sixty.

At the reception, in a very swanky and modish restaurant, I spend about an hour pumping milk in the toilets and sweet-talking the chef into storing it in his fridge. I can't relax for the rest of the day for worrying about a mix-up with the bottles – what if it's rice pudding for dessert and some witless sous-chef uses my EBM? It's not that I care if other people are squeamish – I just don't want anyone touching my hard-won milk supply. I'm like an alcoholic jealously guarding the last few drops of meths.

Monday 27 June

I've just got round to reading the Saturday papers, and I dreamily pull out the travel section just to torture myself. We won't be going anywhere for a while.

I'm hoping for exotic beach shots, luxury hotel interiors. Instead, this week it's dedicated to 'Holidays in the UK'.

There's a whole feature on the Isle of Wight – how great it is, how 'unexpectedly good' the crab salad is, how the beaches are fabulous and the waters shallow enough for families to enjoy. It sounds crap. I'd rather hang myself than go on holiday in the UK. Pity the poor sods who are either too poor or too frightened to go abroad where they have good food and nice weather. Then I realize with a lurch that this feature is aimed at people like us – people with young kids for whom the logistics of buggies/travel cots/laps to sit on on planes is just too tricky and who have to opt instead for an over-packed car and a wet campsite not more than three hours' drive from home.

Is this our holiday future?

Our new three-week nanny arrives today. She'll be living with us six days a week, day and night. Deanna is Dona's niece, so we are keeping it in the family. She is twenty-three and over from Canada to earn money in her college vacation. She is laid-back, laconic and not phased when we ask her to do the night feed.

'I'm not scared,' she says. I guess it'll look good on her CV.

It feels strange having another adult living in our house. I don't like it, even though Deanna is really nice. But Rich is on his knees with exhaustion after doing *all* the nights since Dona left. I haven't spent one night with all three babies yet.

Shhh. Don't tell anyone.

Tuesday 28 June

I wake with a searing pain in my left nipple. I'm hot and cold at the same time. Shit. Is this the dreaded mastitis? I nip round to the doctor and she confirms that the hard, red patch on my breast is indeed a blocked milk duct. More antibiotics. At this rate, I won't have any biotics left. Whatever they are. I go to bed shivering and wake two hours later with a splitting head-ache. I can't lie on my left side because the pain is so bad, and I've been told that even though it really hurts I'm to carry on breastfeeding to clear the blockage, even if the milk starts to go green. Yum. Once again, I am incapacitated and have to watch Saoirse playing on her own. I want to freeze her in aspic so that I can preserve this fabulous toddler phase and enjoy it when there aren't three babies vying for my attention.

I can feel her slipping away from me into her own little world – a world where every surface is an easel, and biscuits and juice flow thick and fast all the livelong day.

A representative from Cow & Gate arrives with a 'donation'. She is from Nigeria. 'In my country, we say to anyone who has more than one baby "God will provide."'

She brings eighteen cartons of formula.

I've found myself thinking a lot about the night I got pregnant with three babies, and how random life is. I was on tour with *Puppetry of the Penis* while we were moving house, and our moving in day coincided with a gig in the midlands. I put pressure on everyone to drive back after the show so that I could spend the first night in the new house with Rich and

Saoirse. We sped down the motorway at 3 a.m., me dozing on the floor of the transit van, just so that I could get back to my new home, and my romantic gesture resulted in a little celebratory 'christening' of our new bedroom. If I had known then that there were two eggs waiting to be fertilized, would I have done anything differently? Would I have begged to stay put in the damp Tamworth B & B? Would I have refused Rich's advances that night? I don't think so. Never look back. It's pointless. Good things will come from every situation. We hope. We have to hope. And also, I really didn't think I could fall pregnant, mostly because I didn't have any libido to speak of and I somehow thought that if you don't really want to have sex, then surely you won't get pregnant. Mad. I blame Mariella Frostrup. I'd recently read her problem page in the *Observer* magazine, where she told a 'frigid' woman to adopt the Nike attitude to sex – 'Just Do It' – for the sake of her marriage. Well, I 'just did it'. And how. So within an hour of crossing the threshold of our new, mortgaged to the hilt, two-and-a-half-bedroom house, I was pregnant with triplets. That's what comes of reading broadsheets.

We have applied for planning permission to have our loft converted. This house was hideously overpriced, but the local schools are great so we have become the catchment-area cliché. We need more space already, and the babes are only tiny. The triple buggy alone takes up the entire hallway, and we have to squeeze past it to get to the loo. Today we find out that our plans have been turned down because of a 'Juliet' balcony. 'Juliet' balcony? What were we thinking? When are we going to get time to stand around in the garden asking 'what light through yonder window breaks?'

The plans go back in with a modified boring window suitable for a family of six. Fingers crossed. We want to stay here.

Friday 1 July

Deanna is exhausted already. The babies only sleep in one-hour bursts through the night. She heads up to bed for 'a nap' when I relieve her at 6.30 a.m. and doesn't come back down until 1 p.m. So much for all the cleaning, ironing, cooking and childcare we hoped she could help with. The problem is she has been doing nights for about ten weeks and this is her last job. 'I wish I'd come to you guys first,' she says. 'I've just got nothing left.'

Still, she'll be back at uni soon, and we'll have the rest of our lives to be woken up all night, so I try not to feel too sorry for her. She's nice to have around, though, and the sleep we get is invaluable. I busy myself during the mornings trying to get everything organized – making up feeds, sterilizing, washing and so on – and I get a curious pleasure out of it. I don't know why. I've never been a practical person – I once spent four days trying to hang a mirror – as I live mostly in my head, my hands hanging uselessly by my sides.

Deanna has been fantasizing about her own practical solution to the problem of feeding three babies at once. 'Wouldn't it be cool to invent a baby-feeding device for triplets? We could fit those water bottles they have for rabbits and guinea pigs to the side of the cot, then have a hydraulic lift on a timer, with a mechanical burping arm programmed to go off after twenty minutes—'

She really is very tired.

Sunday 3 July

We've made it to a barbecue party that seemed like a distant dream back in the gestational days. D, Rich and I set up triplet camp in a side room near the drinks table. Our lovely hostess sees us unloading the babies and shouts, half-excited, half panic-stricken, 'Triplets! Triplets!' Within seconds, we are mobbed. Media luvvies and flicky-haired girls down their Pimms and rush over to have a look. We sit in state and greet the file past. It's like a state funeral. Or an Indian wedding.

'Ooh Mummy, I want one!' squeals a nineteen-year-old Trustafarian.

'Don't be silly, of course you don't,' barks Mummy, her Botox-infested forehead signalling that she is not yet ready to become a granny.

'There's the Triplet Mum!' people exclaim, as I walk past, on my way to get a drink. I feel like a Victorian freak show – the Bearded Lady, the Elephant Woman, the Triplet Mum. 'Roll up, roll up! Come take a look at the super-ovulator! The woman who had a litter of kittens! You will not believe your eyes!'

I feel miffed. This is the sort of party where I used to be someone. 'I used to have a name!' I feel like shouting, like some sad old pop star usurped by a much younger and cuter act. 'I never even particularly wanted children,' I grumble to a group of adoring mums. They laugh. I don't.

It's not that I don't love them – I do, completely – but it's hard getting used to being the centre of attention for something totally random and out of my control, a trick played by my ovaries, rather than something I've actually worked really hard for. I've spent eighteen years acting, singing, presenting on the radio, sweating my tits off in beery comedy clubs doing solo shows and yet this is the biggest I've ever been. My ovaries have made me a star.

Tuesday 5 July

A photo shoot for Discovery Health. The photographer has me and Richard posing with all three babies, deadpan and dummies in our mouths, toys scattered all over the floor. He takes a few Polaroids to check the lighting and shows us. It's utterly shocking to see myself holding three babies. It is final proof that we have triplets. As if my eye-bags weren't testimony enough.

Yesterday was my first weigh-in after starting my diet. I had lost two pounds. Big deal. Only another fifty to go. At this rate, it will be Christmas before I see my toes again. My belly still looks like a balloon six weeks after a toddler's party. Wrinkly flaps of skin hang down around a curiously brown-stained belly button, the linea negra running the full length of my abdomen. Well, I suppose it's a look.

Friday 8 July

I escape to a local cafe for a quick cup of coffee. I have been juggling screaming babies for three hours and it's only 9 a.m. I need a break. When we moved here, I imagined us breezily sipping cappuccinos all day long, but this is the first time I have managed to live the dream, such as it is. Wanstead is a leafy East London suburb peopled by a mixture of hoop-earringed Essex girls and middle-class professionals buying up the 'charming' Victorian terraces. On the High Street you can pay too much for an almond croissant while reading Proust and have acrylic nail extensions all in the same morning. I sit and watch the white souped-up Escorts nudge bumpers with the pristine bull-bars of 4x4s on the school run.

I have a pile of admin as long as my arm and no time to do it in. It's not my strong suit at the best of times. Months fly by without me noticing that the car needs an MOT, that the meters need reading or the TV licence is out of date. I normally either forget to do really important things or do them twice without realizing it. I once had three house insurance policies simultaneously without realizing. But lately things have got really out of hand. I am having to play the triplet card mercilessly. Begging letters are written appealing against long-forgotten parking tickets and fines for non-registration of a vehicle.

Today I must decide what to do about my scooter. It is a beautiful powder-pink custom-sprayed Vespa 125 and it has sat unused for two years. It's shiny flanks are now covered in cherry-tree detritus and bird shit. I should sell it – what does a fat woman fast-approaching forty want with a Barbie Doll motorbike? But somehow I can't bring myself to. It represents my hedonistic, silly-girl past – before babies, before Rich, before a simple trip to the shops involved chartering a double-decker bus. In my head, I still zoom around Soho having important meetings and caffè lattes. What need do I have for it now? We're on the very edge of London – I estimate it would take a good hour to scooter into town and an hour back. Put in an hour for coffee and that's a three-hour round trip. I'll never have three hours off again. It'll have to go. Or maybe I could just let the kids climb all over it.

As I sit in the cafe making one cup last an hour – like the tramp in *Streets of London* – Deanna walks past with the triplets in the buggy. We have only eight nights left with her, and then we're truly on our own again. There is no more money to pay for any more help. Maybe we should all run away.

Passports! I remember with a jolt that another of my admin tasks is to get our passports sorted out so that we can try to have a holiday some time in the next year. I run out and grab the buggy from Deanna. A local mum has tipped me off that the pharmacy does passport photos. I've been stalling because I had no idea how to get three babies into a photo booth, but the nice man simply has me hold each baby up against a white wall while the whole shop looks on in amusement. All three babies look exactly the same in the photos – shocked, floppy, like they're about to be plucked – but apparently their passports will be good for five years. We could have great fun swapping babies' identities. Really, what is the point? No one is going to be able to say who is who from the passport photos, not even me. I might as well have doodled an aeroplane or a vase of flowers in the space where the photo should be.

Wednesday 13 July

Saoirse has taken to following me around the house doing non-specific whining, like an absent-minded toothache – she's pretty sure she should be causing me some pain but she can't remember at times what it is I've done or not done for her. I can't stand it when she whines. It's the last straw. On the whole she has been amazing with the babies, but when she starts to crack we all do. She is our happiness lynchpin. I have to cut her a lot of slack. It must be the definition of existential angst to be the happy, centre-of-the-universe only child and then be inundated with three siblings all at once. How is a girl – even a really cute girl – supposed to compete?

I am trying to sort my way through a mountain of donated baby clothes. We are buried under them. Every available surface is littered with them. Bin bags spill from crammed-shut cupboards, tiny vests and sleep suits sprout from every drawer. The clothes vary in quality enormously – from the puke-stained Asda hand-me-downs to the never-been-worn designer labels. Some of the stuff is from total strangers, donated via friends of friends. It's very touching, but bloody impossible to organize. Each bag contains a variety of different sizes and I can't face sorting them all out. I did try, before the babies were born, to develop a coded storage system in a vain attempt to stop myself from feeling like a pot-bellied branch of Oxfam, but I quickly conceded defeat. These days, we just grab whatever falls out and stick it on the nearest baby. Frank is just as likely to be swimming in a pink, 'age 6–9 months' all-in-one as he is to be wedged into a blue low-birthweight vest. Normally, we just dress them in the stuff that's downstairs under the change table – the things we were given when they were first born. We force their little legs into even littler sleep suits, jamming their bony feet into toe-crunching foot wells. The result is that they have to lie with their knees up around their bellies, their feet retracted up into the legs of the suit, giving them a strange chubby frog appearance. I considered cutting the feet off (the suits, not the babies) but we already get so many funny looks I couldn't stand the extra pity.

Thursday 14 July

Alex and Maddy, Rich's nine-year-old twins, are here. It's the first time they have met their new triplet half-brothers and sister, and they rush in without saying hello to me and grab a baby each. The bond is instant. Maddy is the most naturally nurturing, and jumps up at the slightest whimper they make, while Alex is quiet and tender and careful with them all. I was worried that they might feel put out – being twins is pretty special, but here is their dad with one 'better' – a set of triplets. I needn't have worried. They are just delighted that there is one each plus a spare. So under our already crammed rafters we now have: a toddler, nine-year-old twins, eight-week-old triplets, a narcoleptic Canadian student and two tired adults. And a dog. Today we are taking them all to Howletts Wild Animal Park. It will probably be a bit less crowded.

And smell nicer.

In the evening, we go to see *Mary Poppins – the Musical*, and I marvel at the good old-fashioned nanny. Your modern nanny is nothing like 'Practically Perfect in Every Way' Mary, and is more likely to be found bitching about her employers at the swings than realigning Father's parenting priorities and offering a spoonful of sugar. We need a Mary Poppins, but we can't afford one. A quick scroll through some nanny websites leaves me shuddering. Nannies for just one child ask for around £400 a week, but nannies for young triplets charge in excess of a £1000. A WEEK! Competition for nannies is fierce. Most of the families advertising for help sound like they are offering an extended leisure break, not a job. Gym membership, own car, separate flat. There is no way we can afford or attract the right sort of help. Our advert would read something along the lines of 'Lactating dogsbody sought by skint clueless couple with four kids under the age of two. Own teabag supplied.'

It occurs to me how some couples spend almost all their earnings on childcare rather than stay at home and look after the children themselves. I've heard about women who go back to work and have to do overtime in order to earn just enough to pay the nanny. It's such a huge undertaking, looking after someone else's babies, but I can't help thinking that nannies these days are raking it in on the back of parents' horror at the whole childrearing process. We'd rather pay a fortune to someone else than have to spend all day with them ourselves. It's not that I judge anyone who works after having children – I hope to be working again soon (especially if Mr Blobby needs a body double). It's just that it strikes me as bizarre that we go through all the agony of pregnancy and childbirth only to palm them off on a stranger as soon as possible. It's like taking up a

very expensive hobby – you get all the gear, the club membership, the shoes, only to discover it's not really for you, so you
stuff it all in the back of the shed six months later.

Friday 15 July

Eva visits and I tell her that Orla has started screaming while
feeding. Deanna and I sit and discuss with her what the problem
might be.

'It might be wind,' says Eva.

'She's just burped,' says Deanna, on top of her game.

'Then maybe she's just not hungry,' says Eva. 'You might
have to put her on a different schedule to the boys.'

I see Deanna's face crumple. This would be a disaster, as it
would mean that feeding would take up even more time.
Running two different schedules simultaneously would mean
we would spend a further four or five hours per day (and night)
feeding.

'That really sucks,' says Deanna when Eva's gone.

'We'll not do it, don't worry,' I say. 'She'll just have to
catch up.'

'But what about her crying?'

'I don't think there's anything wrong with her, so we'll just
have to get used to it. She'll stop eventually.'

I've never subscribed to the modern belief that babies should
be 'contented' at all times, that they are somehow 'fixable'.
Sometimes babies just cry, and should be left to do so. Attending to them every time they cry is a luxury we cannot afford,

and in my view I think most of us would like a good cry now and again – infancy is the only time we can get away with it without being prescribed Prozac.

My old Ozzie friend Simon arrives. In typical 'bon vivant' style, he takes us all out to dinner. I get carried away and drink too much, for old time's sake.

'You'll have to pump and dump,' says Deanna, as I reach for the breast pump.

So midnight finds me hiccoughing while I express my breast milk down the loo. I don't mind breastfeeding a baby when I've had one or even two glasses of wine, but right now I've probably got a cheeky little Chablis coming from one nipple and a full-bodied Merlot from the other.

I am terrible. I had a great time.

Saturday 16 July

Thady has white spots on his tongue, and is fussing around a lot when he feeds. A quick check on the Internet reveals that he has thrush, which means that the other two probably have it as well. We're not too good on oral hygiene, passing one dummy around if the other two have gone to Saoirse's Bermuda Triangle of Special Things. It would be nigh on impossible to keep bottles and soothers separate, so we don't bother. I buy some ointment from the chemist and spread it onto their tongues. It looks foul, but it does the trick apparently. Saoirse is very quiet in that suspicious way only toddlers can be, and I find her happily destroying my make-up. While I have been busy sorting out the next feed she has striped the babies' legs with a deep vermilion lipstick, an expensive purchase because of its indelible quality. They now have angry red welts around their ankles. They look like we have been shackling them. Saoirse then tips an entire carton of apple juice over Orla, who sits quietly dripping until her bottom lip trembles.

'Uh-oh!' says Saoirse, like a maniacal Teletubby. She has taken to leaving small 'offerings' like this for her little sister. Yesterday, I found a cocktail sausage tucked neatly behind Orla's ear. The day before, a fold of ham under her knee. It's the only evidence of any malice she has shown, and it is almost always directed at Orla, who must, in Saoirse's eyes, pose the most direct threat.

The house is full. Alex and Maddy are busy helping Rich make a cake. It's so lovely to have them here. Far from being an extra burden, they make it feel like we are a traditional extended family. They add a different note to the disharmony, and somehow change the chord to a more tuneful one. It makes more sense to have all these babies with two other children here. In for a penny . . . Saoirse is utterly devoted to her big half-sisters. The first thing she says every morning is 'Ali? Maddy?', as if I might have taken them away in the night. It breaks her heart when they leave. I hope she grows as fond of her little siblings. If she doesn't choke them with finger food first.

Sunday 17 July

Deanna has gone. It's hard to believe her three weeks is up and she almost skips up the path back off to her real life. I can't work out if I'm jealous or not. From what I remember, being twenty-three is pretty shitty. The insecurity, the fear of taking the wrong path, the lack of stability. I watch Deanna walk up the road and feel very sad. She played a very important role in the babies' early life, sitting with them through the night with great patience and care. They will never know – that phase of their life is already over. Orla smiled right at her this morning, and as she was saying goodbye to the boys they stared at her as if to say, 'Don't leave us with that other one, she's rubbish!' Deanna had a middle-of-the-night intimacy with them that I have yet to experience. I think it's a good job she's going. Last night we took her out for dinner and she got dolled up – nice top, make-up, hair down. She looked stunning, emerging from her sick-stained tracksuit.

'I don't know what she'd done to her eyes, but it really brought them out,' said Rich this morning.

'Did you fancy her?' I asked.

'Erm' is all he needed to say. We've always joked that if we ever get an au pair she'll have to be twenty stone and Ukrainian. Trouble is, I really don't think that would stop Rich. If he can fancy me when my waist measures five feet and I smell of Gaviscon he can fancy anyone.

The babies are about nine weeks old, but really they are only six weeks because their development is adjusted to their due date. So far, all we have really done is complete the third trimester outside the womb. The fun is yet to come, and it will be just me and Rich to cope.

Orla spends most of the day screaming. It sounds so angry and accusing, and I can't help taking it personally. The house quickly falls into disarray now that there is no Deanna to pick up the slack. By 9 p.m. I am exhausted and need to go to bed, but I can't. I sit and have a quiet cry while the girls entertain the triplets upstairs. I've been kidding myself that I've been coping well. Rich has been busy with the girls and I have been left holding the babies, like the crap half of a plate-spinning double act.

Tuesday 19 July

I have lost my triplet night-feed cherry.

This is how my night went.

10 p.m. Last feed of the day. We are in Kearsley at Rich's mum's house, so we each feed a baby. They have decided on a go-slow, and it takes an hour to feed them. I'm doing the next feed on my own, so if this is the new regime I will get precisely one hour's sleep between feeds.

11.30 p.m. Crawl into bed. Asleep before my head hits the pillow.

1.20 a.m. Awake to crying. Frank has lost his dummy. Bugger. I probably won't get back to sleep now.

2 a.m. Awake to Frank and Thady crying. Feed time begins. I prop them up on the pillow. It takes forty minutes to do two, by which time Orla is awake. Frank pukes all over me, but I'm too tired to do anything about it.

3.05 a.m. All back in bed. I lie awake worrying that they will wake me up.

5.20 a.m. Frank crying again. Maybe he's got some more puke he forgot to give me. I put him into bed next to me.

5.30 a.m. Thady in bed now too.

5.40 a.m. Orla is the third in the bed with me. We lie and stare at the ceiling waiting for the magic 6a.m. feed. I get up and express six ounces of milk and warm two bottles of formula. I feel like a farmer with orphaned lambs, shoving bottles into hungry little mouths all around me.

7 a.m. Babies tucked up in bed again. It feels like me and my shipmates have just spent a stormy night at sea. I sterilize the bottles and rinse the vomit off my nightie. Rich gets up for work at the factory. He didn't hear a thing, and I make light of my disturbed night to save his guilt. He seems to have taken on total responsibility for the night feeds, and acts as though I've done him the most enormous favour.

I'm meant to be doing tonight as well, but Rich sees how tired I am and volunteers himself. I bite his hand off and go to bed.

Thursday 21 July

I take Alex, Maddy and the triplets to the Trafford Centre for some retail therapy. On the bus. Mad. I want to buy something to wear, as Celia, Rich's mum, is going to babysit for an hour so that we can go to the pub. Hooray! Except all my clothes are vile. Boo. We go into Morgan and I finger the flimsy gypsy tops.

'I don't really think you'll suit anything in here,' says Alex tactfully.

'Why not?' I ask, paranoid about my weight. I am still in denial about my size, looking at the rails of size ten clothes as if they are within my reach.

'They're a bit swanky.'

'What do you mean?'

'Exhibit A,' says Alex, holding up a sequinned halter-neck.

'Am I not swanky enough for that?'

She holds up the corner of my baggy maternity T-shirt covered in sick.

'Exhibit B,' she says.

'Good point, well made,' I say, and we leave. I have a bad case of body dysmorphia – but, unlike anorexics who think they are huge even as the bones are poking out of them, I still see myself as a slinky hipped girl in tight jeans and stilettos. Shopping can bring me up short. Bowing to the nine-year-old's wisdom, I buy some size sixteen maternity trousers from Asda. They are the only things that will fit over my forty-five-inch belly. I am beginning to despair that I will ever see my knickers from above. Where is that foxy, fun-loving girl with forty pairs of high heels? Who is this bulky, heavy-arsed middle-aged woman, her greying hair pulled back in an unwashed ponytail? Only three years ago I would never go out without make-up and I certainly wouldn't go more than three weeks without getting my roots done. Now I'm lucky if my hair gets washed once a week, and all my high heels are in the loft.

Sunday 24 July

Rich is up and dunking biscuits in his tea while all three babies feed away happily. He is euphoric. He has invented a system for feeding the babies which is hands free. He props two babies up on a pillow, places a second pillow on their laps then balances the bottles on top. The third baby gets put in front and has his bottle propped on a third pillow. It's a landmark. We run around the kitchen shouting, 'Look – no hands!'

It doesn't actually save much time because we still hover in attendance in case someone chokes or the bottles fall, which they do about every two minutes, but it still feels like progress. The boredom of eighteen bottles a day gets to you after a while. I have tried tying the bottles to soft toys and balancing them on the babies' chests, but they kept falling off. Anything but sit with another bottle in my hand.

Feeding time rolls around with alarming speed. We suffer from constant déjà vu. 'Didn't I just do this?' we ask each other. The answer is always 'Yes, and now you have to do it again.' The babies are ten weeks old and at eighteen bottles a day that's 1,260 feeds, most of which have been given by me or Rich: around 400 hours bent over a feeding baby, willing the ounces down. Six ounces per time. Rich likes to make the feeds up, as it involves counting six ounces of formula into six ounces of pre-boiled water, and he finds it reassuring that no matter how tired he is, he can still count to six. There's little more satisfying than a fridge full of ready-to-go feeds – and little more terrifying than an empty shelf. I fall into an irrational panic that the babies will starve if the feeds aren't ready at least an hour in advance. After an agonizing few weeks,

I have started to reduce my breastfeeding and pumping by one session every three days, so the formula milk has become a big focus.

Don't they ever get sick of milk? We can no longer stand the smell of it, and we're only the pushers. Bottles with curdled dregs lie scattered across the floor like cider cans after a teenage party, and still they want more. We joke about giving them a treat – a Mars bar cut into manageable chunks – but they prefer the Milky Way.

Wednesday 27 July

Battle of the bath. To bathe three babies and a toddler you will need:

- A bath
- Warm soapy water
- Nerves of steel

The howling starts when you take their clothes off. Young babies hate being naked. How they ever got those cute shots of naked babies cradled in muscled arms I'll never know. My three scream their indignation the minute I go near their vests. I try to minimize the screaming by keeping them wrapped in a towel until the very last minute, then putting them straight back into the warm towel as they get out. Rich is much more gung-ho, preferring to let them scream and just get on with it.

Saoirse is fascinated by the whole ordeal. We put her in the bath first and she presides over the triplets' ablutions with great gusto, slapping a wet flannel on each baby's head as they come in. She likes to direct proceedings – 'Thady next!' – as if it's all an elaborate charade for her amusement.

By the time Rich is ready to take over with talc and bum cream I am soaked and the babies are apoplectic with rage. They lie on the bed squawking until we feed them calm again, the floor littered with wet towels, soggy cotton wool balls, dirty nappies and weed-on bed linen. No wonder that in ten weeks we have only bathed them four times. Shocking, I know, but how dirty can babies get? It's not as if they're up the chimney all day. Yet.

Thursday 28 July

The babies have hit the ten-pound mark, and would now make quite respectable turkeys for a small family on Christmas Day – and still leave enough for sandwiches the day after. I am worried about their development, though. They are not smiling yet, even though the books say they should be. Maybe they don't find life very amusing. Maybe they're Goths. Or maybe they are developmentally challenged. Eva says to stimulate them with toys, lights, music – a bit like mental patients – but most days it's all we can do to keep them all alive. I spend the morning constructing a play triangle with soft toys suspended between three bouncy chairs. At one point, there is an elephant playing 'Imagine', a cow singing 'Hush Little Baby' and a mobile playing a manic 'Teddy Bears' Picnic'. I put the babies into the chairs. Thady and Frank start crying and Orla vomits all over herself then falls asleep.

I never had these worries with Saoirse because she was on the road with me from three months old. There was always something to look at, someone new to study. I peruse the message boards and find that there is a lot of talk of developmental delay. I don't understand why it should be that because a baby is born early, or in sets of two or three, they should necessarily be behind their full-term peers. Surely all babies only learn things like coordination, balance and adaptability after birth, so why should it matter when they were born?

The Tamba newsletter arrives and there is a feature on multiples and development. It's quite a frightening but informative read. It charts the various reflexes that stimulate behaviour, and details the impact prematurity has on those reflexes. The Moro reflex is activated at birth to initiate breathing, but if babies have prematurity-related breathing problems at birth this reflex may not kick in, which in turn can lead to lowered immunity, balance and coordination difficulties, visual and perceptual problems, low self-esteem and mood swings!

I peer at my three for signs of Moro reflex retention. They look OK to me, but really – how would you know?

Friday 29 July

I am at work in a recording studio. I call Rich at 4 p.m. to see how he is coping on his own.

'You're not going to be very happy with me,' he says.

'Why? What's happened?' I panic.

'I took them all to the park, and Saoirse's had an accident.'

'What? What do you mean? Is she OK?'

'She's fine now – she's got some chocolate. And she'll get new ones.'

'What do you mean? New what? You're scaring me now!'

'She went on the rocking horse and I was rocking it with one hand and pushing the buggy to settle the babies with the other, and I just looked away for a minute and she came forward too fast and hit her front teeth on the metal.'

'Oh my God! Is she all right? Did her teeth come out?'

'No – but they're quite badly chipped. The woman in the chemist said you're going to kill me.'

Of course, it's not Rich's fault – it could just as easily have been me struggling with four kids in the park – but I can't help feeling guilty that I wasn't there. Maybe it wouldn't have happened. Now my poor baby has chipped front teeth and her first school photo will be tight-lipped. I start to cry and continue for the rest of the day.

By the time I get home Saoirse is already asleep. I try to prise her top lip back to have a look – I can't tell if Rich is underplaying or overstating the damage – but she rolls over and pushes me away. I can't believe how much it has affected me. I'm not a person who flaps, I don't overdramatize, I try to take the long view, and yet where the children are concerned I am a complete wreck. I don't like it one bit, and it's only going to get worse. It's hard enough trying to keep one two-year-old out of harm's way – how will we manage three?

I speak to my mate Donna on the phone.

'It's awful when they hurt themselves, isn't it?' she says, shuddering at the idea of Freya, her daughter of the same age, in Saoirse's shoes. 'But what will we do when they're older and someone else hurts them?' she asks.

'We'll fucking kill them,' I say. And I mean it.

Motherhood is too visceral for me. Too real. You can't be ironic about it, you can't distance yourself from the feelings. If loving your children means having a constant ache in your heart from all the hurt that has been and is to come, then I'm not ready for it, thanks. If being a mum means losing a night's sleep over some chipped teeth because you're scared your daughter will get teased, and lisp, and not be able to eat toffee apples, then it's not really for me.

Only problem is it's too late. Times four.

Sunday 31 July

I am so bored of the questions and doom-laden comments. So bored of people who rush over and let their children poke sticky fingers all over the babies. I have started to give evil answers.

'Are they all yours?'

'No, I stole them for a laugh.'

'Was it IVF?'

'No, it was MFI.'

'You wait till they start walking!'

'We're not going to let them walk. We're having lead shoes made.'

Lou and Anouska have both commented on how irritating it is to walk with me and the babies and get stopped every five yards.

'You always have to smile and be polite, don't you?' says Lou. 'Don't you ever feel like saying, "Leave me alone, I'm not in the mood"?'

'Of course.'

'You should wear a sign saying, "Just because I've got triplets, it doesn't make me a nice person."'

I like this idea a lot. As a habitual sneerer and closet shy person, having triplets has been a big strain on my personality. It's not easy fielding the public attention when you feel like telling everyone to piss off. This is what it must be like to be very famous. You can't nip out for some bin bags without causing a commotion in the street. Horrible. I am the Madonna of E11, except I am bad-tempered at the moment and somehow a sullen face looks wrong with three babies in a row. I think the rigid schedule is starting to get to me. Structure is not something I enjoy very much. I prefer to be a 'fly-by-the-seat-of-my-pants' mum, letting Saoirse fit in with us. I am starting to realize that this will be impossible to pull off with four kids. We can't mess with meal times and bedtime now or all hell will break loose. Not that we are ever invited anywhere any more. No, like it or not, I am going to have to have Gina Ford babies. Ford says that babies fare better when they know what is coming next. They crave routine. Gina Ford babies sleep through the night earlier, they always finish their feeds and never run you ragged crying for no good reason. Gina Ford babies grow up to be tax inspectors, company auditors and traffic wardens.

I'm feeling really blue today. I've only expressed two lots of milk and I feel full of sadness at giving up. It has just become too exhausting. My breasts don't seem at all bothered though. I expected at least a little leakage, a bit of buxom overfullness, but nothing. It's all a bit of a let down – no pun intended. Still, there's no use crying over spilt milk. I take Saoirse to the City

Farm and we have a great time – until we pop into the cafe and interrupt a breastfeeding support session. About a dozen mums cradling one baby each sit in a circle nodding earnestly while a gruff-looking woman talks them through the rudiments of lactation. I duck out quickly. I feel jealous and scornful, a sure sign that I am feeling guilty at stopping.

Rich is also down today. It's very disconcerting when we both hit the floor at the same time. He says he feels the days and weeks and months stretching out before him. I try to put things in perspective by cruising the triplet websites. I find a section for bereaved parents and read some very sad posts about pre-term labour, late miscarriages, dead babies. A lot of the women have been through the painful experience of IVF, then fallen pregnant with triplets only to lose them all late in the day. I sit and weep, trying to count my blessings. I feel morbid and voyeuristic, but I console myself with the thought that even though things are hard here at least it is three live babies we are trying to cope with – not three dead ones. That must really be hell. I pour myself a big glass of wine and resolve to be more appreciative tomorrow.

Wednesday 3 August

It is difficult to count your blessings when you've done three night feeds on the trot. Rich reached the end of his energy reserves at the weekend, so I am stepping into the breach and am now exhausted. But there is a strange satisfaction in being up in the middle of the night with the babies. It's like a version of the Stockholm syndrome, where hostages fall in love with their captors. In a bid to cope with the extreme circumstances, we start to empathize with those who are torturing us – hence falling in love with your newborn. I feel closer to the babies now that we have lived through these past three nights together – like veterans from a long-forgotten war.

The babies have a theatrical agent. We have signed them up with a lady called Sandra who specializes in twins for filming. It seems that identical twins are very popular with directors because babies are only allowed to 'work' for two hours a day, so when one is done he can be swapped for his twin and hey presto – four hours in one day. The boys have already secured a casting for a TV drama. Rich comments, with only passing bitterness, that they will probably be more successful than us. The idea of hanging around on a film set is bad enough when it's your own gig, let alone when you are waiting to shove a reluctant baby into a stranger's arms. I don't know what we're thinking. Still, the money can go straight into their therapy fund.

Thursday 11 August

Rich is out all day erecting a greenhouse, so it's me and the babies, home alone. I feel like the inept babysitter, way out of her depth, nodding that she'll be fine and not to worry as he heads off at 6.30 a.m. for his long drive to Kent. I resolve to just go at it like it's the easiest thing in the world. In fact, I've decided, why not make today a special project in being one of those 'trying too hard' supermums, the ones who endlessly bang on about having it all and still baking their own scones? It'll be fun. The house is in chaos, I've got a huge pile of urgent paperwork and an even bigger mound of ironing that Rich has not got round to for a week now. I'll do it all *and* look after the kids.

By 10 a.m. I've fed all three babies and Saoirse, filled in the child tax credit forms, organized three quotes for the loft extension, had a depressing conversation with my accountant and finished the ironing. I'm supermum and Daddy Head of the Household today. I'm quite enjoying it, even though I'm aware that a large proportion of the pleasure comes from the novelty factor. I keep thinking, 'Ooh, look at me doing the dishes and everything!' I feel like Marie Antoinette with her toy farm – 'Let them drink milk!'

Time for the next feed before heading off for lunch at Linda's. She's a great collector of other people's kids, so the garden is full of toddlers bashing each other and eating sand. We mums sit around ready to adjudicate. It must seem like chaos to everyone else, but at least here there are some other arms ready to hold and feed a baby. The triplets can at least get a cuddle while they feed – so much more soothing than having a pillow on your tummy propping up a dripping bottle.

Feeling buoyed by the extra help, I decide to put Saoirse in the front of the triple buggy and strap Thady to me so that we can all go to the High Street. The car needs taxing, cheques need paying in and prescriptions need collecting.

'I can do this,' I say to myself as I set off across the park.

But the buggy has other ideas. Loaded up with three 10lb

babies, it's just unwieldy, but with two-stone Saoirse as the figurehead, it's impossible to steer or lift up kerbs. I keep veering off the pavement, and a nice lady has to help me get the buggy back up the kerb after a near miss with a van. I end up charging down the middle of the road, ignoring the staring and pointing, sweating profusely. By the time I get to the shops, my back is dripping and Thady has started up a low-level whining into my chest. I edit my plans to have an I-am-so-coping cappuccino and head straight for the post office. Inside, it is so aggressively air-conditioned that the babies instantly wake up and start crying. Saoirse takes advantage of her new position five feet away from me at the front of the monster buggy and grabs anything and everything at her level. Toothbrushes go flying, hair gel hits the deck and a whole stack of leaflets advertising travel insurance goes skidding across the polished floor as she bellows a cheery 'Hello!' to the now gawping post-office queue.

'Are they all yours?' asks a posh lady with thinly veiled disgust. It's quite a shock to see myself as she must see me. In my mind's eye, I'm a working-class girl doing a pretty good impression of a suburban middle-class mum with an accidentally large family, but to Mrs-Shampoo-and-Set-Ideas here I'm one of those brawling harridans she sometimes glimpses on 'Trisha' while she's flicking channels before 'Cash in the Attic' comes on. She might even be wondering why I still have teeth but no tattoos.

'Yes,' I say, trying to do my 'harassed but still smiling' routine. Give them what they want.

'Good gracious!' she tuts. I reach the front of the queue just as a basket full of hairbrushes clatters to the ground.

'Saoirse!' I warn, conscious (not for the first time) of her unusual Irish name. Great. Now they're going to think I'm a traveller.

'Hello, Mama!' she smiles, delighted at the attention.

A few women smile at me sympathetically and it's enough to stop me running from the shop. I get to the counter, ignoring the high-pitched screaming coming from the middle of the buggy. Orla has decided to join her brother in the scream-fest.

'I will get this done!' I mutter darkly.

'She must be a glutton for punishment!' chuckles an old lady in the queue. A few people titter and I feel my cheeks start to burn.

On the surface a jovial, flippant remark. 'She must be a glutton for punishment.' But that simple phrase offends me on so many levels that I feel like turning on her and stuffing her pension book right down her wrinkly throat.

The assumption that I planned to have all these children all at once, that I have somehow been 'greedy', makes me fume. Why does she not think that perhaps the triplets are a result of a natural accident? An accident that (on a good day) I would now describe as happy? And in any case, how can one ascribe motivation to a biological function? Ovaries can't be greedy, or frugal, or anything else for that matter. They don't have a consciousness with which to exercise any will whatsoever. They just release eggs on the command from hormones every month. My ovaries happened to do it twice. They're not greedy – just highly functional.

And 'punishment'? Again, that casual assumption that we all share the same adversarial, negative view of childrearing. It amazes me how many times I hear comments of this nature. Triplets bring these submerged, angry feelings about the difficulties of bringing up small children to the surface. Surely a child is always a blessing, not a reprimand?

That's the trouble with being the local freak show – it turns you into the sort of person who uses words like 'blessing'.

Instead of punching the crone, I finish my business and perform a 180 degree turn, allowing Saoirse a farewell swipe at a shelf full of deodorant bottles. They scatter like skittles, the din only drowned by the screams of all three babies now.

'Bye! Bye! Bye!' yells Saoirse, waving manically like a car-winning game show contestant.

'All together now, *one*, *two*, *three* – "You've got your hands full!"' I shout to the throng. Except I don't. I just scuttle out and buy a big cake.

Back home, I'm now counting the hours until Rich gets home. Saoirse is a star, plonked in front of Cbeebies scrutinizing the intricacies of the 'Ballamory' plot for the second time today. She even remembers which colour house they are going to, and I feel shame that she watches so much TV. Cbeebies is the first thing she asks for in the morning, and she marks her day out by its schedule. Still, her language is coming on in leaps and bounds. Today I tripped over her toy bus, stubbing my toe hard.

'Fucking hell!' I snapped, without thinking.

She comedy-timed her echo with Perrier Award precision.

'Fucking hell, Mama!' she chirped, delighted with this tooth-some new cuss.

Yesterday it was her turn to trip up.

'Whoopsie Daisy Maisie!' she exclaimed, as she picked herself up.

'Whoopsie Daisy Maisie? Is that what you just said?' I laughed.

'Whoopsie Daisy Maisie!' she repeated, pleased with herself.

I can't remember saying that very often, if at all, so I was impressed by her memory for idioms. I boast to Linda.

'Whoopsie Daisy Maisie? Oh, I say that all the time!' said Linda.

Deflated, I analyse my response. Firstly, it's galling to find that she is learning things from other people when I'm not there. Of course, every child picks things up outside the home, but Saoirse has been palmed off on a lot of people since the triplets came on the scene. Her development is a patchwork quilt of a lot of influences. I feel as though it is taking place mostly when I am not there and this feels very sad. Where did she learn the word 'rhino'? How come she knows where to put her dirty spoon when someone says 'sink'? These aren't things I've taught her and for some reason it breaks my heart. She will never not know 'rhino' again. It is gone forever, that window of opportunity to teach her what the big grey thing is that has a funny horn on its nose. Still, look on the bright side. There's always 'hippo'.

7 p.m. Rich is back from a twelve-hour day inside a sweaty glass box on the hottest day of the year so far. He's exhausted after three night feeds on the trot and is thrilled to discover that not only have I done all the ironing but I've also cooked dinner (well, Lou made a potato salad and forced me to look up a tuna

steak recipe, and I've thrown some leaves onto a plate). We indulge in a little traditional family improvisation before I tentatively broach the subject of tonight's night shift, trying to keep the exhausted desperation out of my voice.

'I'll do it, ducky,' he says.

'But you must be shattered. And I'm doing a late radio show tomorrow – you'll have to do it tomorrow too.'

'That's OK,' says Rich, with no hint of bad feeling.

Ten minutes later, he's in the kitchen washing up. I put my arms around him from behind and bury my face in his sweaty back. He smells of honest toil and petrol.

'I love you,' I say.

'Do you, ducky? Or are you just grateful?' he smiles.

'Bloody good question. Goodnight.'

Tuesday 16 August

We are on holiday in Anoushka's mum's house. She has kindly offered us her seaside home, knowing that there is no way we will get to go anywhere this summer. All she wants in exchange is a picture of the babies for her guest book. If the babies have closed a lot of doors for us, they have at least opened this one. The garden is directly on the beach, and we have a lovely time paddling while the babies doze inside like Victorians convalescing. It feels very liberating to stare at the sea, although it seems to move very fast here. I wonder if that is just a reflection of my inner state? Time has never gone so quickly and yet dragged on for so long. The summer is almost over, and a new phase in the babies' lives is about to begin, and yet here we are still exhausted, still lucky to get three hours' sleep in a row. Rich and I spend most of our time together and yet I miss him terribly. We are both afloat, trying to steer our individual courses through these extraordinary days, and we are drifting away from the mainland fast. I want to reach out and grab his hand but I can't let go of my raft. So I content myself with keeping him in my sights, and hoping that we'll find ourselves washed up together at the end of it all.

I am sick with exhaustion.

Saturday 20 August

Lois's fortieth birthday. A gathering of several old lesbian friends. Lois, a fellow hasbian, is now married with two children. We walk in the private woods attached to her massive Sussex house and laugh out loud about how times have changed. When I think of how fundamentalist we were, how suspicious of men and how entrenched in our feminist principles we were, it seems incredible how things have turned out. I think we would both agree that we have not really changed at all – it's just the backdrop. Some lesbians hate women like me and Lois, calling us 'traitors' and 'scabs', like we are defectors from some cause. They find us very threatening – life should be travelled on a fixed path and change must not be tolerated. I am even more guilty than Lois because I didn't do it quietly, instead performing a whole show about it. I was voted 'Most Disappointing Lesbian' in a dyke magazine. To begin with, I was quite delighted with the accolade, but recently it has started to pall. I have written several features about the triplets already, but today Sophie hands me a copy of *Now* magazine which includes an alleged interview with me – an 'ex-lesbian and mother of triplets'. It is full of inaccuracies and out-of-context quotes culled from old interviews. It's horrible, salacious and misrepresentative. I am shocked, and feel stupid for believing that I could control the coverage of my extraordinary life. I can't. My interesting, complicated, unusual life is reduced to tabloid headlines and lowest-common-denominator tittle-tattle.

Tuesday 23 August

I have a twenty-four hour pass to Edinburgh. The Fringe is on, and I have spent some if not all of every August up in Auld Reekie. This year will be no different, triplets or not. I leave Rich in charge and fly off to get drunk and make merry. I have recently been featured in the *Scotsman*, so everyone knows me when I arrive. Everywhere I go people shout: 'Jackie! Who's looking after the babbies!' I meet up with Al, Deidre, Dave and Ben, and we lurch from one bar to the next, finally ending up at a piano bar singing Sinatra songs until 5 a.m. Deidre is enjoying her break from motherhood too – everywhere we go she shouts, 'Let us in – we're mothers!' I know I will pay for this tomorrow, but I don't care. I need to let my hair down – even if it is greasy and my roots haven't been touched since January.

Wednesday 24 August

Urgh. Never again. Someone kill me, please.

Having a hangover is horrible, even when you don't have kids and you can just lie in bed all day feeling sorry for yourself. It's another torture entirely when you have four babies needing your attention. It's the cruellest trick that parenthood is the time when you most need to drink, and the time when you are least able to tolerate it.

Saturday 27 August

We are triplet-free for twenty-four hours. My big brother is getting married today in Southampton. The wedding reception will take place on a boat, which sets sail at six and doesn't dock again until midnight. Now, I'm a landlubber at the best of times, but triplets on board a moving vehicle surrounded by water for six hours? I don't think so. Richard's agent Maggie has volunteered herself and her husband Nelson to stay at our house and babysit the trips. They arrive for a briefing and it is only now that I realize what a control freak I have become. They smile benignly as I go through the long list of dos and don'ts. Sterilize all the bottles in this way; make sure they finish every drop; don't put them down without winding them; don't give Orla the fast-flow teat, she can't handle it; if you take the buggy out, make sure you use the hoods if it's sunny, and be sure to load up from the back. Oh, and when you're making the feeds up, rotate the bottles in the fridge in strict order. Maggie and Nelson have had four children between them and been through it all, but they indulge me anyway.

The babies are all lined up on the bed, present and correct when we go to kiss them goodbye. Bang on cue they all smile. It is the first time all three have smiled at once. Even Thady unfurrows his brow specially for the occasion. You'd swear they know we are leaving them and want to make it as hard for us as possible. It must be a survival instinct. I suppose this is the point at which I'm supposed to cry and decide to stay at home. But I don't. I wave them a cheery goodbye and we set off to get plastered on a boat.

Sunday 28 August

We go to Meera's for tea and she has collected lots of lovely mums together. Some have toddlers, some school-age children and two of the women are heavily pregnant. They are all in awe of us. Saoirse stalks the other – older – girls happily, while they are equally happy to ignore her. 'Hello, girls!' she says cheerily. They don't even look at her.

'Please, can you say hello to Saoirse, girls? She thinks you're all so cool because you're older, so if you could just say hello back—'

They stare at me nonplussed. Don't I understand the rules here or something?

Finally, one of them speaks.

'No,' she says flatly, before carrying on with her game of feeding the dollies.

'OK,' I say quietly, before sloping off back to the adults.

'You're so calm!' one of the pregnant ladies says. 'You're not normal!'

I never really know what to say when people say this. Am I calm? What am I supposed to be doing, running around the garden screaming with poo in my hair? I suppose it's an option. I can't help feeling like this appraisal is an accusation, like the other mums need me to crumble so that they don't feel so bad about struggling with their babies – 'Look, just *lose it* a little bit, will you? You're making the rest of us look bad!'

I find myself becoming an unwilling baby guru in these situations. I get asked all sorts of questions about baby care, and I hear myself bleating on about various things and I think to myself, 'Who is that git with all the opinions all of a sudden?'

The mums lap it up. They all want to hear it – freshly dispensed advice from the supermum. We're all expected to be baby experts these days. In my mum's day, you just stuck your head in the nappy boiler and got on with it. You were deemed to be doing an excellent job of bringing up your children if you didn't stick your head in the gas oven by the end of the summer holidays. Nowadays, mums can't move without some child expert or supernanny or baby whisperer telling them that they are doing it all wrong and that swaddling/controlled crying/co-sleeping is the new cod liver oil. We are expected to read up on all the major players. 'Is your Eliza a Gina Ford or a Furber baby?' is the latest battle cry in NW3. No wonder so many mums are scared witless of the little tyrants that come into their lives. Add this enforced perfectionism to the modern phenomenon of women wanting to 'have it all' and you have a potent cocktail of frustration and disappointment. Women don't seem to like their babies any more. They're 'hard work', they're 'demanding' and 'trying'. These verdicts are delivered with a hint of surprise. But surely it's in a baby's job description to be all these things and more, and just at the very time, post-pregnancy, when you are least fit for it? Did they not read the small print, these weary women at the swings? These droopy-eyed ladies in the ball parks and paddling pools? In between the flash cards and the Mucky Pups and the Tumble Tots sessions, did we forget to enjoy them? It's not that difficult. They're just babies we're dealing with here, not nuclear reactors. I try this out on the mothers' meeting. They listen, nodding their agreement. There I go again. I hate people who bang on about their opinions. Now I am one.

Another mum arrives with her two-week-old son. She looks shattered, and heads straight for the sofa to breastfeed.

'You should talk to Jackie!' says one of the mums. 'She can tell you all about breastfeeding!'

The woman looks up wearily. 'Are you having problems?' I ask, ready to leap into gear.

'He's feeding for four, five hours at a time and I'm exhausted. I'm on the verge of giving up and just giving him the bottle,' she sighs.

And I'm in. I can't help it. I know stuff now.

'Well, if he's at the breast for four hours he's not feeding, he's sucking for comfort. There's no way he can be eating for that long because (a) his stomach is only the size of a walnut at the moment and (b) your breasts are probably empty after half an hour and it takes a good hour and a half for them to refill.'

'Really?'

'Yes. Babies often need to suck in addition to the time they spend eating. It depends whether or not you mind being a human dummy.'

I've used the D-word. They are all listening now.

'I do mind. I'm shattered.'

'Would you use a dummy?'

'I think so. But he needs to feed for hours because he falls asleep a lot while he's eating.'

'So wake him up!'

I'm getting good at this. I know all the answers.

The mums look at me with new curiosity. Wake a sleeping baby? Are you mad?

'How do I do that?'

'Pinch his toes, unwrap him, take his clothes off. Otherwise, you'll just be there all day, a human dummy cum pillow. Great for him, a bit crap for you.'

But she looks so tired and fed up, I just give her my phone number because I don't think she is listening any more.

Or maybe she just thinks I'm the biggest git ever.

I go to give Rich a cuddle before saying our goodbyes.

'We've decided. You're *definitely* not normal. You're still cuddling each other and you've got four babies,' says a twinkly mum.

'Yes. And we've had sex,' I say. There's a sharp intake of breath before they all burst out laughing, presuming I am having them on.

Monday 29 August

The film crew have arrived. We have agreed to take part in a celebrity edition of 'Who Rules the Roost?', a BBC 'fly-on-the wall' programme about childcare responsibility in families. For the first week, Rich will be at home while I go out to work, and for the second, we will swap and he will go out driving a lorry. They were very keen for us to take part, expecting plenty of fruity language and domestic disharmony – surely a house full of triplets and a toddler to boot would throw up some viewer-pleasing rows? I arrive home after the first day's filming. The director looks worried.

'Is it all OK, Marie? We're not too boring for you, are we?' I ask.

There's a telltale moment's hesitation. 'No! No!' she lies.

How on earth is she going to make this anything other than a pukefest? Rich was baking bread when I got home! It's not at all what they were expecting and I feel immensely proud that we are not only coping but thriving. Not drowning but waving. Saoirse hasn't really got a handle on the whole fly-on-the-wall thing and keeps mugging at the camera. She's already learnt everyone's names and greets them with a chirpy 'Hello, Jo! Hello, Paul! Hello, Al!' each time they switch the camera on. It's as if she wants to establish dominance. She won't be the passive subject of gloating reality TV. I've had a great day sitting at my computer in a borrowed office writing various features and columns. It feels like old times. I'm so glad to be home though, and I hug each baby in turn like they do in the movies. This is what it's like to be a dad. You get to stay out all day and then come home to a cooked dinner and kids who are excited to see you. It's the easy bit. No grinding monotony of changing, washing, feeding, consoling and adjudicating. Just bath time and bedtime and an evening of relaxation. I'm already dreading my week at home. How on earth will I cope with four babies all on my own? I've done it for the odd day here and there, but not six days in a row. It's not possible, is it?

The crew shadow us all evening and pretty soon we are tired of the constant questions.

'So Jackie, how do you think Rich has coped today?' asks Marie for what feels like the twentieth time.

What does she want me to say? That I think he's rubbish? That he is a real let-down and that I could do so much better myself?

'Really well. I knew he would.'

'Oh,' she says, hoping for more. 'But he hasn't done the three things you asked him to do.'

In an attempt to inject some TV-friendly conflict into our lives, they asked us to come up with an agenda for each other for the week. I said I'd like Rich to tidy up more, to play with Saoirse and to interact with the babies more. Now, these are genuine wishes of mine, but I am not in the habit of giving Rich a list of instructions to follow. I've always gone with the policy of if it ain't broke don't try and fix it. He already does the majority of the housework and childcare – why would I want to make extra demands? He already plays with Saoirse a lot – just not in any traditional sense. He talks to her a lot, and will happily spend an hour over the five-minute walk from the park to let her look closely at spiders, leaves, aeroplanes, whatever it is that catches her eye on any particular day. It's true that I worry about the fact that he finds it harder to play with the triplets, treating them a bit like a problem that has to be dealt with every few hours, but when I look back I remember that he found it equally hard to play with Saoirse when she was tiny. Little babies just don't interest him very much. I'm sure that when they start sitting up, babbling and clapping their fat little hands together with glee he will melt and start to play with them more, but for now I am content that he looks after all their practical needs. They have each other, and Saoirse, and me to goo-goo ga-ga at them.

I look around at the surfaces littered with dirty plates, empty bottles, bits of broken crockery and piles of ironing.

'No, I suppose it is pretty untidy in here,' I offer, aware that my desire to please her is battling it out with my loyalty to Rich. Marie nods furiously from behind the camera. 'But I suppose it is quite hard to tidy up when you've got four babies to look after,' I add, catching Rich's eye as he kneads the dough for his bread.

Marie looks a bit crestfallen.

'But do you not think he should have tried a bit harder?' she says, trying to draw me out.

I think for a minute, trying to work out if I am indeed harbouring some resentment. Somewhere near the bottom of my stomach I notice a small knot. It feels a bit like humiliation. I realize with a start that she has planted – or watered – the seed of some unrest here. But I'll be damned if I'll let her know it. I don't need the amateur relationship-counselling these programmes have to offer.

'Yes, I suppose he could,' I say evenly. I busy myself picking up the slack, feeding, winding, changing the babies, trying to work out what is niggling me. Eventually the crew slope off and we sit in the living room exhausted.

'I do feel a bit miffed,' I say.

'Why, ducky?' says Rich, channel-hopping.

'You could have done a few things I wanted you to do—'

'But I didn't get time, ducky!' he says, smiling.

'So when the programme comes out, it won't be full of shots of you in your pants sunbathing and doing Sudoku?'

'Me, ducky? No, ducky!' he grins.

Right, so that's what he's been up to.

'It's not that I particularly want you to do all the tidying and get the craft table out for Saoirse – it's just the fact that you didn't is being turned into an act of deliberate defiance by you. They will make it look as though you don't care about what I want.'

'I do care! I made some bread!'

'Because *you* wanted to! It's not what *I* wanted.'

'You ate it!'

'That's not the point! The point is you were fulfilling your own agenda, not mine, and the fact that I was made to tell you three things I specifically wanted, and the fact that you then chose to ignore them will be made significant in the programme!'

'How?' says Rich, amused by my sudden paranoia.

'Oh, come on! You've seen those shows! They'll have a voice-over of me going, "I want Rich to play with Saoirse more", over the top of loads of images of you doing the crossword in the park while she picks up dog poo.'

'I didn't do the crossword today!'

'And then they'll have me saying, "And I want Rich to interact with the babies more" – cue shots of them all crying while you watch the cricket.'

'Cricket's not on till next week.'

'Oh, you know what I mean. I give up.' And I flounce off to bed. It's the closest we've come to a row in three years.

That's how they work, these documentary makers. They get under your skin just by being there all the time. I've often wondered how they manage to find so many dysfunctional families and bad-tempered couples, but now I realize that it's not necessarily that the families are like this to begin with – it's the process of being filmed all the time that makes them crazy. Having a camera up your nose from morning till night is very stressful. You become unhealthily self-conscious, viewing your life and its little peccadilloes through a third-party filter. I defy anyone to be 100 per cent pleased with what they see.

Tuesday 30 August

A new day, a new resolve. Rich says he will tidy up and get the PlayDoh out for Saoirse to show that he is doing what I would like. If it's not a sunny day. I get home from the office to find my brother Adrian, his partner Silvie and their son James helping Rich out. Despite all the extra hands, there is chaos in the house. Half-empty bottles of curdling milk formula are scattered all over the floor, Saoirse is filthy and the babies are crying. Rich and Adrian are making caraway-seed bread rolls to go with the huge pan of pasta he has cooked. I clock an opened bottle of red wine, half empty.

'Have you been drinking on duty?' I say from the kitchen door.

A camera flies at me, eager to catch the moment I crack and let rip with a stream of abuse.

'I needed some for the pasta sauce!' says Rich, flour smudging his nose like a fifties advert for home baking.

'Oh, give us a glass,' I sigh, stepping over the toys, pram and mini-golf set littering the floor.

The table is laid and we all sit down to eat. There is a lot of noise – children shouting, good-natured joshing between the men, laughter from Silvie and me as we watch the kids shovelling ropes of spaghetti into their tomato-stained faces. We resemble an Italian extended family in some naff pasta sauce commercial – 'Hey, ees crazee 'ere, but we larve everybardy!'

The crew slope off looking disappointed again, and I realize that the wine bottle is half full.

Friday 2 September

Rich is exhausted but making a show of being OK. He is being trailed by the crew constantly this week and he says that they keep filming the babies when they are crying. They also manage to catch him every time he is sitting down with a cup of tea or sunbathing in the garden. We are beginning to feel as though they might be making a very different programme from the one we signed up for. 'Britain's Worst Parents'? We imagine the knock at the door the day after transmission.

'Hello, we're Social Services – we've come to collect the neglected triplets.'

I run this past my comedian friend Dara.

'I don't think you've got any worries there – it's not like they get loads of calls from families eager to rehome *triplets*, is it?'

It's my turn to be at home and look after them all next week. I think I'll mock up some teats for bottles of vodka and leave them lying about. A few well-placed syringes here and there – give them some contentious cutaways.

I'm determined to cope. Our pride will not let us reveal the true extent of the impact the triplets have had on our lives, and as a consequence our relationship with the film crew has become quietly adversarial. The questions keep coming thick and fast, endlessly repetitious – 'How do you think Rich is coping? How do you feel about being a stay-at-home mum? Do you think you'll try to do the things he asks you to do while he is at work?' I know they want particular answers, probably along the lines of 'He's useless and I'm going to show him a thing or two when I get my turn', but I refuse to buckle. I feel like I'm in an interrogation room. Rich and I start fantasizing about confessing to imagined crimes. It's easy to see how the police get false confessions out of people. After a while, you are just so fed up with being pecked at day after day. It would be very tempting to just say, 'All right, all right, whatever you say, where do you want me to sign?' You get to the stage where anything, even life-imprisonment, would be preferable to trying to find a new way to say the same thing over and over again. I could quite easily let the small irritations with Rich bubble to the surface for public consumption but (a) it's very undignified and (b) I made a decision long ago not to be a nag. It's very dull and unattractive and most of the time the things people nag about are relatively unimportant. If something really bugs me I'll say so, and that will be the end of it. At the risk of sounding like an old hippy, I confess that I subscribe to the Gestalt maxim: 'I am me and you are you and if we should happen to meet in the middle then so be it. If not, then that is just the way things are.' It's not a cop out, and it doesn't make me a walkover. It just means that I don't spend my time going on and on about things in the hope that the other person will somehow decide to do exactly as I wish all the time. Such victories are pyhrric anyway, and I want my victories to be real. So I just can't get that worked up about the tidying and the PlayDoh. When quizzed about it by the director, I just shrug and say, 'Oh well.' I'm not about to turn myself into Andy Capp's wife just for a TV show.

So it is even more galling, given my magnanimous approach this week, to find that Rich has told them that he wants me to do all the washing and ironing, take all the children out every day for some fresh air and cook his dinner every night. He knows I hate ironing, I can't cook, and going out with all four children on your own is like doing a fun run in full deep-sea-diving gear. The worst of it is, he knows I'm such a goody two shoes and respond so eagerly to any pathetic challenge that I will probably do it all and more. I must try to get some help, though I don't know from whom. My usual aides are all out of action. Linda and Anoushka are on holiday, and Lou is in the middle of her own baby dramas.

Poor Lou. She's in hospital having suffered an ectopic pregnancy. She didn't even know she was pregnant. She's had keyhole surgery and has lost one fallopian tube, the embryo having implanted itself inside it. Apparently, the ovary is still there, and it might compensate by passing the eggs around the back to the remaining tube. She sounds tearful and uncertain. She doesn't know yet what her chances are of conceiving another child. She needs to speak to the consultant but he's not there now. I feel so bad for her. It's her third miscarriage this year.

'All I want is one more baby,' she says from her hospital bed. 'Then I'll stop.' She sounds weak, depressed and tearful – not at all like the robust, cheery public-school girl I love to take the piss out of.

She's at Whipps Cross – the same hospital in which we discovered we were expecting triplets. Funny old world. Mother Nature has a perverse streak. There's Lou – good, middle-class girl married to her first-ever proper boyfriend, Tom, with their sweet blond son Harry, Saoirse's sometime punchbag and best friend – struggling in her attempt to have a second child; then there's me, one-time lesbian, reluctant working-class suburbanite and accidental multibreeder. It's just not fair. I really hope she gets pregnant again soon and can put all this behind her.

Sunday 4 September

My first day of solo childcare. The triplets are either on a growth spurt or they are conspiring against me. Every time I put Orla down she screams. Eventually, she falls asleep, then Thady decides to give it a go. Once Thady's cried himself purple, Frank takes the baton and runs with it. Saoirse jumps around enjoying the misrule. By midday I've done a pile of washing and ironing, and I'm deciding what to do with all the bits and bobs Rich has left unhoused all over the kitchen surfaces. It's half past one by the time I work out what to do for dinner. I've put Saoirse to bed for her nap, and she won't be up until two, by which time she will need feeding. The triplets' next feed is at three, and I need to go to the shops, and the shops shut at four. It'll have to be a trip to the local shops, as apart from some left-over chicken limbs I can't see anything resembling the ingredients for a meal in the fridge. Normally, Rich has it all sorted on the catering front and the house is full of meat, fish, vegetables and cheese, but last week's filming meant he wasn't able to go to the big supermarket and get a big shop. He's been going to our local convenience Somerfield and buying stuff day by day. He likes doing this. He's a good cook, and likes to buy fresh things from the greengrocer on his way back. I hate food shopping at the best of times – in an air-conditioned food emporium with wide aisles, plenty of parking and no kids in tow. This is not the best of times.

To get the ingredients for a meal I will have to strap one baby to my chest, put Saoirse in the front of the triple buggy and the remaining triplets in behind her. This is not fun. I refer any doubters of this fact to my entry for 11 August, now known in this house as PostOfficeCountersGate. Only this time, it will be worse. This time I will also have a film crew in tow. As if we weren't enough of a sideshow. Never mind – since Rich has asked me to get the babies out in the fresh air every day, at least I will be killing two birds with one stone.

I calculate that I'll have to either run to the shops without feeding Saoirse or risk getting there after the triplets' feed, which should be over by about ten to four. What to do?

'I know – we'll have a picnic!' I declare. I hurriedly make a rubbish cheese sandwich for Saoirse and stick the cold baby bottles into the buggy. I'll feed them all outside. It's a nice Sunday afternoon. It'll be fun. And that way I can get to the shops first.

I strap Orla to me – she is the lightest – and load up on the front path. The cameraman, Paul, runs backwards in front of me, almost colliding with a few trees and several lampposts as I stride down the road with renewed purpose. All the way through the park the local youths, normally not that interested in the triplets, start running at us and jumping in front of the camera shouting, 'What you filming? Can I be on telly, mate?' I ignore them – and the knot of tension starting to form in my left shoulder. Once at the supermarket I am faced with a problem. How do I manoeuvre a five-foot buggy round the narrow High-Street supermarket aisles without comedy results involving unplanned shelf rearrangement? Plus where do I put my shopping? I have no hands free to carry a basket, and the buggy handles do not allow for hanging things. The film crew look on amused as I try to steer my way around the fresh produce to the dairy section.

'This is impossible!' I mutter.

'So Jackie—' starts Marie. Not a great time for an interview. I try glaring, but she persists.

'What's it like doing the shopping with the children on your own?' I swear she is smirking.

'Oh, it's brilliant,' I say coldly. 'This is ridiculous. I don't know how Rich manages it.'

'He does it quite differently,' she says mysteriously. What does she mean?

'Oh?' I say, trying not to sound too interested. 'How?'

'He leaves the babies by the front door next to the salad veg and picks them up at the end,' she says casually.

Does he now?

'Would you not consider doing that?' she says, angling idly.

'I think we're already in danger of being accused of child neglect. I don't want to encourage anyone,' I say, shunting the buggy round a difficult corner. I will get all the things we need and get out of here with all the children in tow, not just dumped in a corner, prey to any passing loony.

And then I shall have words with Rich.

I emerge from the shop having kicked and dragged my groceries around the store. I have three full shopping bags. Where do I put all the stuff? I am so unused to shopping in the High Street that I have completely overbought and have nowhere to put all the groceries. I kneel on the pavement trying to stuff the three bags into the small basket underneath the triple buggy, but it is already full of blankets, nappies, the change bag, the bottles for the next feed and the lame picnic I've prepared in lieu of Saoirse's lunch. I push and I shove, desperately trying to get the bags into the tiny space left. I cram the first bag in, then the second, but the third will not go. I give it one last heave and the first bag pops out the other side. A small crowd has gathered. The combination of triplets, a camera crew and a moderately overweight sweaty woman on all fours trying to pack her shopping away is just too much to resist for even the most discreet goggler. We all watch as a sad little nearly ripe avocado rolls into the road and is flattened by a passing 4x4. Quickly, I round up the escapee items and stuff them one by one into the corners of the buggy. Orla is now bright purple in the sling on my chest after having been almost upside down during my fumblings.

'So Jackie—' starts Marie, but I am off. I make it across the zebra crossing without stopping and I'm into the park before the crew can catch up with me.

This buggy is impossibly heavy with Saoirse in the front. She can get out and walk for a bit now that we are in the safe confines of the park. I go to lift her out and notice for the first time that she has no shoes on. In my rush to get her out of bed and into the buggy I have forgotten her shoes. A camera zooms in on her bare feet. Did they know? Did they deliberately not tell me so that they could get some good footage of her naked, neglected feet? I look at the path. It is peppered with tiny fragments of broken glass.

'Walk on the grass, Saoirse!' I say, as if it's some fantastic new game I've just invented. Bugger. Bad mother.

In the distance, I spot my neighbour Carey and her ten-year-old daughter Georgia.

'Hello!' shouts Carey. 'Need a hand?'

'Yes! Help me feed the babies!'

Georgia's eyes light up and Marie is thwarted once again. We sit on the grass and each baby gets a one-to-one feeding experience – quite rare these days. It must feel like the baby version of silver service to them. Saoirse eats her sandwiches and for ten minutes all is well with the world. I suppose the crew think I am cheating, getting emergency assistance like this, but I can't help living in a nice place where people look out for one another. I'm not turning down any offers for the sake of their story. I am not a martyr. Yet. And so what if Rich did it all by himself? It's only because he's a typical hairy-arsed man who'd rather eat his own gonads than admit he could do with a helping hand.

But there is no time for complacency. It is half past four and I have dinner to cook. I rush home. Rich has left two organic chicken legs in the fridge. I eye them suspiciously. I have no idea what to do with them.

'How do you cook chicken legs?' I ask, apparently hypothetically but rather hoping for an answer from Paul, the cameraman, who looks like he knows his way around a spice rack. No one responds. I've got a house full of people but I'm on my own here.

I grab a baking tin, slosh in some olive oil, chuck the chicken legs on top and garnish with some garlic cloves and a few sprigs of rosemary. As an afterthought, I chop two leeks up and throw them in to bake. It looks good. I am acting like someone who knows what they are doing and it's working. I put the chicken in the oven, then boil some potatoes for a salad. By the time the leaves are on the plate and the potato salad is made, the chicken is crispy and smells delicious. The crew even do a close-up as I serve it up. Rich walks in to find me placing two steaming platefuls of quality tucker on the table. The babies have been fed and they lie kicking in their cot. I've done it. I've done it all. I stand back and wait for the accolades to roll in.

'You didn't cut all the green bits off the leeks, did you?'

asks Rich, peering at my offering and looking in the bin. 'That's the tastiest bit.'

'Would you like what's left shoved where the sun don't shine?' I ask sweetly. Big close-up.

He then plonks a large bin bag down in front of me.

'Have a look at this,' he says proudly.

'What is it?'

'It's veg. I met a man with an allotment and he'd grown too much so he's given us some. Look.'

He opens the bag and it is full of green things. A huge bunch of basil, peppers, two massive comedy marrows and armfuls of spinach.

'What am I supposed to do with this?' I say, brandishing the marrow.

'Stuff it,' says Rich.

To my astonishment, he then spends the rest of the evening doing whatever he fancies. He plays the piano for a bit, he mooches around, he makes no attempt to help feed the babies or do the washing-up or anything. I pull him to one side.

'Why are you behaving like the bloke in "Bewitched"? I hiss. 'This is an extreme situation here – it's an all-hands-on-deck job. You can't just come home and expect your pipe and slippers!'

'Darren,' he says.

'What?'

'The bloke in "Bewitched". Darren. Goodnight, ducky.' And he kisses me sweetly on the lips.

Monday 5 September

I am in hell. Last night I had to sleep in with the babies. It's the rules. Whoever is going out to work needs a good night's sleep, so whoever has had them all day also has to do the night feed. It seemed perfectly reasonable to me last week, when I was swanning in at 6 p.m. and popping off to bed at 10 p.m. for a good eight hours' sleep. This week I think it stinks.

'It's not fair!' I tried whining, but to no avail. So last night I bedded in with my three little babies for the first time in a while. All was well for the first two hours – they had their 11 p.m. feed and slept, well, like babies. But come 1 a.m. it all changed. I was awoken by what sounded like a bad remake of *Creatures from the Swamp*. Or a medieval enactment of judgement day. Gargles, groans, farts, strange screeches filled the air all night until I finally caved in and fed them at two and again at six. I was exhausted when I went to bed. Now I am beyond exhaustion. The crew arrive like vultures circling for road kill. Once again, I am behind the ironing board. I am ironing bored.

'So Jackie—' says Marie.

'I'm in a really bad mood. It's just too hard, this. I can't do all this on no sleep.'

I know I sound dramatic but I mean it. I need to get some sleep or I will die. Tomorrow, for sure.

'It's not that they were crying or anything – it's just that they make all these noises and I can't sleep through it. It was like waking up in a zoo.'

Happy with my misery, the crew go off for lunch while I plan how to make things easier.

'Here are the problems,' I say to myself out loud. 'One of

us has to sleep near the babies in case they cry or need anything during the night. The other has to sleep out of earshot of all the noise to ensure a good night's kip. Until now we have had the babies downstairs as it's cooler and nearer to the kitchen for the middle-of-the-night feed. The 'sleeping partner' has been upstairs. What if we swap? The babies can sleep in the cot in the main bedroom and I can sleep in one of the bunk beds across the landing. I'll be able to hear them if they cry, but not all the rest of the noise. They'll wake me up when they cry for food; other than that I'll get some sleep. Rich can sleep downstairs on his own.'

Pleased with my new plan, I think about what else I could do to experiment with their sleep routine. Until now we have been swaddling the babies in fleecy blankets, which worked in the early days but is now the subject of a bitter management dispute between Rich and me. The triplets are bigger and stronger now, and they often wake because they have wrestled free of the covers during the night and are cold. Upstairs we have three brand-new baby sleeping bags hanging idle in the wardrobe. It's time to roll out the big guns. Rich has resisted this until now because he is essentially conservative and would rather keep things as they are even when they are clearly no longer working. I am essentially radical and like to shake things up just to see what happens. Now that I am in charge on the home front it's time to implement some essential changes in the running of the triplets' sleep for the good of the family as a whole. I am the time-and-motion mum, the sleep shop steward, the mummy management consultant brought in to modernize and streamline. Rich is going to hate this.

When he gets home I hit him with it.

'Right – this is what's happening tonight. The babies are going upstairs in our room. I'm sleeping in the spare room and you're down here.'

'OK,' he says suspiciously, waiting for the catch.

'And they're going in their sleeping bags.'

'They'll be very warm—' he starts.

'The bags are only light. I just think that part of the reason they are waking up so much is that they are cold, and it's too bright down here. Upstairs is much darker. And I'm giving them Stage 2 Hungrier Baby milk at bedtime. That way, I'm hoping they will sleep longer. I'm not going to wake them up at eleven. I'm just going to wait and see what happens.'

'OK,' says Rich, knowing it's a lost cause. 'We'll see.'

The night of my experiment is to be captured on a nightcam carefully installed in the corner of the bedroom. It is on time-lapse so it can record up to six hours of activity using an infrared light. The crew hope to catch the chaos of a night feed with three small babies. They want shots of me in and out like a fiddler's elbow, seeing to one baby then the next. I imagine they will cut the footage together and speed it up, then play some jaunty music underneath in a kind of 'Oh my God, what a nightmare!' kind of a way. As Rich says – we'll see.

Tuesday 6 September

I am triumphant. I put the babies to bed as planned at 7.30 p.m. They looked about a bit at their new surroundings, then fell fast asleep, three in a row, their arms flung up above their heads like extras in a western shoot-out. They remind me of those decorative wall ducks. We sat and had our first baby-free evening, drinking wine and chatting. The crew knocked about a bit looking bored then left us, promising to be back bright and early to witness the carnage after the storm. But there is no carnage. I turned in at around 10 p.m. half expecting to be woken by plaintive cries of triple hunger an hour later. I wake with a start to hear one baby whimpering a bit. I look at my watch. It's 4 a.m.

'Four!' I almost shout. So I feed them, put them down and hope for the best. The next thing I hear is tapping on the front door. Have I left a baby in the buggy outside? Is everything all right? I look at my watch. It's 7 a.m. I am almost hysterical with laughter. They did it. They had a solid sleep, interrupted only once to feed. I feel smug. Smugger than smug. I am Mrs Smuggins of Smugsville Avenue, Smugland. I peep in at the babies who are just stirring, before rushing down to let Marie in.

'So . . . how did it go?' she asks nervously. It's very bad news for her, if it worked. I keep her waiting a bit. I'm not going to spill the beans till the cameras are here. But I can't resist a quick thumbs up before I get the bottles ready.

'It worked,' I say, once the boys are here with the gear. 'I think the combination of the darkness, the Hungrier Baby milk, the warmth and the sleeping bags made them much less fidgety. I didn't hear a thing until four o'clock!' I gloat.

'So how many times did you go into the room after we switched the nightcam on?' asks Marie, obviously worried now.

'Erm . . . none,' I say. 'None times.'

'So you didn't go into the room until four?'

'Nope. They were fast asleep.'

'What time did you switch on the camera, Paul?' asks Marie, biting her bottom lip.

'Ten,' says Paul flatly. We all stand in silence for a bit as they let it sink in. They have hired, at great expense, a camera that has just filmed six hours of solid nothingness. When they look at the tape, instead of the farce they anticipated, they will see three babies sleeping peacefully – and quietly – until exactly the point at which the film ran out. It'll be like those live-feed pictures from the Big Brother House that insomniacs watch in the middle of the night – hours of people just sleeping.

'So . . . that's that then,' says Marie letting out a sigh. 'But how are you feeling?'

'I feel *great!*' I say. 'Totally rested. Unbelievable.' They go off for breakfast and a quick regroup. How is Marie going to make anything of this rather peaceful new household? Part of me feels sorry for her – she's got to make an interesting programme out of us getting on pretty well. Not classic reality TV. But I'd rather have a good night's kip than a shouting match on the telly. Call me old-fashioned.

I ring Rich at work to tell him the news.

'So she'll just have a totally dull tape of last night,' I finish.

'No, she won't,' says Rich, laughing. Now it's me that's worried.

'Why – what have you done?'

'I went in after you went to bed and did a funny walk with my pants off.'

Friday 9 September

The crew have finally gone. We race around the house cheer-ing. It's been a long hard two weeks, this last week being especially trying for me. I have cleaned, I have ironed (and supplied the requisite shot of me trying to figure out how the hell to put up an ironing board), I have cooked – yes, COOKED – every night. I loathe cooking, but this week I have produced stuffed marrow, home-made pesto (Delia Smith) and fresh spaghetti, lamb steaks with bacon and white wine sauce and red snapper Creole with crushed rosemary potatoes and a medley of baby vegetables (Nigel Slater). Rich has been astounded. On the red snapper night he roared with laughter when I put the plate down in front of him.

'What's happened, ducky? Where've you gone?'

'Shut up and eat it. Sorry I'm not wearing gingham,' I sneer, but I am secretly proud of my achievements. I've looked after Saoirse and the triplets, I even plumbed in the dishwasher, which has been sitting idle for the past month, and cooked five great meals. I am, for one week only, a domestic goddess. Lou pops in and quizzes me about my week so I boast about my cooking. She's a proper wife who is always knocking up great meals for Tom when he gets back from work. She will be impressed.

'Why on earth did you make such elaborate dinners?' she guffaws.

'What do you mean? I thought that's what you do!' I say, defensive now.

'No! Sometimes I'll do a nice meal, but only once or twice a week – I might do some roast chicken one night, then the next we'll have cheese toasties or a takeaway! I haven't got time to be messing about in the kitchen all day!'

'Oh.'

'You should have just knocked up something nice and simple.'

'But that's the point – I wouldn't know where to begin! I had to go to recipe books just to find out how to do things. That's why I ended up doing such fancy stuff.'

'Oh, come one – you do know how to cook really!'

'I don't! Last week I blew up a boiled egg! An *egg* for God's sake!'

Heaven only knows what sort of programme they will make about us. I hope it's not something that will embarrass the kids later in life.

'We'll not watch it, ducky,' says Rich. 'We'll put the DVD on a shelf and get it down on the triplets' eighteenth birthday. Then I can say, "Look at me when I had hair", ducky!'

'And I can say, "Look at me when I was really slim," I say, imagining myself as the thirty-stone pensioner I often fear I will become. Hopefully, by the time the babies are eighteen the DVD format will be totally obsolete and we won't be able to watch it anyway.

Saturday 10 September

We are in Suffolk for my dear old friend Julia's fortieth birthday. She has rented an enormous country house and filled it with all her friends and their children. We ummed and aahed about coming at all before the babies arrived because we just couldn't imagine orchestrating such a massive organizational conundrum. We really thought we would not be able to leave the house until they could all walk to the car — or better still, drive it. And it is a long drive with triplets and a toddler, but we are so elated that we can actually do anything at all we grab most opportunities that come our way to go out as a family.

Saoirse spots the other kids, who are mostly a little older and therefore infinitely desirable, and becomes feral almost immediately. They roam the grounds as a pack, shouting down rabbit holes, spreading paint all over the lawn and pulling raspberries from the canes in the kitchen garden. It is heaven for her, while I'm stuck in a back room feeding the triplets and Rich is helping in the kitchen. At one point, she disappears for two hours with a mum called Mary who has two children herself. Mary takes them to the beach to look for crabs, and when they return Saoirse doesn't even bother to come and find me. Instead, I find her sitting naked on the front steps with three other little girls.

'Hello, Bubba!' I cry, delighted to see her having such fun but wanting my baby back at the same time.

She turns casually, only momentarily distracted from impressing her older friends.

'Hello, Jackie,' she says, before resuming her pre-school pow-wow. A triplet is crying, so I go back to my post and feel sad that I wasn't there the first time she saw a crab. I taught her how to imitate their claws a few weeks ago, and it would have been nice to see her watching them for real. It's just another small tragedy in this multiple-birth saga. I'm destined to miss out on a lot just by sheer volume of baby. Other parents see us with four kids, feel sorry for Saoirse, then whisk her away to help her and us out, and before you know it she's had some epiphanic experience involving shellfish and I'm weeping onto a baby's head in a stranger's stately home.

Later that evening, all the children are being put to bed so that the adults can have a sophisticated dinner. We weren't going to be here this late but have managed to improvise a cot on the floor in the study for the triplets, and Saoirse is put to bed in the travel cot. She goes down fighting but by 7.30 p.m. they are all asleep. We sit patiently in the parlour waiting for the other parents to wrestle their over-excited children into bed. There are screams, protests, footsteps along corridors above our heads, threats, demands, bribes. The parents do a relay of whose child is out of bed now, and the dinner is delayed while mums lie down with toddlers in a vain attempt to get them to go to sleep. Rich leans in conspiratorially.

'All our four are asleep, ducky.'

We smile. And they tell us we've got it hard.

Monday 12 September

We visit our parish priest, Father Pat, to arrange the triplets' baptism. He is an old-school Irish priest – slightly forbidding, not remotely happy clappy and very nice indeed. He visibly balks when he sets eyes on the triplets.

'God Almighty,' he says. I'm shocked. Is he allowed to say that? It's delightful to hear a priest say this.

'It's a good job I'm a priest. I wouldn't be able for children at all,' he says, shaking his head in wonder.

Triplets – they make blasphemers of us all.

Wednesday 14 September

We need more space. The house is full to bursting point with
stuff. We have got so much stuff. And I've always hated stuff.
I've never been the sort of person who buys, collects or covets
stuff. Even though I am a major music lover, and can tune in
to any radio station at any time and be relied upon to join in
with the second verse of whatever is playing, I don't even own
a working stereo and I don't have many CDs. Just because I
love music, it doesn't mean I feel I have to own it personally.
Oh God, how bloody hippy do I sound now? I might as well
be quoting Sting – 'If you love somebody, set them free.'
Anyway, the point is that having children brings not only joy,
sleepless nights, worry and beauty to your door in equal
measure, but it also brings stuff. Having triplets is even worse
on the stuff front, because you need three of everything all at
once. At least when you have your children one by one, the
sensible way, you get to reuse the stuff for each child at the
appropriate developmental point. We have three baby bouncer
chairs, three cots, four high chairs, four buggies (two singles, a
double and a triple), three baby slings, two sterilizing units,
twenty bottles, two change stations, six sets of baby towels, four
baby car seats, two playpens, three baby gym play mats, three
travel cots, three musical cot mobiles and a partridge in a pear
tree. On top of all these practical items we have about a
hundred cuddly toys. Our small terraced house looks like some
soppy teenager's bedroom, there's that many pink bears, purple
bunnies and stripy elephants lying about the place. I hate it.
Where is the minimalist pad of my dreams? As I survey the

wreckage, I have a small weep over the white leather daybed I will now never own.

We have to either move or make more space. As we've only been here a year, it will have to be the latter. I didn't give Gordon Brown £10k in stamp duty only to move a year later (and what can anyone possibly want with £10k's worth of stamp? I could post him the bloody house for that). We've already had planning permission granted, but we don't have the money to do the work.

Remortgaging is our only option – unless I take my mate Alan up on his generous offer of an interest-free, long-term loan.

I meet Alan for lunch and spend an age trying to broach the subject. I hate asking anyone for money. I feel greedy holding my hand out for my own change in shops. But I take a deep breath and start.

'We're thinking about getting our loft done—'

'Oh yeah?'

'Yes . . . and you know you said ages ago that if we needed any help financing it you might—'

'How much do you want, Clune?'

I'm blushing.

'Erm, well, we've had a few quotes done and . . . erm, it's about twenty—'

'Fine. I'll write you a cheque.'

And that's it.

'Are you going to put the babies up there?'

'No, it's going to be for us. We're thinking about making it a rule that the kids aren't allowed up there at all. We might not even tell them it's there.'

'Good idea. You could get a secret panel put in behind a false bookcase. Get the floor soundproofed. Get it all sound-proofed.'

So we're going to have our haven after all. I have such lovely, generous friends. I am very lucky. I think again of the poor girl on the fifteenth floor of the tower block, pregnant with triplets and newly single. I hope she has good friends, if not rich ones.

I am so happy that we are going to have a bedroom together again. If we stand any chance of surviving these next ten years with our relationship intact, we need at least a little attic room to retire to together. I think it'll be the best twenty grand I never spent.

Monday 19 September

Saoirse is bored. She knocks around the house picking up things she knows she's not allowed to just to get the attention a telling-off will bring. I feel so guilty that she gets so little stimulation, so this week I have decided to give her some toddler time and take her to the many playgroups that are run locally. I meet Lou at the group up the road. It's in a draughty old church hall – they normally are – that's filled with donated toys, equipment and grubby dollies, and a nice old lady who makes tea and gives you biscuits if you promise to sit in the 'hot liquids' safe zone. Lou and I chat while Harry and Saoirse run around making mayhem. There are little craft tables where children are quietly engaged in making substandard greetings cards to be lovingly pinned to kitchen appliances later on.

'Oh whassis?' says Saoirse, her enthusiasm aping my attempts to get her interested in things. The craft lady has some clock shapes cut out. She is helping the children to stick little weather symbols on to the clock faces.

'It's a *clock*, Saoirse,' says Lou.

'No, it's a *barometer*,' I say, doing my competitive parent routine. Lou and I like this game. She won't let me teach Saoirse to count above ten because Harry can.

I like this club. Today I meet the woman who had her baby at twenty-eight weeks. We first met when we were both twenty-weeks pregnant and laughed about the fact that I looked ready to drop and she still looked tiny. Her little boy is with her and is adorable. Everyone asks after the triplets.

'When you gonna bring them babies in?' they all tease. But how can I? It's hard enough running around after Saoirse, let alone having three babies to tend to as well. And how would I get them all there? It would take me longer to load and unload them all again than the group lasts.

Tuesday 20 September

The local Catholic Church has a mums and toddlers group on Tuesday afternoons. There is no formal structure but plenty of toys, bikes, prams and noisy things to send the twenty or so children mental. It starts at 1.30 p.m. – right in the middle of Saoirse's nap – so, after loading the triplets into their buggy, I drag her out of bed and we head up the road. She will play whether she likes it or not. The hall is packed with little Catholics beating each other up while their mums stand around chatting and drinking tea. Since most of the grown-ups are of Irish extraction, at least you get a *decent* cuppa, and *chocolate* on your biscuits. None of the thin, 'fair-haired' Protestant tea with a dry old cracker on the side that you get in so many places. Saoirse's chubby cheeks are still flushed with sleep and she clings to my leg, not wanting to join in. She doesn't look frightened or shy – just mutely appalled. I know how she feels. I park the babies up along the side and try to stop the bigger children from driving straight at them in their toy fire engines and police cars. It looks like a very serious road traffic accident is being attended to by a pack of dwarves in Gap casuals. One little girl keeps poking her head first into Thady's seat, then Frank's, then Orla's, before starting at the front again. She cannot believe her eyes. The other mums seem nervous of me. They daren't include me in their moaning about how hard their lives are – maybe they think I'd laugh in their faces.

'What day is it tomorrow?' asks Carol, a pregnant mum of two. Her first born is now at school, so she's used to this play-group racket.

'Wednesday,' I say, pretty sure I am right.

'There's a group at the Methodist centre next door—'

'See you there,' I say.

Is this what you're meant to do – ferry them from one group to the next, filling up their week with a social diary that would put Tara Palmer Tomkinson in the shade?

Well, if I'm going to do this properly . . .

Wednesday 21 September

'Playgroup, Mama?' demands Saoirse, when she sees me reaching for my coat at 10 a.m. She's getting rather too used to this.

'Yes, playgroup,' I sigh. It all seems a bit pointless. It's not as if they even play with each other at this age. They do what the experts call 'parallel play' — i.e. ignoring each other and carrying on in their own little world. I suppose at least it's good training for marriage.

The hall is the requisite ten degrees below freezing, but there are dinky tables and chairs set out. Bright blue beakers and plates of biscuits are ready for break time, and around forty children are ignoring each other very noisily all around the hall. A decrepit piano sits forlornly in the corner with a sign that reads, 'Keep away from radiators.' I can't tell whether this is the piano's top tip for life or if it is the piano itself that is in need of careful placement. It is shoved right up against a massive double radiator.

Saoirse takes one look at the other children and heads straight for the biscuits. The atmosphere in the room changes. Suddenly, like a shoal of fish, all of the children spot the snacks and race to the table, instinctively aware of the threat to supplies my daughter poses.

After tucking into four or five biscuits and two miniature boxes of raisins, she stands up and says, 'Home now, Mama.'

I wheel the buggy out again and bribe her to hold my hand all the way up the busy road. I can no longer carry one baby on my front and push Saoirse with the other two babies. It's too difficult to steer. It takes twenty minutes to do a five-minute walk because Saoirse keeps collapsing her legs in protest, but I've watched 'Supernanny' and I will not give in. By the time we get home I am sweating heavily and have to wrestle a screaming Saoirse up to bed for her nap while the babies scream for their feed outside in the front garden. We often leave them there while we get ourselves organized inside. Our neighbour from South Africa thinks we are mad.

'We would never do that in Cape Town,' he says. Good job we're in East London then, isn't it? Over here people dump their babies, they don't steal other people's.

Thursday 22 September

I think Linda mentioned that Tumble Tots is on today, but I can't remember. I think I've blocked it out. I sit hiding behind the curtains, drinking tea and letting Saoirse watch Cbeebies. At 9.30 a.m. there's a knock at the door. Linda and Carol are in the street with their buggies loaded up and ready to go.

'We're heading off – you coming?' says Linda, whose energy astounds me.

'I'm not sure . . . I don't think I can . . . the babies are all asleep and Saoirse hasn't had any breakfast yet.'

They go off and I immediately feel like a slacker. I shove some cereal down Saoirse as she sits slack-mouthed in front of Linda Barron in 'Come Outside', then load the sleepy babies into the buggy. Their heads still loll to one side and they shiver as their hot bodies cool in the almost autumn air. We race across the green to the hall, where I wrestle with two sets of fire doors to get the buggy in.

Inside, I can see mums leading their children over, through and along a miniature padded assault course. There is a lively but focused atmosphere as the little faces contort in concentration. It looks fun, and Saoirse is already running for a trampoline she has spotted in the far corner. Linda and Carol wave from the parallel bars. I recognize at least five other faces from all the other playgroups. Don't these people do anything else except play? I suppose it beats sitting in the house. Marginally.

'Have you booked?' asks the smiling lady in the Tumble Tots T-shirt.

'No,' I say, my heart sinking. People only say this when they are about to turn you away. I feel like playing the 'Don't you know who I am? I'm the triplet lady!' card.

'We're full up, I'm afraid,' she says.

'Oh no! Don't tell me that!' I say, glancing down at the pram. 'It's been a massive effort to get here!'

The lady is of the nice variety and sees Saoirse's excited face. She has a peek at the babies and softens.

'Look, stay for today, but we have no more spaces, so she won't be able to join,' she says sadly.

It's better than nothing, so we stay and have great fun, apart from when we have to sit in a circle and sing songs. Saoirse likes to sing songs but not until she's ready. The other children sit happily in their mums' laps and giggle when, in a particularly hilarious number, the mums have to tickle their noses.

'Get *off*, Mama!' shouts Saoirse. She looks at me as though I'm mental. She's so used to playing on her own that my sudden hands-on approach is freaking her out.

'That was great. Thanks for letting us stay,' I say, a bit

gutted that we're not allowed to join. If I hadn't been stuck in with triplets all summer I might have got my act together and joined a few things before term time. Oh well.

The nice lady sees my 'poor me' face.

'Look,' she says quietly. 'We've had a few dropouts, so you can have a place if you want one.'

'Really? Great!' I say, stupidly pleased.

'But if anyone asks,' she says almost whispering, 'you were on the waiting list.'

Blimey. This child's play is serious business.

Friday 23 September

Saoirse puts my trainers on and says, 'Bubba playgroup?'

'Not today, Bubba,' I say from the sofa. 'I can't take it any more.'

'Can't take it any more,' echoes Saoirse, nodding sagely.

She knows I'm a lazy mum, and I think she likes it that way.

She'd better.

I remember that the admissions secretary of the local school is in the office this morning so I call. I have been paranoid about getting Saoirse on the list for the pre-school nursery. Our Lady of Lourdes has a good reputation and subsequently places are highly sought after. We need to get the family name on the books because a year after Saoirse starts nursery, there will be three more bringing up the rear. I've read terrible stories about triplets being rejected or split up and sent to different schools because they are just too much of a burden, especially in districts like ours where there is a high call on limited places. Even if you do get all your children into the same school, there are no guarantees that they will all be in the same session – pre-school hours are either five mornings or five afternoons a week. The logistics of ferrying four children to and from school for morning and afternoon sessions are already giving me a head-ache. After requesting an application form for Saoirse, I broach the subject of the triplets.

'And the other thing is, we have triplets,' I say nervously.

'Right,' says the lady without a flicker of horror.

'I was just wondering – would you take three at a time? And do you split them up? Or do you keep them all in the same class?'

'Yes, of course we'd take three, and it's up to you whether they stay in the same class or not. We decide that with the parents when we have twins in the school. Normally, we put one in each reception class and see how they get on.'

Now for the biggy.

'But would you make sure they were all in the same session – morning or afternoon?'

'Of course,' she laughs. 'It would be a bit unfair to do any-thing else.'

Saturday 24 September

Rich is out putting a greenhouse up, an occasional job that helps fund his twins' schooling, so I am alone with all the kids again. I brave the park by leaving Saoirse with Carey and her daughter Georgia across the road. Saoirse was desperate to go once she found out that a new rabbit had taken up residence. She couldn't have been happier if I'd told her that Georgia's house was made of chocolate ice-cream. So it's just me and the babies in the park and I'm getting the usual amazed glances when a man walking with his two-year-old daughter stops in front of me.

'Triplets? No!' he says, mock-shocked.

'Oh yes!' I say, trying to fend off any potentially negative remarks. I'm tired, having been up until 3 a.m. doing a radio show, and I just can't take it today.

'Look, Hannah!' he says, grabbing his little girl and pointing at the buggy. 'Do you know what that is?'

'No,' she says, looking intrigued.

'Hell on wheels!'

He is very pleased with his little non-joke. I want to kill him.

I leave the park smarting, and bump into a dad I often see in the park with his son.

'How are you getting on?' he says, making an 'it must be hell' face.

'Fine, thanks,' I say brittlely.

He raises his eyebrows in disbelief.

'You look like you've reached a sort of Zen-like calm,' he starts, chuckling to himself, but I head him off at the pass and explode. There is four months of suppressed anger ready to spew out and he is just in the wrong place at the wrong time.

'Do you know I am *sick* and *tired* of people telling me what a nightmare my life must be. I don't remember asking for anyone's opinion! I don't walk around pointing at people and saying, "Your children look like monsters", do I? It wouldn't be acceptable even if it were true, so why do people think it's OK to say it to me? And actually, no, my children are not "nightmares", they are very good, they are sleeping well and we're very very happy!'

'OK,' says the dad meekly before hurrying off.

I pick Saoirse up and relate the story to my neighbours.

'Those sorts of comments really upset you, don't they?' says Simon, Georgia's dad.

'Yes, they do.'

'That's the second time I've heard you say something like that – and I don't think it's that offensive.'

'Oh, don't you start!' says Cary.

Maybe it's a man thing.

Rich arrives back so we all go home together.

I shout at the babies for the first time. I am exhausted from trying to work late and manage all day on my own, and all three have been crying for an hour, solid.

'Oh, just *shut up*!' I scream.

Rich jumps. Saoirse looks aghast. I have never shouted. I don't like people who shout. We don't do shouting in our house.

It doesn't make me feel any better, and it makes the babies scream louder. I'm on the verge of picking up my coat and walking out. For half an hour anyway. Rich leads me out of the kitchen where the mayhem is in full swing. He sits me down with a glass of wine and puts everyone to bed before cooking me a lovely dinner. When order is restored like this, I feel silly for losing it. They are only babies. It's pointless to take their crying personally. It's the tiredness that has made me feel so defeated. I can't work late at night any more. I'll have to give up the radio job, much as I love it. It's just too hard now.

Sunday 25 September

When do babies grow? I woke up this morning and suddenly they are bigger.

I wish I had a time-lapse camera, like the ones they use in nature documentaries where they show you flowers erupting into bloom and shoots pushing through the earth in a matter of seconds. I have a huge pile of donated clothes that are now far too small for these three fifteen-pound monsters we suddenly have. Saoirse is dressing her tiny dolly in one of Orla's first vests. It seems ludicrous to think that Orla used to wear it. It's a toy vest surely?

I post a message on the Tamba board about the rude man and his hilarious 'hell on wheels' comment. I am particularly interested in whether people think it's as offensive as I do, and whether they have experienced similar nasty remarks. The responses I get astound me.

One woman recounts the story of how her twins were introduced to a friend's father who happened to be a clinical psychologist. He asked if the twins were identical and when told that indeed they were, he remarked, 'My colleague Dr Mengele would be interested in them!'

Mengele was, of course, the Nazi doctor who performed inhumane and brutal tests on identical twins in the concentration camps, injecting them with fatal diseases to see how they responded. The comment was particularly offensive to the couple as the twins' dad's grandfather was Jewish and had been among one of the last groups of children shipped out of Germany in the Kinder-transport.

Another woman took her triplets to the zoo where they met a paediatrician who asked if they had been born as a result of IVF. As the man was a professional, the woman didn't mind the intrusive line of questioning and told him that, yes, they were born after fertility treatment.

'You should sue the hospital,' said the paediatrician.

'What for?' asked the stunned mum.

'Ruining your life,' he replied.

Suddenly, 'hell on wheels' doesn't seem quite so bad.

Monday 26 September

We have reached several important milestones. Firstly, for the past ten nights the babies have achieved that Holy Grail of parenthood, the event of all events that is the light at the end of the newborn tunnel.

They have slept through.

Count them. Ten nights. All three of them. From 7 p.m. to 7 a.m. Not a peep.

We allow ourselves some hearty congratulations. I'm sure it's my new sleeping plan. Rich says he broke the back of it by weaning them off the 2 a.m. feed all those weeks ago. He just toughed out all the crying until 6 a.m. when the next feed was due, giving them dummies to get them through. Together we have done it. Yesterday I was reading a baby magazine (they'd sold out of the FT . . .) and someone had written in to Gina Ford's baby advice page asking why her four-month-old daughter was still waking three or four times a night. Gina said she would not expect a four-month-old baby to sleep through on only four feeds a day.

Ours are four months old – three, adjusted – and they are now on four 7–8oz bottles a day. They are defying Gina Ford. Hah! Our babies are more Gina Ford than Gina Ford herself! They are the ubercontented. We still cannot believe our luck. Saoirse was an extremely good sleeper from day one, and would go through from 11 p.m. until 6 a.m. when other babies were waking every hour through the night. But even she took about six months – and a few hearty solid feeds – to sleep all evening as well.

In the absence of sleep deprivation, I am now worrying about how much they sleep. They feed at 7 a.m., and even then sometimes we have to wake them. Then they go back to sleep for a couple of hours. This morning, they slept until the next feed at 11 a.m. Lou came over to help and they were still in bed. They normally then stay awake for a couple of hours and I put them in their chairs, sing to them, put them in the baby gym or just rush around doing things which seems to keep them quite entertained. Then they will be a bit crotchety between the 3 p.m. feed until the 7 p.m. night feed. In all, they seem to be fully awake for only about four hours a day. This doesn't seem right.

Maybe they're bored. Maybe we should be hothousing them. Gina says they should only be having two naps during the day – one shortish nap in the morning and a long one around lunchtime. Once again, they are defying her. Have they not read *The Contented Little Baby Book*?

The second milestone is that within three days of each other the babies have found their thumbs. This is a very big deal. Saoirse is almost two and is still totally addicted to her dummies – or 'diddos' as she calls them. She has about a dozen scattered around the house. We have tried to limit her access to them to bedtime only, but she is like an alcoholic who squirrels way half bottles of vodka behind radiators and down the back of the sofa. She will leave the room empty-mouthed only to return five minutes later with a dummy hanging petulantly from her lips. The minute she hurts herself, or is denied something, or is overtired, she will set up a furious chanting of 'Diddo? Diddo? Diddo!' until one of us can stand it no longer and caves in. She wasn't meant to still have them, but we just decided that, with triplets on the way, it would be pointless to wean her off them just at the point when three new little ones were arriving. 'We'll do it when she's two' we promised ourselves, deep down knowing that if the babies still had dummies by then we would not have the heart to do it. It has proved a very interesting decision to give our children dummies – or 'sooth-ers' as they say in the USA. There is a distinct class divide between parents who use them and those who don't. The semiotics of soothers fascinates me. What I have learnt, albeit in a highly coded and underhand way – a little comment here, a disapproving look there – is that people who give their baby a dummy are signalling their unwillingness to 'listen' to the child. This school of thought says that a child who isn't hungry, dirty or tired may cry because they need a cuddle or some attention. If parents choose to ignore this by sticking a dummy in – making a dummy out of? – their child, then they are obviously extremely lazy.

But worse than this, they are probably quite . . . how can I put this? No, there's no other word that will do.

Common.

There is a received wisdom among the middle-class circles I now move in that dummies are for chavs or single mums on benefits whose drug habits and/or inept parenting make them reliant on the little bits of rubber on a plastic base designed to simulate a nipple. No one with any education or breeding would give their child a dummy. It just looks, well, so *working class*. It's the children of these anti-dummy brigade parents who are always the most whiny, irritating little poppets you could ever wish not to meet. The ones who never stop crying, whingeing and generally spoiling a potentially nice coffee morning. The ones who, later on, get to leave a 'cute' message on their parents' answerphones – 'Mummy and Daddy aren't in at the moment . . .' In short, the ones who really need their gobs stopped with a nice juicy soother. I wouldn't mind but the anti-dummy mummies are the ones who've always got one breast hanging out with the baby hanging off it. The minute the baby starts fussing, out comes the maternity bra, down go the flaps and on it goes – not eating but chewing. The mummies become human dummies. Far better, surely, to pop a little soother in and get back to your cappuccino, both bra straps in place and no one looking at your stretch marks?

We gave Saoirse a dummy when we realized that she wanted to suck rather than eat. Distressed and exhausted by her constant demand for the breast all evening, I talked to the health visitor who told me that most babies need to suck for many more hours than they need to eat. In days gone by, women would wrap a small lump of butter in a cloth and give it to the babies to suck on. If this failed, there was always gin. Alcohol abuse aside, this information was so helpful to me as a first-time mum. I hadn't realized that wanting to suck did not always mean wanting to eat. As a lifelong orally fixated border-line compulsive eater, quite how this eluded me I don't know. The dummy was a godsend, enabling me to put Saoirse down for hours at a time, eat a meal without slopping it all over her head and stretch both arms out at once. Simple pleasures only a new mum or someone recently out of a full-body plaster cast will understand.

Our daughter's dummy-filled face was greeted with much disdain, however. 'Oh, you've given her a dummy,' people would say, as if it was a tattoo. 'It's not that we disapprove,' they'd say, detecting my defensiveness (it's hard not to feel a little shame in the face of such hostility). 'It's just that our Josh won't take a dummy,' they'd say almost proudly.

I never believe this. I hate the inferred superiority. For 'He won't take it' read 'We're above that'. Pah. 'He won't take it' indeed. They're just not trying hard enough.

It wasn't without its problems though, the dummy decision. In the months before she was able to find it and put it back in her mouth during the night, we would be woken several times by her crying when her dummy fell out. I would wake to the sound of the bloody thing hitting the wooden floor and lie there tense, waiting for the inevitable wail. Then there have been all the times when, despite having around twenty at any one time, we searched high and low while she cried only to realize that all the dummies had entered the soother vortex that is our house. But in all, the dummy has been a lifesaver, enabling me to take her to work on various occasions, safe in the knowledge that she would be quiet while I recorded radio programmes or read for rubbish parts in bad TV dramas.

Anyway, we started by giving the triplets dummies, even though we shuddered at the prospect of the night duty times three. We got the same disapproving looks, and I resisted the urge to say, 'Well, *you* come and juggle four babies under two and let's see how long *you* can stand the crying!' It's not very often that they all cry at once, but when they do the dummies have eased things so much. But for some reason, perhaps by silent triplet committee (a sub-group of the 'let's sleep through' caucus), the babies have decided to suck their thumbs instead, spitting out any other object apart from a bottle teat. This is exceptionally good news. A thumb is, barring some terrible accident involving digits and a careless moment near the tiger enclosure, always readily available, doesn't need washing and (hopefully) doesn't fall to the floor in the middle of the night. We couldn't get Saoirse to suck her thumb no matter how hard we tried, but the triplets are mad for it. They fuss around a bit trying to master their fine motor skills, like drunks at closing time, but eventually they manage to get their thumbs in and pretty soon their eyes are rolling back in their heads with pure ecstasy. We are delighted. Now we have no excuse not to get Saoirse off them.

★

I've just looked in on the babies. They're asleep again. They've got triplet narcolepsy. It's like a game of grandmother's foot-steps. Every time I turn around and look at them they close their eyes and freeze. They're probably pulling faces and stick-ing their fingers up behind my back as I write this.

Wednesday 28 September

I'm at the doctor's family planning clinic. I was dissuaded from having a sterilization during my C-section and I really don't want to take the pill as my hormones have been messed about with so much already, so I have arranged to have a coil fitted. I arrive and the nice lady doctor asks me to go for a pee to empty my bladder. I go into the consulting room and she asks me when my last period was.

'I haven't had one yet,' I say.

'Are you breastfeeding?'

'Not any more.'

'Oh. Well, is there a chance you could be pregnant?'

'I don't think so.'

'Have you had unprotected sex?' she says, looking a bit concerned now. I suddenly feel like a naughty schoolgirl. Which is exactly what I am.

'Well . . . a bit,' I say, hugely embarrassed.

The doctor and the nurse look at one another.

'You'll have to do a pregnancy test tomorrow, then another in two weeks before we can fit the coil. I'm sorry, but we have to do it by the book.'

I feel really stupid now.

'Please use a condom,' she smiles.

'Or abstain,' I say. 'I wouldn't mind but I haven't even got any libido anyway. I only did it to be polite.'

The doctor and the nurse explode with laughter.

'That is *very* polite – the definition of politeness,' says the doctor.

And it's true. I still hadn't recovered my sex drive after Saoirse's birth, but Mariella Frostrup made me.

And now look at me.

Thursday 29 September

I'm heading up the High Street to Boots with all four children in tow. I have to get a few essentials plus the double pregnancy test. Then it hits me. All the women in Boots know me. They are very friendly and chat to me all the time about the babies. They let me park the triple buggy in the middle of the aisle while I grab what I need. One of the women is nice but very gossipy – and I am about to walk in, with four children under the age of two, and purchase a pregnancy test. I will be the talk of the town. Bugger. Linda suggests saying that it's for Saoirse. Helpful. How am I going to do this without everyone knowing?

In the end, I bury the kit under a pile of other stuff and distract her just as she is swiping it through the till. But I know she's clocked it. Oh, to be a fly on the wall when I leave.

★

I decide to try to entertain the troops back home with a bit of old-fashioned variety. I know most mums, and even some cat owners, like to do silly dances and made-up songs for their little ones, but there's something about having three babies and a toddler that just feels more like a proper audience, with a real expectation about them. I'm outnumbered, so I have to go back to working the room. I sit the babies in their bouncers and set about putting on a show. For the first few songs they just stare and dribble, like OAPs at a regional rep matinee, but then I hit the musicals and discover that Frank likes show tunes. I sing him the entire back catalogue of Judy Garland and he gets very excited. He is so excited he vomits, which means one of two things – he's either gay or he's still got reflux. Thady and Orla can take or leave Judy. They prefer eighties classics. Duran Duran, Culture Club, Kelly Marie. My show is just about to hit the finale – I'm planning a couple of numbers from *Cabaret* to keep Frank happy – when I get a whiff of something horrid. Someone has done a poo. I'm letting rip here but I'm pretty certain it's not me, so I set about sniffing out the offending bottom. It's that charming ritual mums go through when several babies are gathered together – 'Is that yours or mine?' they'll say when they get an ill wind, pointing and laughing when it turns out not to be theirs. It's always mine. With four in nappies, it's bound to be. This time, it turns out all three babies and Saoirse have thick, fudgy shit packed around their genitals. The poo is amazing. It has gone from the greeny-black meconium babies pass for a few days after birth, to black, to wholegrain mustard, to swamp green, then to khaki, then Dijon mustard, then caramel Angel Delight, finally settling at almost-set fudge. Our whole house smells of poo. We live in the poo house. Come to our house – it's the one that smells of poo. I smelt poo all morning and couldn't work out if it was a lingering nappy change or a freshly baked one. Finally, I located a dark brown semi-dry poo caked between the bedroom door and the door frame. I have no idea who it belongs to. I hope it's not mine. Things aren't that bad. I had to chisel it off. It's all glamour.

My days are marked out by who has done a poo and who is yet to drop one. It's one of my small pleasures – as well as costuming the babies. Each morning, Saoirse and I pick outfits. We like to theme them if possible, and because of the volume of clothes we have received, themes are normally highly poss-ible. I like to think of my triplets as a short-staffed Village People tribute act. Today, Thady is a metro-chic, urban squad-die. He's wearing lovely camouflage pants and a green T-shirt. Orla is a Glastonbury hippy chick with stripy woollen leggings in bright colours and a matching baggy top. Frank is the only gay in the village. He's wearing a leopard print, long-sleeved lycra-mix top and black jeans. He looks just like Matt Lucas in 'Little Britain', with his blond eyebrows and big round bald head. It's not half as much fun just having one to dress – that's not dressing them up, it's just boring old clothing them.

Friday 30 September

I am so fat. Today is the first day of my new diet. I am not losing any weight at all by my conventional method – not eating as much cake – because my hormones seem to be all over the place. I might even be going through the early menopause. One minute I'm fine, the next I'm sweating cobs and feeling weepy. I will be forty in December. I weigh – whisper it – fifteen stone. *Fifteen*. Only rugby players weigh fifteen stone, surely? I will be fat and forty and fifteen stone if I don't do something drastic now. Bridget Jones eat your heart out – I am well on the way to being literally twice the woman you ever were.

When I fell pregnant with the triplets, I had about a stone to lose after my first pregnancy. During the triplet pregnancy, I put on so much weight because I was ravenous all the time and couldn't even walk very far by the end. Since their birth, I have lost only a quarter of the weight I gained and I'm finding it increasingly hard to be moderate. I either eat constantly or not at all.

I have always held a very dim view of my body. I was a fat toddler – so fat, in fact, that my mum once took me to the doctor to see if I had a hormonal problem. He examined me, pronounced me simply 'bonny' and gave me a tube of Smarties. As a teenager I was plump, and since university my weight has fluctuated wildly from borderline obese to skinny minny. Part of me doesn't give a hoot. I am a card-carrying Socialist feminist who realizes that the personal is political, that the beauty industry is a racket designed to keep us down, and that I am much more than the sum total of my vital statistics. The other part of me thinks I am a disgusting lazy gluttinous slob. Most of the time I manage to ignore my weight. I am amazed when I read about those poor tiny women with body dysmorphia who look in the mirror and see a much larger person staring back at them. I have body dysmorphia too, but in the opposite direction. I look in the mirror and instead of seeing a blubbery premenopausal jowly librarian I see a foxy eight-stone 25-year-old rock chick. It's only the scales that pull me up short.

But today I am going to make a big change. I have started a food-replacement diet whereby you eat no real food at all, just milkshakes and soups from little packets reconstituted with water.

'That's on-the-moon food,' Anoushka said yesterday, while we tucked into a Last Supper of carrot cake. 'I'm so worried about you doing this – you had triplets only four months ago!'

'Just think of it as me going to the moon. It's only until Christmas,' I say, trying to ignore the inner voice telling me she's right and I'll never do it. I so want to be like all the other mums at the swings with their flat tummies and their tight jeans. Surely a bit of deprivation in the short term will be worth it in the long run? And how long can triplets be an excuse for everything going south?

Tuesday 4 October

Very depressed today. I try to analyse why.
1 It is Day 5 of my diet. At a weigh-in on Sunday I had apparently lost over eight pounds. I was totally amazed, but suspicious. Did the lady plant bricks on me at my initial weigh-in? This is the hardest diet I have ever had to do. I am so hungry I could eat my own head, and I have a constant headache. My motivational methods leave a little to be desired too. Tracy texts me to say well done, and points out that I'd lost the equivalent of four bags of sugar. Instead

of rejoicing, I found myself totting up what I had left to lose. Last time the health visitor came two weeks ago, the babies weighed 15–16lb each. My soul hit the floor when I realized that I still have to lose the combined weight of the triplets. But I am determined to do it. I recently bought some new underwear in an attempt to cheer myself up, but it hasn't worked. There is something just so depressing about a size 18 thong, and I'm of the reluctant opinion that if you have to buy jeans in any size bigger than a 16, then you really shouldn't be wearing jeans at all.

2 I have been reading stuff on the Internet again. It all started when I casually pulled down my much-thumbed copy of *What to Expect in the First Year*, a guide to the development and care of babies. Each chapter goes through baby's development, from newborn to first birthday, and includes a handy checklist of milestones baby should be reaching. I used to love ticking off the boxes when Saoirse was little. This time it makes for depressing reading, even when I look up the checklist that applies to the triplets' adjusted age (three and a half months):

> By the end of this month your baby . . . should be able to:
> • On stomach, lift head up 90 degrees [Nope.]
> • Laugh out loud [Nope.]
> • Follow an object in an arc about 15cm above the face for 180 degrees (from one side to the other) [Possibly. Haven't got the tape measure out yet.]

It gets even worse when I look up what they '. . . will probably be able to do':

> • Hold head steady when upright [They're meant to be upright?]

- On stomach, raise chest, supported by arms [They're meant to be on their stomachs?]
- Roll over [What?]
- Grasp a rattle held to backs or tips of fingers [Note to self – must buy rattles.]
- Pay attention to a raisin or other very small object [Ditto raisins.]
- Reach for an object [Must remember to offer objects.]
- Squeal in delight [Just randomly? Or are we meant to be entertaining them with anecdotes?]

I give up with the next section, 'may even be able to'. As far as my triplets are concerned, it may as well say 'play a mean game of table football and be able to recite the complete works of Shakespeare'. I feel stricken with guilt. Have we been neglecting them? Is this normal developmental delay associated with prematurity?

I look up 'triplet development' on the Web and it throws up some disturbing studies.

The Society for Research in Child Development conducted a survey of 23 singleton babies, 23 sets of twins and 23 sets of triplets over the first year of their lives, matching the groups for social and medical conditions. Using a series of researched tests at 3, 6 and 12 months, the mother–infant relationship was monitored in order to compare development between singleton, twin and triplet families. Particular attention was paid to the mother's ability to read signals appropriately, and to offer the appropriate stimulation. The study had its own expectations:

> We expected that the high stress involved in raising triplets would interfere with the mother's ability to attend to the non-verbal signals of each child, to synchronize with the infant's

communications (for instance, stimulating a child when he/ she looks at the parent with attention and interest or refraining from stimulation when the child averts his/her gaze or shows signs of fatigue), and to pay close attention to the infant's newly acquired skills.

Because the development of infant cognitive competencies is built upon the mother's sensitive approach and timely introduction of new learning material, we expected, then, that triplets would exhibit poorer cognitive outcomes at one year.

Bloody hell. Have I got a 'sensitive approach'? Have I been up to speed with my 'timely introduction of new learning material'? Are we so focused on coping with the day-to-day demands of triplets and a toddler that we have forgotten to stimulate the poor sods? Are they already destined for the scrap heap, unable to socialize, low in self-esteem, slow and withdrawn now and forever? It gets worse. The study concludes that:

At one year, triplets showed poorer cognitive outcomes, both in terms of their cognitive development and their ability to use symbols during free play, such as playing 'mom' by feeding a doll and putting it to sleep.

I am stunned. It has been so easy just to lump all three babies together and unconsciously think that because they have each other it's OK to leave them for large chunks of time. I know that these studies make dangerous reading – it's all too easy to fall into a guilt trap or a competitive parenting milestone trap – but nevertheless. I read random chunks of the study to Rich.

'Load of old rubbish,' he says.

'What do you mean?' I say, keen to hear his opinion but wanting him on side.

'They'll do stuff when they're ready.'

'Not without help, they won't!'

'Look, they're not going to be rolling around on the floor like slugs unable to sit up or walk when they're five years old, are they?' he laughs. I don't think he's taking this seriously.

'They might be, if we don't start playing with them more,' I say, feeling irritated by his nonchalance in the face of such damning evidence of our neglect.

I go back online to find out whether triplets can play catch-up later on in childhood, and find another survey. This time, the 33 sets of triplets under scrutiny are seven years old and are compared to 33 control singletons in terms of their development and behaviour. The study uses the McCartney Scales of Children's Abilities (MSCA) and Achenbach's Child Behaviour Checklist (CBCL), and reassuringly it concludes that there is no significant difference in abilities between the triplet children and the singletons. In fact, in terms of behaviour, triplets are reported to have fewer problems than the controls – hurrah! However, it does note that among half the triplet sets one child has more behavioural problems than the other two. So which one of my three poor rejected simpletons is going to get the first ASBO? I suppose there are some positives about being triplets – at least they won't be lonely in Borstal.

Are we powerless here? Is it a necessary consequence of multiple birth? We are already at full stretch trying to feed, clean and comfort three babies at once. How can we do any more? It's a good week if they get more than one bath, never mind flashcards. Add a lively toddler to the mix and it becomes even more difficult to do anything apart from tread triplet water. I read another Web page and discover that the Australian Multiple Birth Association asked 74 mothers of six-month-old triplets to calculate how many hours it took to look after the babies and do the housework each week. The mothers calculated that it took 197.5 hours – and there are only 168 hours in a week. How am I supposed to be supermum when there really aren't enough hours in the day for the basics? And I thought we were doing well . . .

So I am officially worried and officially fed up. I am trying not to let what I laughingly refer to as my 'career' go down the pan at the expense of my children's development. To add insult to injury, Rich has very narrowly missed out on a trip to Turkey this week to film an advert, and is moping around the house feeling sorry for himself. It's not only the babies who are neglected. I don't even have the time to talk to him about it, and he's too bored with being at home to want to dangle toys in front of the babies. Depressed, I switch on the news in order to count my blessings, only to hear a new report that states categorically that children do better if they are in the full-time care of their mother for the first few years of their lives. Great. OK, so I'll stay at home with four babies and teach them French and piano and poetry while we try to live on the paltry few quid Rich can make from erecting greenhouses while the house is repossessed from over our heads.

Bloody surveys.

I can't even have a bar of chocolate to cheer myself up.

Bloody diet.

Later . . .

This is no time for brooding. This is time for action. I gather all the babies up and take them off to the Catholic Club playgroup. It's as noisy as last week, but Saoirse finds a toy buggy to push around and is happy enough, so I actually do something I have never dared to do at one of these things – I unload the triplets and put them out on the play mats. I dangle toys in front of them as they lie there looking startled. There's a spinning top with multicoloured balls inside that they seem to like, and a rattle with a giraffe on it. They coo and gurgle and smile. Their eyes are everywhere. It's as if they are seeing the world for the very first time. Saoirse comes up now and again to ask for a bit of help with a bike, or to take her coat off, and she looks bemused by my antics, as if to say: 'What's Mama doing with the babies? They normally get parked in the corner.'

Encouraged by the babies' reactions, I turn them over onto their stomachs. Orla immediately pushes herself up with her wiry arms and looks around – yes! Thady follows, only not quite so high, and Frank has a go but the weight of his lovely big fat head seems to drag him back down to the ground. Never mind, he is practising. I place them face down over a mirror set into one of the baby rugs. Their heads bob up and down trying to work out who the looker in the mirror is. They seem very pleased by it all. I turn them back over and Orla does a 180 degree rollover – bloody hell! I am amazed, but I feel even more guilty now. I don't know whether to feel pleased that they can actually do a lot of the things I was worried about or sad that we weren't trying so didn't know. This is how kids in all those Romanian orphanages fall behind in their development. There are simply not enough people to hold them, talk to them or stimulate them. Rich and I must make more of an effort, find the time and play with them more. They need it. I remember one of my friends telling me how she was always fed, fed, fed as a child, when all she really craved was some affection.

How do other mums of multiples cope with this? Rich and I are at home a lot, and we try to make sure the babies get out every day, if only for a walk in the buggy, but it's hard sometimes even though there are two of us. How do sole carers cope? There really should be some help with this.

The babies start to look tired, avoiding my gaze (I am trying to read their cues better!), so I sit back and take a breather. I glance around the room at the children playing. Only one or two mums are engaged in play with their children. Obviously, this is a breather for them, since they probably play all the time with just one or two children at home. They welcome the break. But not me. For me, this is Baby Boot Camp. I look behind me and all the other mums are sitting with cups of tea and biscuits, having a nice chat. They have nice hair, nice clothes and clean shoes. I am scruffy, my maternity jeans frayed and wet at the hem, my hair dirty and pulled back in an unflattering ponytail, and while I have been bending over my elastic waistband has been dragged down, revealing some greying waist-high pants. Some of the mums have been watching my work with the babies.

'Poor you!' one lady calls over to me.

'Why poor me? I'm very happy actually,' I say. Even though

it's a bit of a fib at this precise moment, I am glad of my babies. Even though they are hard work and they stop me from chatting and eating biscuits. Even though by having them all at once they have made me an outcast in situations like this. I just don't fit in. The other mums look nervous of me, as if they are scared of talking to me in case they want to moan but feel they can't. Some of them look as though they think they might catch fertility from me. One or two offer help, and I immediately soften. I think I must look a bit forbidding.

Either that or I smell.

Rich and I are still not sleeping in the same bed. I have grown quite fond of the bunk beds. I lie in bed at night in the tiny box room, thinking about things, and I feel about eight years old. It's a welcome break from the responsibilities of childrearing. Tonight, I offer to sleep in with him. He is depressed and a little bored. We cuddle up and fall asleep, but an hour later Saoirse wakes crying and he gets up to comfort her. I slip into the box room and fall into a coma. I'll worry about our relationship tomorrow.

Wednesday 5 October

Rich is tired and looks depressed.

'What's the matter?' I repeat over and over, only to be given that most infuriating of male responses: 'Nothing.' Eventually, after some expert wriggling on the end of my even more expert line, he cracks and says that he feels fed up with looking after the babies, he doesn't like it that I sleep in the other room and he hates it when I come back home and interrupt his way of doing things.

'Sometimes I think it would be easier to do all this on my own,' he says. I am shocked. I had no idea he had been remotely bothered that we've not been in the same bed. I suddenly feel like one of those frumpy older women who won't sleep with their husbands any more because their intimacy has long since flown the nest. From assuming we were doing very well as a unit I am now having nightmare visions of him just upping and leaving. I panic.

'Don't look like that, like I've just told you I've got terminal cancer!' says Rich.

I try to steady myself. I don't want him to clam up again because he is too scared of hurting me. I need to know the truth here.

After talking for a while we decide that one of the problems is the fact that we both have very strong ideas of how things should be done, and if those methods are not adhered to we both have a tendency to shut off and withdraw altogether. Having four babies to look after is like being captain of a ship in which certain things must get done at certain times or we all sink. This ship has two captains who sometimes want to veer off in different directions – and I think we have just hit a small iceberg.

I'm starting to feel the strain of keeping everything together. I berate myself for not being thinner, sexier, more interested in him. I chastise myself for not paying enough attention to the babies, to Saoirse, to Rich. When we got together, I was a gobby, confident urban fox (or so I thought). Now I am a bloated, insecure domestic cat. Is it any wonder he feels a sense of deflation? How is it possible to be everything to all parties?

'Hang on a bloody minute,' I think, coming to my senses. 'I'm starting to sound like one of those awful bleating chick-lit women bemoaning their inability to 'have it all'. Actually, I'm doing bloody well, earning our living, looking after the kids and keeping the household going. I'm sorry Rich feels down, but he'll just have to get over it and learn to work as a team more. And if he feels a bit neglected now and then, well, so do I! It's inevitable. I am not going to fall into the trap of judging myself as if this was a normal situation. Some things will have to slide for a bit. This whole experience has been hard on both of us, and while I wouldn't mind a bit of sympathy and a wallow in my own sense of lost self, there is no time. Plus it's very boring. Let's just get on with it, make the most of every day and be nice to each other.'

And plan a dirty weekend after Christmas.

Besides, there really is something to say for counting your blessings. A couple of stories I read today put a few things in perspective. A homeless woman gave birth to triplets on the stairs at Berkeley subway station in the US on Monday. People were pushing her out of the way. She was eventually rushed to hospital and had to have a C-section to deliver the other two. All the babies (girls) are doing well. And we think we've got it hard. It's a cliché, but I do feel humbled. I also read a post on the Web from a young woman in Ohio pregnant with triplets who is about to throw her boyfriend out because he has been stealing from her. What a classy guy. She is about to go on bed rest, on unpaid leave. She needs reassurance that she can do it alone.

What can I possibly say that doesn't sound like a platitude?

Back here in the UK, a fellow triplet mum on the Tamba website has posted to tell me how she was physically restrained yesterday by a woman demanding to have a look at her triplets. When she tried to pull away, the woman told her off for not wanting to share! I don't know what the opposite of synchronicity is but it's a shame the nosy woman wasn't on hand at Berkeley subway, or available to gawp at the Ohio woman's babies while she helps to feed and change them.

Thursday 6 October

The triplet's first official photo is back, and it's hilarious. All three babies propped up against a cheesy blue-sky background, their eyes agog with the bright lights. I show it to all the mums, and several brim up. Frank and Thady look so alike, flanking Orla like a couple of fat-faced bouncers. We sit and laugh at it for ages, imagining what the school photos will be like. What will it be like for Orla to be one of three but different? Will she feel less special? Or more? We can only hope that she is close to Saoirse. The babies are starting to notice each other more, but the boys seem especially aware of the fact that they are identical. When we place them face-to-face, they smile, delighted at the reflection. Are they half of the same person? Or will they be totally different, two distinct beings who just happened at one point to be one egg? Today, in the park, I meet an elderly woman who at first asks all the ordinary questions before telling me that she is a twin herself, but that since their mother's death they have hardly spoken. 'And we were so close growing up. Even after we got married. I mean, it was the reason my marriage broke up – we were always on the phone to each other.' She looks sad talking about it, but seems to accept that her twin just appears to need distance now. 'I think my mum kept us close. When she went, it just sort of . . . stopped,' she says, shrugging sadly.

I hope our children are close, but maybe the woman is right. Maybe kids just maintain sibling relationships to please the parents. Maybe there is no reason why we should feel any bond with our brothers and sisters. Yes, we have an upbringing in common (for the most part) but we all become individuals with different lives, and different experiences of that upbringing. Singleton babies come into the world alone; therefore, existentially, there is no good reason why they should be any closer to siblings than to any other children.

But what if your children arrive en masse? From the very moment of conception Frank and Thady have been a pair, and soon after that Orla was in very close proximity for almost eight months. That's got to count for something, hasn't it? Can you share a womb with someone and end up completely alienated from them? Perhaps it's that very closeness that starts to irk with age. Personally, as an overlooked third child in a busy household who learned to show off and be different to get attention, I can't think of anything more irritating and off-putting than having an identical twin. Imagine how completely weird it must be to look at someone who is exactly like you but not you. How infuriating.

A recent newspaper feature about grown-up identicals disproves this, however. It catalogues six pairs of identical twins, all of whom have nothing but positive things to say about the experience. There is the usual stuff about a special bond, finishing each other's sentences, telepathy, but moreover there is a genuine sense of mutual respect. Seeing someone who is your mirror image go through the trials of life right in front of you and alongside you must be very tough at times, but also a great privilege. There can be no better way to learn than to watch another version of yourself encountering life's obstacles. I've read that it becomes very hard to discipline triplets when they hit the toddler stage because they naturally want to comfort each other. If one is crying, the other two will want to console and protect him.

'Perhaps they'll all gang up on *us*, like in *The Midwich Cuckoos*, and when we try to tell them off, they'll just turn and stare at us until we become compelled to beat each other up,' I privately muse. I always loved that story of the blond alien children born into a quiet rural village; they end up almost destroying everything with their telekinetic powers. The idea of children upsetting the balance of power so utterly is a compelling one. What would Supernanny do – put them on the naughty stair? They'd blow it up.

Identical twins are just, well, a bit *spooky*. Who can think of *The Shining* without remembering the scary twin girls, two ghostly figures who stand side by side staring straight ahead?

The Tamba media requests forum recently advertised for

twin boys for a remake of *The Omen*. Although only one boy would be filmed at a time, the idea of two miniature Damiens on set somehow seems even more scary. Children can be very powerful when in packs. Add a pair of identical boys to the mix and the triplets become quite a frightening prospect. When I think about the triplets going through puberty it makes me shiver.

Let's just hope they're not blond.

Sunday 9 October

Today is the second birthday reunion of my NCT group. Saoirse was two years old on Friday, and all the other babies – Felix, Catherine, Lola, Harry, Liam, Dylan, Arthur and the identical twins Jonty and Milo – will be there. Our group was largely made up of geriatric mothers like myself who'd left it rather late in the day to have children. Only two other women have had another baby since. I'm slightly dreading turning up with our three new babies. These people were with us all the way through the latter stages of pregnancy and throughout the first year of Saoirse's life. Many of them report only just getting back on their feet now that the children are two. Feeling tired, unsure about the future and stretched in all directions, I'm not sure I can pull off the PR job required to be a triplet mum today. It's too much like hard work. But what is the alternative? I never know. When people ask me, as they do with fist-gnawing regularity, how on earth I cope, I always say, 'Very well, actually', even if it's the worst day ever, all three babies are screaming in the buggy, Saoirse has covered herself in dog poo and I just want to sit on the pavement and cry. It's partly a matter of pride and partly because I know the enquiry is only rhetorical. No one really wants to know. I'm often tempted to give them an answer they can't deal with, just to highlight the pointlessness of their asking.

'Actually, this is a living hell. I am on the verge of topping myself. One day just bleeds into the next and I can't see any light at the end of the tunnel. Please help me.'

Perhaps I should print this up and laminate it to the side of the buggy. I bet I'd get round the park unhindered.

Tuesday 11 October

The babies have started to change very rapidly. Thady is now almost as fat as Fat Frank, which makes telling them apart even more difficult. Frank is slightly balder at the back than Thady, but otherwise they are a mirror image of each other. They have started to grab at things, and they seem to be able to hold their heads up and control them without headbutting me all of a sudden. It's as if they heard my worries about their develop-ment last week and have decided to pull their fingers out. Maybe this is going to be easier than I thought.

Wednesday 12 October

Hereinafter to be known as Black Wednesday

The day starts well with Rich leaving at 6 a.m. to work on a greenhouse. At 7 a.m. I get up and feed all three babies at once using a version of the pillow propping system, but this time rolling the duvet on our bed up and balancing the bottles on top while the babies lie on the pillows underneath. I'm just congratulating myself on the fact that all three have finished when, as I wind Orla, she opens her mouth and lets forth a cascade of white vomit. It covers me, her and the rug beneath us. Gingerly, I put her on the change station and hose us all down. Richard's mum Celia is here, so I get Saoirse up and leave her downstairs with her 'Ma' while I run a bath to rid myself of the smell. All three babies fall asleep on the bed and I relax for ten minutes in the bath. There is no noise from the babies, so I even get to read two chapters of a book.

Refreshed, I go back into the bedroom to find that all three babies are indeed blissfully asleep – but Frank is covered from head to foot in vomit. He looks like a fat bald lager lout lying unconscious in some Magaluz gutter. Oh dear. It looks like we have a problem. I remember the first time Saoirse was violently sick. I was shocked at both the volume and the ferocity of the projectile puke that issued forth from her tiny body with no warning at all. Terrified she was mortally ill, and inexperienced in the way of babies and tummy bugs, I rushed her to hospital only to have her grin and gurgle at the doctor when we got there. So I know this is probably not serious, but this time it's not just one baby, it's two. And if two have got it, then there's a pretty good chance all three will have it by the end of the day. This isn't a little tummy bug – with triplets, this is an epidemic. I wonder if it would qualify as a national disaster: I imagine us set adrift on a sea of vomit, our raft hastily made from formula milk tins, sodden nappies for sandbags.

Bugger. And today I have to go and have my contact lens

check or they won't give me any more lenses. I've got three pairs of glasses but can't find any of them. All that remains is an arm of one broken pair. Like my house keys, half my make-up and several single socks, they have gone to that great toddler hidey hole in the sky. I have to go to the appointment. I am blind without them and I'm down to my last set of daily lenses. I'll have to leave Celia here with three puking babies. Bugger, bugger, bugger.

Off I set on my scooter and the heavens open. I get to my appointment soaking wet, and halfway through the session the optician says: 'Ah – bit of a problem. I can't fit you with your lenses today because you have to go to Moorfields eye hospital right away.'

'Why?' I panic. 'What's wrong?'

'You have something embedded in your cornea. You need to get it removed right away.'

'What is it?' This is all I need. Four hours queuing in A & E with three sick babies at home.

'I don't know, but it's quite well bedded in. It looks like a piece of glitter – do you put glitter on your eyes?' he asks, shining a bright light right at me.

'Well, I used to do a bit of cabaret singing,' I say, thinking that it might be a piece of my glamorous past come back to poke me in the eye.

'You'll have to get the tube in to Moorfields,' he says, eyeing my scooter helmet.

'Can't you just give me a set of lenses to wear until I get there?'

'No – you can't put anything in. You can't drive.'

'Look, I've got three babies at home who are probably

spewing their guts up as we speak. I'm going to have to be as quick as possible here, so I am going to go on my bike – blind, if I have to.'

I don't take kindly to imposed limitations. I am a bit stupid like that.

Reluctantly, he gives me the lenses, but makes me promise I'll only put one in the unaffected eye. He also tells me off for leaving them in too long every day. I explain that I'm up at 6.30 a.m. and hardly ever in bed before midnight, what with all the babies and the washing and the tidying and my work to do. I need to be able to see for more than twelve hours a day.

'Your eyes are being starved of oxygen. When you've been seen at the hospital, you'll have to come back here and we'll talk about what you can do then.'

I'm tempted to ignore him and just go home to my babies. If the glitter has been in there since my cabaret days, then one more day won't hurt. But he is insistent, and the idea of being a *blind* mum of triplets is not very appealing, so I set off in the pouring rain to Moorfields, obviously having put both lenses in for fear of crashing.

At the triage desk, I am told that the waiting time is approximately three hours. I am soaking wet and worried about the chaos at home. I call Lou, who is on her way round to help Celia with the babies. She is stuck in a tunnel and has been there for forty-five minutes. She is going out of her mind with frustration. Celia says the babies have been sick three times so far, and the washing machine is full of bed linen, baby clothes and her entire wardrobe. I play the triplet card. I walk up to the triage desk again. 'Look, I need to get home as quickly as possible. I have sick triplets!' I say dramatically.

The nurse raises one eyebrow and casts a glance at the assembled motley crew of patients-in-waiting. There are eye-patches and bandages and bloody cloths all over the shop. The waiting room of an eye hospital accident department is like a comedy sketch waiting to happen. Clearly my sick triplets do not cut the mustard here.

'We'll do our best,' she says.

I settle down to steam gently in my wet clothes. Miraculously, just ten minutes later, I am sitting in front of a lovely Nigerian nurse who numbs my eye and extracts the blob from it. I race back outside, one good eye left, and jump back onto my scooter. The ride home is treacherous. Cars skid past me in the pouring rain, spraying me all over. I have one eye closed and the other is streaming. If I get home in one piece, it will be a minor miracle. I know I should pull over, leave the bike and try to find a cab, but my instinct is to get home and make sure the babies are OK. I can't defy it.

Eventually, I get home dripping wet and exhausted. All three babies are asleep and Celia looks ragged.

'How are they?' I ask.

'Frank's been sick three times and he's been asleep all day,' she says.

I check his temperature. The papers are full of stories of dead babies whose mums thought they were 'on the mend' because they were sleeping so much, only to see them slip into a coma and die. His temperature is OK, but he feels hot. I give him water and watch him like a hawk, jiggling Orla on the other knee. Thady, so far, has not succumbed.

Then it's time for my coil fitting. Is it fair that a girl should have this much fun in a day?

I ask the doctor to be gentle, and she promises not to hurt me. She is a fibber. It bloody kills. I feel like I am in labour.

'Well, it's all done now, and it's 99.9 per cent effective, so you won't have to have it changed until 2010,' she smiles.

'I'll be forty-five then. Hopefully, I won't need one any more!' I say.

I hurry back across the green in the rain. I must get back to put the babies to bed. A nagging awareness nips at my heels all the way up the road. What is it?

Then it strikes me. Unless I go and have this coil removed, I won't be getting pregnant again. Ever.

And the maddest thing about the whole day is that this thought makes me want to cry.

Thursday 13 October

We take advantage of Celia being here to go out on a date together. Except we've run out of milk formula and the nappy situation is about to become critical, so instead of a cosy bistro we head for the supermarket.

'Hello, darling,' I say, grabbing Rich's hand as we walk through the car park.

'Hello,' smiles Rich shyly. I can't remember the last time we were on our own together.

We have fun looking at electrical goods and laughing at the men's fashions. Rich buys some pomegranates and we experiment with the new self-service tills. It never occurs to me what a couple of saddos we must look, gleefully lapping up a simple retail experience. It's like being let out of prison.

As we pull into our street, home again after just an hour, I feel happy.

'That was nice,' I say.

'See you again same time next week,' says Rich.

'Don't you want to see me for a week?' I say, mock-hurt.

Rich smiles, joining in the game.

'Erm,' he says, pretending to think of an excuse.

'What's the matter – am I too needy? Is it too much too soon?' I whimper, playing the desperate singleton.

'Let's just see how it goes, shall we?' he says as he pats my hand.

I sometimes bemoan the fact that we never had a proper courtship – just wham, bam, straight into parenthood – but in moments like this I'm glad we cut all that crap. Sometimes you just know it's going to work out, so why not get straight down to breeding?

Friday 14 October

I order the triplets' christening cake. We are already up to our eyeballs in Rich's cakes, but we need a special centrepiece, with three babies on it! I remember seeing a shop in Dalston advertising cakes for special occasions so I nip off on my scooter and go in. The woman behind the counter is bored and stares dully at me as I flick through the catalogue of cakes available as special orders.

'I need a cake for a christening,' I say.

'OK,' she says, turning to a page with some lovely cakes displayed on it.

'It's for triplets,' I say, hoping to cheer her up. It works. Her face lights up and she smiles at me.

'How wonderful,' she says. 'You are very lucky.'

'I know,' I say.

'I had three children, but I lost one,' she says sadly.

'Oh, I'm sorry,' I say. 'It must have been awful. I can't imagine what it must be like for you.'

'He was twenty-one. He died last year. Muscular dystrophy. He was fine one week, the next – dead.'

And we stand there, two mums, and have a little cry together.

Monday 17 October

I spent the whole weekend on my own with the babies. It's been horrible. Whether it's my wildly fluctuating hormones or this bloody starvation diet, I don't know, but I have had the worst time. The babies took it in turns to scream inconsolably from 7 a.m. until 7 p.m., taking it in four hour shifts between them. Saoirse has a terrible cold and is grumpy. At one point, I had Orla screaming in one ear and Saoirse begging me to put the baby down and carry her instead. I stood on the landing and just joined in with the screaming, half thinking it would stop them in their tracks. It didn't. They just screamed louder.

The only respite came when Mum and Dad visited with Gerry and Alan, my mum's sister and her husband, who are over from Australia. As soon as they walked in, the babies decided to coo and giggle. They loved the attention. We went for a walk and Gerry and Mum really enjoyed all the gawping, answering all the questions for me and revelling in the oohs and aahs. I could tell Mum thought I was being a bit short with people. It is in her Irish DNA to be polite and friendly to everyone, no matter how tiresome or idiotic they are. She would describe my attitude today – monosyllabic, sullen, dismissive – as 'very English'. But I can't help it. I am so over being the local talking point. It's got to the stage where I actually avoid going out with the babies because I can't be bothered talking to people, but I don't like the inevitable confrontation if I try to swerve past when they stop dead in front of me.

Perhaps this is going to be as hellish as everyone has been telling me all these months. I'm feeling very low. So low that I even broke my diet last night and swigged vodka from the bottle when I'd put the kids to bed. I can easily understand why parents become alcoholics. Your nerves are so jangled by the end of the day you need something just to take off all the rough edges. I find myself clock-watching near baby bedtime, waiting for the magical moment when I can uncork a bottle of red and unwind, although I sometimes give in early and concur with Audrey Hepburn's quip that it must be six o'clock somewhere in the world. No doubt I should be doing yoga or practising meditation or taking a long hot bath in order to relax, but there are three piles of damp washing to be dried and ironed – this week's sickfest has taken its toll on the washing machine – and bottles to be sterilized and made up. Alcohol is so much quicker. I can't even be bothered to tidy all the toys away. I keep catching sight of Saoirse's dolly lying in the corner and it makes me jump. 'Shit, I've forgotten to put Orla to bed,' I think, every time I look at it.

By the time Rich gets home I am ready to scream.

'Please, can I just go out for a little while?' I plead.

'Yes, love,' he says, seeing the desperation in my face. 'Where are you going?'

'I don't know,' I say. 'I'd like to go and sit in the pub and get absolutely plastered, but I can't because of this diet. I might just go for a walk.'

So I wander out. It's a foggy night, even though the day looked lovely. A beautiful, Indian summer Sunday, glimpsed from the window as I juggled and jiggled three screaming babies and a snotty toddler. The last good day of the year.

So I wander up to the High Street, looking in shop windows and passing restaurants already filling up with people. A couple in their thirties stroll towards me and I scrutinize them. They obviously don't have children. They are strolling. Parents on a rare night out would be hurrying to wherever they were going, keen to pack as much enjoyment into their night as possible. I have a look at the menu outside a new restaurant, fantasizing about having a meal out with Rich.

We really must get some babysitters on board. I just don't know where to begin, and unless I make some time to locate someone good, who is used to babies and cool enough to take on four at once, it just isn't going to happen. Nothing happens in our house unless I do it. I have started negotiations with the builder next door about converting our loft, as the first guy we approached has disappeared. The planning permission has been granted and Gary next door is now available, but it seems impossible to orchestrate taking the job on to completion. We need a structural engineer to provide detailed calculations, we need someone to coordinate the visits from the council's building regulations department and we need to source and buy the new bathroom, the windows, the floor. I can't even get it together to remember that the babies need their third vaccination. Rich probably doesn't even know they need one, let alone that they are already three weeks late for it. I feel overwhelmed with responsibility, and when I try to offload tasks onto Rich he just sort of shrugs and gets on with making cakes. This morning, in an 'if you can't beat them, join them' kind of a way, instead of tackling the huge pile of paperwork I have to get through, I decided to make gingerbread men with Saoirse. I've never done it before, but I thought it would be fun, and might help me relax a bit. I burnt them. Saoirse took one bite and flung hers on the floor. So I threw them all in the bin and left the house in a huff. I hate feeling like this. I'm not normally keen on moaning, but at times I think I am allowed to. Today, the months and the years just seem to be stretching out ahead of me, day after day of self-sacrifice and 'God, isn't it bedtime yet?' I want to run away, but mums aren't really allowed to do that.

I want my old life back.

Wednesday 19 October

I receive a call from a woman called Niki, a friend of a friend, who has just found out she is expecting triplets. Like mine, the pregnancy was completely spontaneous, but because of previous problems she has been scanned early and is only just seven weeks pregnant with what looks like an identical pair and a fraternal. I try to place myself back in those early weeks to remember what exactly I was so worried about. How quickly we forget those things that ate us up just months ago. In some ways, I'm glad we didn't find out until relatively late that there were 'three in there' – the first twelve weeks can be so touch-and-go I would have been on pins the entire time. Niki is very worried and I try to set her mind at some level of rest.

'I'm just worried that they won't all be able to fit in me,' she says.

'How tall are you?' I say, imagining a tiny little thing.

'Five foot eleven – does that make a difference?'

'Oh, you'll be fine!' I say. 'I'm five foot eight and I carried to almost thirty-five weeks.'

'Is it really as simple as that?' she says.

I want to say yes, but I know there are lots of other factors – health, age, diet, the condition of the fetuses, TTTS, etc. 'Well, it certainly helps,' I say.

'But I've just been for a private scan, just to check every-thing's OK, and they told me that the identical pair don't have a separating membrane between them.'

My brain tries to pull any memory of membrane talk to the front. I can't think straight because I am soaking up her distress, but from what I recall I think this is not great news.

'What did they say were the implications of that?' I ask, hedging my bets. It's sometimes not a lot of fun being a lay expert.

'Well, isn't that, like, the worst thing? It can lead to the cords getting entangled.'

'Right. I'm not sure, but I thought it was more the issue of whether or not they share a placenta – the nutrients, the blood and oxygen supply—'

'I don't know. I asked them, but they were so vague I just had to get out of there.'

'You need to speak to an expert really soon. That clinic might not know what they're doing. The thing is, a lot of medical professionals might never encounter triplets in an entire lifetime. It's us who become the experts because we get to see top consultants and we get to share with other mums who know what they are talking about. We form a little advisory body. Join Tamba, post a message asking for advice and you'll get loads of help.'

I am rattled by this conversation. It strikes me again just how ill-prepared a lot of doctors are for a triplet diagnosis. I feel cross on her behalf that they told her something in such a worrying way without being able to refer her directly to someone who could either confirm the diagnosis or not and give her the odds on maintaining the pregnancy.

I jump onto the Internet to refresh my memory about separating membranes and identical twins. What she is describing is called a monozygotic monoamniotic pair – the rarest and most precarious of twin pregnancies. A monozygotic pair is when the egg splits to form identical twins, and a monoamniotic pair is when that split occurs late, usually around the ninth day after conception, thus providing only one sac. Monoamniotic twins occur in only 1 in 1000 twin pregnancies and the outcome is often not good. It's quite scary stuff. There is a support group whose home page I click on with a heavy heart, only to discover some potentially good news. Apparently, 40 per cent of twins initially diagnosed as monoamniotic are actually misdiagnoses. The membrane can be so thin that it is hard to see, especially if the diagnosis is made early on in the pregnancy. Of the remaining, 60 per cent go on to be delivered as healthy babies. The perinatal mortality rate is high, but it is not impossible, with proper monitoring, to sustain and deliver two monoamniotic babies.

I call Niki but her mobile is switched off. I leave a long and garbled message on her voicemail, hoping that she finds the news helpful.

Three hours later and I have not heard back. I am so over-involved now – I cannot hear of a triplet pregnancy without wanting to know all about it and help out where I can. It's part of the legacy – and the curse – of being part of this special group. I think she felt relieved to be talking to someone who didn't ask, 'Oh my God, how did you feel when you found out?'

I think I know how she felt. Been there, done that, had triplets. Not many people can say that. I'll just have to keep it all crossed. The best that she can hope for is that the private clinic was wrong, and gave her a few days of unnecessary torment. The worst? We won't think about that now.

Friday 21 October

I visit the Baby Show at Olympia. It's a three-day expo of all things baby-related. The tube is crammed full of nervous-looking pregnant women and new mums with conspicuous consumption pushchairs. Inside the hall it is a complete racket

– in every sense of the word. There are stalls offering everything from clothing to toys and learning aids. The pregnant women waddle about looking lost and confused, not knowing which of the things being aggressively pushed at them they are really going to need. Credit cards are flying about and the loos, unkindly, are on the second floor.

I'm reporting for the BBC on companies promoting products designed to 'raise your baby's IQ', of which there are many. Since the birth of the Baby Einstein movement, many companies have jumped on the bandwagon and created DVDs of random images accompanied by electronic classical music in order to evoke what they call the 'Mozart effect'. According to the dim but enthusiastic and somewhat sickeningly on-message PR girl I talk to, Baby Einstein was started by a mom (in America, of course) who made a video for her baby using toys as puppets in her garage. Since then, it has become a brand leader and is available in many different languages. I resist the urge to ask the girl why, if they are so effective, she hasn't watched a few herself and improved her own IQ. Instead, I trawl around the other stalls offering similar products. There's Baby Smart, Baby Bright, one is even quite brazenly called Baby IQ. This one at least has the London Symphony Orchestra playing in the background. It's even backed by the Literacy Trust campaign 'Talk to Your Baby'. An interview with their spokesperson reveals that they are backing these DVDs because they are meant to be interactive. It's not just a case of plonking your baby down in front of the electric babysitter then wandering off to file your nails. You are meant to sit with them and narrate the images, encouraging language development.

Apparently, children are starting school unable to hold basic conversations because parents are not talking to their children enough, and this in turn has an impact on literacy skills. The reasons for this quality downturn in classroom chatter are various. We are busier than our parents' generation. A lot of mums no longer stay at home. Many work, and employ non-native-speaking 'cheap' help who cannot offer their charges conversation. We also rely too much on the telly to entertain our kids because we care too much about other things that need doing, or because we are selfish and expect a life alongside childrearing. Someone even posits the theory that modern pushchairs, which are generally designed to face outwards and thus cut off face-to-face contact, are the culprits. Whichever way you cut it, we are not as good at raising our children as our mums were.

I try to cast my mind back to my own pre-school years. I vividly recall my mum making a fish-and-chip shop for my brother Adrian and me. She cut greaseproof paper up into fish shapes, and made newspaper chips. By balancing a step ladder on its side she made a shop counter. We were thrilled with it. It's an idyllic picture, but I think the reason I remember it so well is because it had never happened before. It probably never happened again. She was always bent double over a twin tub, lifting her own body weight in steaming terry-towelling nappies out with wooden tongs. With four children under school-age, she rarely got time to play. If we had had wall-to-wall children's TV in the sixties, I'm pretty sure she would have used it too.

I feel grumpy as I mooch about. There is so much pressure to be a better mum, to buy this, have that, make sure you're not neglecting this or that aspect of parenthood. I'm turning into one of those old bags who say, 'It wasn't like this in my day and I turned out all right!' I try to analyse the feeling and I think it's because having triplets magnifies the issue of how much attention and energy one puts into one's children. Mums and mums-to-be of singleton babies are trudging dutifully around the whole hall, their eyes flicking hungrily from one thing to the next. If they feel the pressure with just one baby, then how can I not, when stimulation has proved to be so important in triplet development? I am thrown back into my paranoia about the babies' development. I will take a few DVDs home and sit with them saying, 'Look at the clown! Funny clown! Fell over!', while Chopin tinkles benignly in the background. I'll even switch the language option to Italian – why not up the stakes a bit? If we're going to obsess about IQ from before they can even wipe their own bums, we might as well go for it and have trilingual triplets. If they can't recite Dante's *Inferno* in the original by the time they are at nursery, I'll ask for my money back. I will do this because everyone else is. And besides, I might get a chance to flick through *heat* magazine uninterrupted.

I interview an American academic, Professor Joseph Garcia, who has developed a sign-language system for babies. He is passionate about how really young, pre-language babies can learn basic signs that make communication much more sophisticated. Frustration is a key problem in pre-verbal children, and signing can improve life considerably. I tell him that I have triplets so will not have time to teach them.

'If you have triplets then it will be even more important for you. It will be a godsend.'

I get a copy of his book but know that I probably won't bother. I don't want them to discover how to sign things like

'I feel neglected'. I'd rather not know. Sometimes ignorance really is bliss.

Back home, Maddy (here with Alex for the christening) and I experiment with the DVDs. We put the babies in their boun-cers and sit them in front of the TV where glove puppets and train sets cavort to classical music for their viewing pleasure. They slump, dribble and generally look unimpressed. Then Alex comes in and puts a video of 'The Simpsons' on. The babies perk up quite a bit.

Philistines.

Sunday 23 October

The triplets' baptism day. We spend all morning trying to find the cakes Rich has spent a fortnight baking. He has squirrelled them away in various tins and Tupperware, and can't remember where he has put them. He is becoming very eccentric these days, wandering about in his pants calling out for Dundee cake like a geriatric in a care home. Maybe he's got 'baby brain', that well known new mum affliction, by proxy.

Alex and Maddy set about buttering bread for the sand-wiches. I love it when they're here. They grab a baby at the slightest whimper, and will spend ages just jiggling and cooing. This is the best kind of interaction. Forget DVDs.

People start arriving at the house as I'm upstairs dressing the babies with the girls. We bring them down all together in their robes – Thady in a beautiful handmade gown Celia made for Rich and his sister Fiona, Frank in my niece Grace's raw silk christening dress and Orla in Saoirse's taffeta number. At least we think that's the right way round. There's a hairy moment upstairs when we have to take a long look at Thady and Frank to make sure we've got it the right way round. Maddy swears she's got Frank but he's wearing Thady's gown. I check who has got the biggest bald patch (Frank's baby hair has rubbed away at the back) but they seem the same today. Oh well. We head out to the church and I take a moment to look back down the street. My mum and dad, Gerry and Alan, my sister Maggie, Tim and Jeanne, Ray, Tracy, Grace, Adrian, Silvie and James and assorted godparents – and three fat babies in drag being paraded up the road. It's a lovely sight.

The service goes really well. The babies don't cry even when the priest pours a huge shellfull of water over their heads. I'm surprised – not because they are particularly easily startled, just because they get bathed so rarely they really aren't used to water at all. At the end, the priest raises each baby up high for us to applaud. He asks us to pose with him for the parish newsletter – its very rare that he gets to baptize triplets.

Back at the house, everyone gets plastered and the babies have a great time being passed from one set of arms to the next. Silvie, Frank's godmother, tells me that she had the wrong baby at the crucial point. She thinks that either the boys were baptized with the wrong names or she just lost track of who she was holding. There was a lot of shuffling around the font, what with six godparents, three babies, two parents, Saoirse, Alex and Maddy. So as far as the Catholic Church is concerned, Orla might now be 'Thady' and Frank 'Orla'. That's what happens when you make boys wear dresses. We have champagne and high tea. The christening cake is magnificent – three little babies nestling under an icing blanket. Rich makes a brief speech when we cut the cake, thanking everyone for coming, and I decide I need to say a few words too. I want to mark the occasion. My speech ends up a bit like something out of a Richard Curtis movie.

'I just want to say that it's been a pretty interesting year, as you can imagine (*cue indulgent laughter*). Many of you know how frightened I was when we found out we were having triplets, and I just want to thank you for all your incredible support and kindness over the last ten months. You've been bloody brilliant, and there have been times when I really think I couldn't have done it without you. Thank you for turning a potentially terrifying thing into something really rather wonderful. Now I know what community and friendship really mean. Thanks for your time, your gifts, your help and your support.' At this point I start crying and can't speak any more.

I feel great.

Monday 24 October

I sit and write thank-you cards to all the people who brought gifts. We have a huge pile of money boxes, cute booties and commemorative bowl-and-cup sets in triplicate. While I'm writing, there's a documentary on called *Having a Baby Ruined My Life*. It features several families who say that having children has destroyed their quality of life so much they wish that they could turn back the clock and make a different decision. It's full of footage of women sighing and shouting and wrestling disobedient toddlers into bed. Lots of them say they can't wait for bedtime so that they can get some peace. One woman makes me laugh in recognition when she says sometimes she is too tired to get up and find the remote control so that she can switch Cbeebies off. There have been a few nights when *I've* sat, defeated, unwilling and unable to turn the telly over once the battle of bedtime is won. Another couple appal me by discussing how much they regret having their son, now five and fully cognizant of what they are saying, *in front of him*! And they wonder why he is sullen and uncooperative! I don't mean to be one of those 'holier than thou' mums but, really, it's not hard to make the link, is it? If the parents are so unhappy and insensitive as to say these things in his presence, then they have no right to expect a happy, life-enhancing child. You get what you pay for. It's true in commerce and it's true in parenthood.

The poor bastard, having to sit there and listen to his miserablist parents bemoan his very existence. He'll probably turn a gun on them when he's eighteen and everyone will say, 'He was always so quiet.'

As I watch, I get more and more cross. Another mum tried to conceive for years before falling pregnant with twins after IVF treatment. She sat whingeing about how hard it is, how she longs for her husband to get home from work so she can get out.

What is the matter with these drippy mums? I know it's hard – I'm not saying it isn't; believe me, I've had better days than the one I spent recently clothed in vomit while Saoirse screamed the house down (see my entry for 17 October) – but the bottom line is, no matter how bad your day is, *they are only babies*. The way some parents talk, you'd think they were being asked to diffuse the world's biggest atomic bomb on a daily basis. Why do they moan so much? What were they expecting? Are they so fed up because they are too perfectionist, and can't let go of their old high standards? Some mums seem to find it a real struggle to get out of the house because everything has to be just so. At a children's party recently, I got laughed at by another mum with just two kids because my change bag was a tenth of the size of hers. Some mums seem to pack for a two-week land safari just for a quick nip to the swings. What would really be so bad about going out without a change of clothes/a nappy/milk? We took all four to McDonald's today. We stuffed them in coats and pushed them there, with no change bag, no spare clothes, nothing. When they started crying, we got them out and they stank of poo. All three had let rip on the short journey there. But no one died. Saoirse got to run around in the play area, then we all went home. (We won't do it again though, but only because I remembered that I hate McDonald's.)

Am I too slack? Is that why we are coping so well? Am I so out of kilter with the rest of the mothers in the UK? I hate programmes like this. I start to feel like I must be doing something wrong not to be as grumpy and miserable as everyone else seems to be. Once again, I count my blessings that Rich is at home a lot. I think the other main difference between me and these mums is that I have an ally most of the time. I am not lonely. Or at least, I am not as lonely as some of them seem to be. Even though we are side by side, looking after triplets and a toddler breeds its own kind of busy loneliness. Too busy to chat. Too busy to sit down and look at each other. Too busy for intimacy of any kind.

I get so cross with the programme that I switch channels and catch an item on the news that shocks me to the core, not least because of its juxtaposition with what I've just seen. The Chinese government has started 'penalizing' women who have broken the one-child-per-family law. A reporter has infiltrated a small village where, six months ago, communist soldiers went in and attacked pregnant women they had been tipped off about. One woman, eight months into her second pregnancy, was taken to a clinic and injected in the stomach. 'When the baby was born he had thick, thick black hair. He was dead. They put him in a bucket of water to make sure he was dead. Then they threw the body in the bin.' The mother can barely talk about it. I bet she wouldn't moan that having two children has ruined her shag pile carpet.

Tuesday 25 October

I'm on a BBC Radio 4 programme, 'The Learning Curve', to discuss the Baby Show. The presenter, the wonderfully jolly hockey sticks Libby Purves, is fascinated by my triplets. She tells me of a friend who has grown-up triplets who, as children, were hardly ever invited anywhere en masse as it was just too much chaos for most people. Libby would get the whole family to stay over, even if it meant sleeping them all like sardines on the dining-room floor. 'Bath time was fun – it was just a question of grabbing a child, sticking it in the tub and then in its PJs. A child in pyjamas is money in the bank as far as I'm concerned.'

My kinda gal.

Wednesday 26 October

I get an email from Niki, the woman newly confirmed as pregnant with triplets. She was so worried about the fact that the private clinic told her she had a monoamniotic pair she went to see Professor Nikolaides, the acclaimed baby doctor. He scanned her and said he could see a dividing membrane 'clear as day'. She is hugely relieved. I almost cry with joy.

Thursday 27 October

I am packing. The girls are going back to Bolton, and Rich, Saoirse, Orla and I are going to visit Rich's sister Fiona in Barcelona. Thady and Frank are staying with Celia. The original plan was that we would all go, but I ran into a couple of problems. Firstly, we would have to take a third adult to accommodate the third baby. The rule is one baby per lap. Secondly, and more importantly, the airline does not accept premature babies until they are six months old because of the risk to their lungs that flying poses. Although Orla was born at the same time as the boys, she was not intubated so I feel much more comfortable taking her on a plane.

'We could just take them all,' says Rich. 'How would they know if a baby was prem or not?'

'I think turning up with three of the buggers would be a pretty big clue. And I don't want to be turned away at the departure gate. Plus the rule is probably there for a good reason. The boys' lungs might not be as strong as Orla's, so it's best not to risk it.'

So for four whole days and four nights we will be posing as a family of four and not six. We will have Saoirse and Orla only. We will pass as normal. No staring, no questions, no triple-buggy inaccessibility. We will be able to saunter up Las Ramblas anonymously, just like every other family. I can't wait.

Although if we ever get there it will be nothing short of a miracle. The girls have packed their own cases, but I am left packing one for the boys and one for me, Rich, Saoirse and Orla. There is stuff everywhere, and where is Rich? In front of the telly crying his eyes out over a 'fantastic' black-and-white movie on TCM called *Goodbye Mr Chips*, which seems to be about a silly old sod teaching in a public school. When I point this out, I am told I have no heart. I am frantically trying to remember nappies (enough for the boys, spares in the hand luggage), formula milk (in case we can't get the same brand in Spain), enough bottles, the sterilizer, clothes, sleep suits and grow bags, the travel cot, three buggies, favourite toys, dummies for emergency use only (about ten – they have a habit of evaporating the minute you need them), passports, keys, phone charger, etc. The house is a mess and we have arranged for the builders to start work on the loft while we are away.

This is bloody ridiculous. Why am I bothering? I just thought it would be nice to have a little holiday. We've not been anywhere for a year. But this is really not worth it. I am so stressed by the whole process of packing and splitting up the family that only a stay in a lunatic asylum would be a worthwhile destination.

Monday 31 October

Barcelona. We drag Orla and Saoirse out of bed at 4.30 a.m. in time for the 7 a.m. flight from Liverpool. We are pre-boarded as we have young children and I can see people looking on with pity as we wrestle two kids, two buggies and our hand luggage onto the plane. I want to say, 'This is only the half of it – we're travelling light today!'

'Thady? Frank?' Saoirse asks once or twice. She's confused, not used to so few babies around. When one of the stewardesses admires Orla, Saoirse says 'Thady, Frank' very solemnly, keen they should not be left out. The stewardess asks me what she means, but I play dumb. Too early in the morning for the triplet conversation. For now, we are just a family of four. But I feel guilty nonetheless, as if I am denying the boys' existence. It feels like lying by omission, not volunteering the information that, yes, Orla is very cute, and she has two cute little brothers from the same pod at home. It's a typically Catholic response – to cast myself as St Peter denying Christ three times before cockcrow rather than just enjoy a bit of singleton baby chat for once.

Barcelona is wet and overcast. Bloody cheek, after my five-day packing nervous breakdown. Fiona and David welcome us warmly. They love having visitors from back home bearing gifts of decent newspapers, magazines and Fry's Chocolate Creams. We decide to go for a walk around the fantastic market off Las Ramblas. Leaving Saoirse in bed for a nap, we put Orla in the baby sling facing outwards and she is in heaven. Her eyes pop out at the sight of the still-live twitching lobsters on ice.

She gobbles up the smells and noises of the pre-siesta rush. Strangers come up and coo in Catalan and she grins obligingly. They seem to love babies here even more than in Italy. It's a good job we don't have all three here or they'd declare a national holiday in celebration. The only negative looks we get all afternoon are directed at Orla's feet, which are bare. We hardly ever bother putting socks on any of the babies because they just kick them off, and babies' shoes are just ridiculous. The Spanish don't approve, clearly. People look at her face, smile, look down at her bare little toes, then back up at me to frown. All the Spanish babies we see are trussed up like Christmas turkeys in white frilly socks, matching accessories and coordinated outfits. We have neither the time nor the patience to hunt pairs of tiny socks down and keep them on thirty little toes.

When we get back, I feed Orla and put her to bed and there is hardly a murmur out of her. She wakes an hour or so later and is all smiles. She is like a different baby. No screaming for attention, no yelling to be picked up. I was afraid she might miss her brothers, but not a bit of it. She seems to be revelling in all the focus. I feel delighted for her, but also very sad that this is just a little holiday from being a triplet. I am missing the boys. Unexpectedly. I thought I'd be giddy with the comparative freedom. Whenever I think of their big fat currant-bun faces and the cheesy, hardly ever washed folds of their necks, it makes me want to weep.

Tonight we were all to go out for pre-dinner drinks but at the last minute I've opted to stay in and babysit Saoirse, Orla and Fiona and David's sixteen-month-old baby, Miranda. I've put them all to bed and I'm sitting alone. Maybe it's because

I'm very tired, or maybe it's the fact that I'm teetotal at the moment, but I just didn't want to go out. I feel like I've lost a bit of confidence. I can't remember how to go out for a drink. All I know how to do is look after loads of kids. Besides, I'm still in my maternity jeans and my new hairdo has reverted to its normal frizzy fright wig, so it's not as if there's anything to show off. Here I am in Barcelona, my favourite European city, free of two babies but sitting in alone nonetheless. Things have changed. My life bears no resemblance to how it used to be, so why try to claw my way back? Why deny that things are different now? I never thought that I would be one of those dreary women who say things like, 'My priorities have changed since having children and I just don't see the appeal in going out any more', but look at the evidence. I can't shake off the exhaustion of caring for three just because I've only got one here. I am a triplet mum. The old cliché is true – wherever you go in the world, you take yourself with you. If not your triplets.

Wednesday 2 November

Fiona and David have insisted that Rich and I go out for the evening while they babysit. We get dressed up – both of us get to shower and wash our hair! – and head out into the avenues and alleyways of Barcelona, weaving in and out of seedy back streets and noisy thoroughfares.

We head for a favourite haunt – Vildsvin, a champagne and oyster bar. Rich orders half a dozen oysters and champagne while I sip a mineral water. Bloody diet. If I'd known how much weight I was whacking on every time I sent him out for a party pack of Belgian buns and a paving slab of Galaxy, I might have thought twice. Except I know I wouldn't have. It really felt like I had no choice but to eat constantly. I was so hungry and also so bored from the immobility. So now I'm forced to sit and watch him scoff his head off on our so-called 'hot date' while I pretend not to mind.

I rummage around for conversation topics but everything I think of revolves around the babies. I've fallen into that parent trap, and our world as a couple seems to have shrunk to being solely about our progeny. We end up talking about the relative merits of early mortgage repayments. Hot stuff. I try to remember the flirting tips I once saw on one of those dating makeover shows. You're supposed to lean in, play with your hair and make casual physical contact. But how are you supposed to make 'casual physical contact' seem electric with someone who has seen you inflate to the size of a big top? How can you flirt winsomely with someone who has seen right up your clacker? There's no mystery between us. Now I know why they used to ban fathers from the delivery room.

The evening ends with Rich trying to order a large whisky and me persuading him not to. It seems to be my role of late, taming his excesses. It's become a habit – how can you look after four babies with a shocking hangover? So that's me then. A great big fat damp squib.

Friday 4 November

I keep feeling sick. Rich keeps saying I might be pregnant and then laughing maniacally. My hormones have calmed down a bit now, so the idea of another baby has become terrifying again, thank God. I think about what it is that might be giving me this constant puky feeling and I realize that it's because I keep remembering what was happening this time a year ago. As the anniversary of the triplet discovery draws near, I find myself playing out the preceding weeks. 'This time last year we were in Brighton and I found out I was pregnant – do you remember? I was going out drinking with Julie Burchill and I didn't know I was expecting triplets!' Or: 'This time last year we went to Southport for the night when I was on tour – remember? – and I puked all day the next day and had to go to hospital.' Or: 'This time last year I kept crawling up the stairs to bed and I thought I was going mad and you kept chopping wood in the back garden and it was all I could do to drag myself downstairs and watch you.' The memories make me queasy because the overarching recollection is of how sick as a dog I felt. I have never felt so awful in all my life. I felt poisoned with hormones, awash with them. It was dreadful, and it went on for weeks. I would go to bed at 9 p.m., exhausted after having done nothing all day, with only another day of retching and vileness to look forward to. At one point, I went to an NHS walk-in centre and told the doctor I felt desperate. He looked at me like I was mental.

'Why are you desperate?'

'I just feel so awful,' I cried. He told me to take Gaviscon.

My friend DJ had been so concerned about me he'd offered

to pay for private care. I decided to sit it out, thinking it was just ordinary morning sickness and treatment would just be a waste of money. Imagine if I'd gone for a private scan and found out at six weeks that I was expecting three! Although the worry might have been more intense – it's not uncommon for one of the embryos to die early on – at least I would have had an explanation for why I was feeling so dreadful, which might have helped me cope. I remember saying to Rich, 'I just want to die.' It really was that bad. Even now the memory of it makes me heave. I can't smell certain things – ginger biscuits, Gaviscon lemon-flavoured tablets, wet laundry (oddly) – without feeling thrown back in time. I can't even hear the theme tune for 'Bobinogs' on Cbeebies without my stomach turning because Saoirse used to watch it a lot as I lay on the sofa moaning. Just seeing the name 'Southport' written on a map makes the bile rise in my throat. I feel like I am reliving a traumatic experience sensorily. I didn't start to feel better until I was about twelve-weeks pregnant, just before we found out about the triplets. I can still remember having fish fingers and brown bread and feeling deep joy that I didn't want to vomit.

We head back from Barcelona and I am really excited about seeing the boys. I can't wait. I rush in as soon as the car stops and Celia raises her finger to her lips.

'Ssshhh!' she says, clearly in charge. 'They're just dropping off.'

But I need to give them a big fat squeeze so I burst in and grab both of them for a cuddle. They stare up at me, sleepy-eyed and snotty-nosed. They look delicious.

'Thank you so much,' I say to Celia. 'You've done a brilliant job.'

'Honestly, it was my pleasure. It's been lovely,' she smiles. She looks almost sorry we are home.

Within five minutes all three babies are screaming their heads off. Perhaps we ought to head back to Spain. It doesn't take long to remember the reality of three little babies. I realize that the extra spare time I've had has allowed me to romanticize my real life. In truth, although we both said it wasn't much of a holiday having a toddler and a baby to look after, it was so much easier just having one baby to feed on schedule, one baby to settle at night, one bottom to change. It's the repetition of triplets that's the killer, the 'haven't I just done this?' feeling you get every time you pick up a bottle or pat a windy back. I feel deflated. Back to life, back to reality. It's pissing down outside, and we are shattered. It's been exhausting, and it's only given us a taste of what life might have been like had we not heard the news we heard at that fateful first scan.

Perhaps we shouldn't go on holiday without them all ever again for fear that we'll only want more freedom. Although right now I can't imagine how we would cope taking four young children away. We'd need a removal lorry, not a suitcase. OK, so maybe we just won't go on holiday. For eighteen years. Good plan. That's cheered me up. Rich and I will just have to become SKIers – Spending Kids' Inheritance. We'll wait until they've left home then say, 'Right, the house is sold and we're buggering off for a few years. See you later.'

There are so many places we both want to see that are now on hold indefinitely. Russia. China. Rich wants to revisit India. I want to drive a Winnebago across Australia. Bali. Japan. The southern states of America. Canada. We want to mooch around Europe all summer one year. The thought of any of this with four kids fills me with The Fear. We are confident, capable people; I'm sure if we really put our backs into it we could do at least some of these things, but the expense would be prohibitive (six air tickets to Indonesia!) and the enjoyment ratio would be severely compromised. It's just not that relaxing taking them all anywhere, so it wouldn't justify the cost.

Roll on 2023.

Monday 7 November

The builders are here. The house is covered in scaffolding and there is an exciting tapping noise coming from the roof. We will be in our new loft bedroom by Christmas. I ask Gary and Terry to plumb in pipes for a bath.

'Are you having an en suite?' they ask.

'No – I just want a nice roll-top bath under the big dormer window so that no matter how shit my day has been I can sit and soak and look at the stars.'

'You can't have it by the big window – the neighbours opposite will see everything!' laughs Gary.

'Gary, if they are so desperate for thrills that they get pleasure looking at my saggy old body heaving itself out of the tub then they are welcome,' I say.

The new room is not a home improvement, it's a necessity. We need space desperately. The babies are still all sleeping together, but we can't put them in one cot any more because their heads are bumping against the railings, so we have taken to putting them to bed on the lower bunk in the spare room. This is fine for the moment because they are not rolling or moving much, but very soon it will not be safe to leave them unfettered. The problem is we have no space to put up the spare cot. Not even a scrap of hallway. I read a report recently about overcrowding in British homes. It seems that about a third of children are sleeping in makeshift beds at night because of lack of space.

Once the loft is done, we will move up there and turn the main bedroom downstairs into a nursery. Down will come the expensive tailor-made curtains I bought before I knew I was pregnant again, out will go the heavy pine furniture, and it'll be all systems go on the primary-coloured plastic front.

I have been advised that we should have our house checked over for child safety. This is always a good idea, but with twins or more it's a must. When you have more than one inquisitive toddler on the move things need to be nailed down and attached to the walls. A singleton trying to open a top drawer will probably be frustrated and not end up emptying it onto his head, but two or three determined tykes will find it child's play. Triplets, I am reliably informed, work as a demolition team. Something's out of reach? Easy – form a human pyramid with your sisters and that glass vase is within your grasp. Want to get behind that wardrobe to retrieve a raisin you can see? Put your brothers on either corner and wiggle it until it topples over. This sounds cute and clever in theory but in practice it is terrifying – and potentially tragic. Last year there was an accident reported in the press where twins suffocated to death inside a chest of drawers while their parents thought they were quietly napping in their cots. The twins had helped each other climb out, opened the door and pulled the chest on top of themselves in the next room. Horrible. I can't begin to imagine how those poor people felt that night. I am such a slacker when it comes to preventative measures, but we really must knuckle down and sort it out.

Lou arrives. Today we are leaving Harry and Saoirse at a local pre-school for the first time. As we get into her car (leaving Rich making a Christmas cake while he ignores the triplicate screams from upstairs), she casually announces that her house is on the market. They want to move out of London. Lou – who comes over a few times a week to help feed babies. Lou – whose son Harry is Saoirse's best friend, the only kid she knows who laughs at the word 'dungarees' as much as she does. Lou – who will change all three babies' nappies without me even noticing let alone having to ask. Lou – who lives five minutes away and is my saddo Ikea lunch buddy ('They've got a great play area!').

What am I going to do without her? Some people are so bloody selfish. I toy with the idea of using her spare keys to do the old 'prawns in the curtain poles' trick so that potential buyers will be put off by the inexplicable smell. In the end, I content myself with telling her that it will take ages to sell because the market is always slow at this time of year.

We drop the kids off and wait a while to make sure they are settled in. It's a big step, but they both seem fine so we leave. Saoirse needs this interaction. She's started to become very possessive of things, although she gets confused with her possessive pronouns, shouting 'Yours!' angrily when she means

'Mine!' Last week in the optician's, a woman sat on a chair Saoirse had just been playing on and she roared up to her screaming, 'No, lady – yours!' I put it down to the stress of having to share her parents with three babies all at once. Either that or she's a brat. This pre-school playgroup will help her negotiate and share.

We skip into the car park, giddy with the freedom. Lou can go back to an empty house and do something exciting like the hoovering without interference, or do some paperwork. It doesn't sound like much fun, but when you are used to being trailed by a toddler tyrant all your waking hours it is absolute heaven just to be on your own in the daytime. I get to go home to three babies and a mountain of Rich's washing-up. The Christmas cake smells amazing as I walk through the door. I give it a stir for good luck. We need it.

Two hours later, we head back to pick up the kids. We spy on them from outside. Harry is playing nicely at a table. I can't see Saoirse. Then I spot her, standing in the middle of the floor wearing an army hat and repeatedly slapping a boy around the head. It appears he has committed the heinous crime of attempting to peep at the car she is holding. Oh well. It's only day one.

Thursday 10 November

A visit from Eva, the health visitor. With her is a very sweet trainee. Her eyes pop out of her head when she sees what chaos we live in. I like these visits because Eva is lovely, and tries to help as much as she can, but I always end up feeling like I'm doing something wrong. The babies are all asleep when she arrives so we sit and chat for a while. She asks me about their development, their schedule, their health.

'Thady and Frank are pretty laid back, but Orla is a bit of a screamer. She screams herself to sleep a few times a day, which is a bit stressful, but we just put her down and let her get on with it. She's also much more advanced than they are. She needs stimulation. She won't be left in the buggy for long. She doesn't eat as much as the boys though. They are quite happy just to eat and sleep.'

'How are they doing on their tummies?'

'They don't like it. They cry. But Orla can roll over already.'

'Have you started weaning them yet?'

'Well, we've tried them with some baby rice and a bit of apple – they prefer the apple.'

'Keep them on savoury for the first month – carrot, broccoli – or they'll develop a really sweet tooth.'

'Oh.'

'How much milk are they having now?'

'Well, four feeds of eight ounces – that's thirty-two.'

'They should be down to sixteen ounces at six months.'

'Oh.'

'Try to reduce their milk as you give them more solids.'

'OK.'

I've been dreading the whole weaning thing. With just one baby, it's a welcome transition. Solids mark the arrival of the second stage of babyhood, the bit where they start being more fun, feeding themselves and smearing gunk all over the place.

They can sit up, hold a spoon, entertain themselves a bit more by making a mess. But with three? How the hell are we going to feed three at a time? We've only just mastered the art of three bottles at once. I feel reluctant to give up our hard-won routine. We cling to it. Whatever is happening we know that the babies get a full belly four times a day and they are sleeping through the night. Why should we change? This is ridiculous thinking, I know. A baby cannot live by milk alone. I feel a sense of dread. The early stages of weaning are quite tough. Babies have to learn to take food from a spoon without pushing it out with their tongues. I remember getting quite frustrated with Saoirse at times. Most of the carefully prepared gunk would end up all over her clean clothes or on the floor. Trying to wean three at once is going to be extremely time-consuming and very messy. So far, we've just been playing around with a couple of spoonfuls a day. Now we have to get down to business.

I find myself thinking about feeding time at Howletts Wild Animal Park in Kent. We often visit Donna there where we play at being animal keepers for a day and help feed the gorillas. It's brilliant fun. Crates of mangoes, legs of lamb and whole baked potatoes are shoved through the roof of their enclosure and they all scrabble around in the hay for their dinner. Why can't we just do that with the triplets? Create a special environment with a food chute and a hosepipe-friendly floor? We could even put a glass frontage on it to satisfy the triplet curiosity of the general public, thus killing two birds with one stone. Instead, Rich goes out to the shed and retrieves the two extra high chairs we have been given.

Saoirse's high chair is still by the table, although she considers sitting in it to be completely beneath her these days. Of course, when I put Frank in it, she screams blue murder – 'No, Franky boy, *yours* chair!' – but we placate her with a yoghurt and put Thady and Orla in the other two.

I make up some revolting sludge that looks like wallpaper paste (baby rice and milk formula – yum) and we try to coax them to slurp at the spoon. The boys are too busy trying to get their thumbs in their mouths and Orla pulls the most disgusted face I have ever seen. I think Orla is a princess and is going to bypass the whole puree phase and sit things out until she can eat shellfish in fancy restaurants.

I go from one baby to the next, a spoonful each, then back to the beginning, despite Eva's instruction that I should leave the bowl down in front of them so that they can 'play with it a bit'. Yeah right. The babies' hands, faces, clothes and chairs are now covered in a light film of chunky white spew. They look cute, but quite cross. Frank's head is so fat and heavy he can hardly hold it up long enough to get the food in. Thady has slipped down to one side and Orla is fiddling with her bib – we've been given a batch of comedy bibs with 'hilarious' slogans such as 'I've got genius genes', a claim that Frank has already disproved by attempting to eat *it* rather than the food. The whole process takes about an hour.

We then have to wait a bit before giving them half their normal milk feed at midday. This is going to take forever. If we have to give them three milk feeds and three square meals a day, we will be in negative-equity time by nightfall. If I had only one baby, it would just be a case of propping him up on my knee and spooning some food in. We could be anywhere. In a cafe. In the park. But this is impossible with three. They need to be properly propped up. Far from being the liberating moment it is for a singleton baby, weaning is going to imprison us in the house even more.

Mind you, according to the American triplet website message boards we shouldn't be going out anyway because of RSV – respiratory syncytial virus. RSV seems to be yet another bog-eyman in America. It's basically a cold-like virus that most babies will get before they are two years old, but the implications for premature babies can be very serious, especially if they have had lung problems at birth. Triplets, due to their prematurity, are obviously at risk. The advice is to keep babies at high risk away from crowded places in what they call RSV season ('fall to spring'), don't share toys or pacifiers (like that's possible with four kids) and wash everything all the time (ditto).

Several women on the message board say that they have not taken their triplets out ANYWHERE for six months for fear of exposing them to RSV. How do they manage this without going crazy? Presumably, they don't allow anyone in either in case they are carrying infection. On the one hand, I admire their dedication to keeping their household germ-free; but on the other, I just think, 'Oh, come on. It's not THAT dangerous unless the babies are on oxygen or severely compromised anyway.' I can hear the collective gasps and cries of 'Bad mommy!' as I write, but I cannot live my life imprisoned in order to protect the babies from colds. Yes, it's been a bit snotty in our house of late, but they are doing fine, even though the boys did have mild RDS at birth. Thank God I don't live in America or I'd be drummed out of town.

I'm either very slack or they are very paranoid. I read a post recently by a woman who was asking people how they manage to load up the car with all three babies without leaving one alone briefly in the car and thus prey to any passing paedophiles or child-snatchers. I thought the replies would laugh her off the board, but instead people responded with their own crazy schemes for car-loading which involved various door-propping techniques and buggy ferrying. One woman puts all three in their triple buggy in the garage then wheels it to the car ten feet away *on her own driveway* so that she can load them up without letting them out of her sight. I was going to ask if she'd thought about the possibility that the Monster from the Deep might come and nick the car when she went to put the buggy back in the garage but thought better of it. I remember an incident recently where a British couple were reported for leaving a sleeping child in their car while they nipped into a shop in the USA. It makes me shudder – if the triplets fall asleep in their buggy while we are out with them, we routinely leave them parked outside in the front garden until they wake up. If we've been out in the car and they are asleep when we get home, it has been known for us to park outside our house and keep an eye from the front window until we see an arm or a leg flapping. We'd probably get death by lethal injection for less in the States.

Saturday 12 November

I have spent all morning pureeing. Two bags of apples, a bag of pears, a huge bag of carrots and five whole broccoli heads all steamed, mashed, mixed with milk and scooped into ice-cube trays ready for freezing. When we weaned Saoirse, I just could not be bothered and was quite shameless about her 'packets and tins' existence. I sneered at other mums who boasted about their home-cooked baby gunk. Why bother when there are jars available? Growing up in a poor household, we thought that anything 'from the shops' was posh – why eat Mum's home-made cupcakes if you can afford Mr Kipling's? But weaning this time will require a crippling personal loan to keep the triplets in parsnip and potato mash 'from the shops', so I have bitten the bullet and invested in a steamer. It took me two hours to peel, slice, steam and puree about a hundredweight in fruit and veg. The buggers had better eat it – I had to undergo a complete personality change to create it. The freezer is now full of mini-meals ready to be spewed all over the kitchen floor and pooed all over their freshly washed vests.

Thady and Frank are taking very well to the new food regime, gamely sucking any old rot off the spoon, but Orla continues to clamp her jaw shut and curl her lip if we do manage to get anything down her. She's going to be trouble, that one.

Rich and I continue to operate as a semi-sullen double act. When he comes in from working or shopping or taking the babies out, I take my cue and head off out for a couple of hours to clear my head of all the crying. We are having a silent war over who is suffering the most. Today, I put all three babies down in the same room for their nap and Rich is cross because that's not the way he does it. Orla always wakes first and if she cries she wakes the boys, so he puts her in our room at nap times. He is trying to slip in a crafty lunchtime kip himself and Orla has indeed woken crying, which has disturbed the boys. I head out of the door and leave him to sulk. He always gets cross when his half-hour toilet sessions or his little sleeps are interrupted, as if they are his inalienable right, but when do I get half an hour to myself during the day? Never. Not until the babies are in bed. And sometimes not even then.

I take the triplets out of his way and we go for a nice walk. I pop in and out of shops while they doze. Well, I say 'pop', but that's rather an elegant word for an ungainly operation involving lots of sweating and swearing as I try to lug the five-foot long and now very heavy buggy round tight corners and irritating little steps. After the third shop, I decide to leave them parked outside. I nip in to buy a paper and a woman sticks her head through the door.

'Are these yours?' she says.

'Yes,' I say.

'Ooh, aren't you worried, leaving them outside here?'

'Not really. I can see them, and it's not like anyone would want to steal triplets, is it?' I laugh. The woman looks uncertain about my mental state. She's not wrong to.

I'm worried about me and Rich. Sometimes our dovetailing is so effective we scarcely seem to notice that the other is there, and although our home life is largely very peaceful I don't want to wake up one day and find that I am running a mini-crèche with a virtual stranger. The relationship section of our report card is marked 'Must do better'. But when?

Sunday 13 November

We take the babies to see Mum and Dad. Orla cries all day, especially when we try to feed her solids.

'Maybe she's not ready for it,' Mum says, staring in horror at Rich forcing the spoon into her mouth while she screams. They look at us as if we are torturers.

But what can we do? The boys are starting to get the hang of it really well, and we can't have two different schedules. She will just have to pull her socks up. Her crying is becoming quite stressful. She has become a screamer, the sort of baby about whom other people quietly say, 'Thank God mine isn't like that.' She screams herself to sleep. She screams herself awake. She screams when she's hungry. She screams when we feed her. She screams when she's understimulated. She screams when she's overstimulated. Lou says Orla's the loudest baby she's ever heard. When Orla screams, it's impossible to hold a conversation in the same room, even if you shout. Last night, when Rich was putting them all to bed, a neighbour came to tell me we'd left the car lights on. When I went to switch them off, I could hear Orla from a hundred yards down the road.

Maybe she's ill. She sounds husky throated, but then maybe she's just screamed herself hoarse. We give her some Calpol – that infant cure-all – and I decide to take her to the doctor in the morning. Sometimes it gets so that you actually hope they are ill rather than just sociopathic.

The boys continue to eat, burp, smile and sleep. Their cheeks are massive and it's all I can do to stop myself from taking great chunks out of them with my bare teeth. They are very easy to look after and very passive. People respond so warmly to them because they just look so simple and unassuming.

Poor Orla. She gets a bad press and it hurts me. Despite my aching eardrums, I don't feel anger towards her. She's a complicated little person, and she needs careful handling. There's nothing wrong with that. I'm sure she'll cheer up once she starts moving around. And if she doesn't, I'll just put it down to triplet-induced anxiety.

Monday 14 November

Fanny the Nanny is here. I met her through a mum at a playgroup and she is coming to work for us on three afternoons a week. She is a lovely, smiley Bolivian lady and she speaks Spanish with a few words of English. She has agreed to come and just pitch in wherever needed, so I steel myself and ask her to clean the bathroom. It is covered in filth from the building work going on overhead, but I have not had the time, the will or the strength to do it myself.

She sets to with great gusto, and I feel so guilty I have to go out. I return an hour later and she is sitting with a very smiley Orla on her lap. That in itself is worth its weight in gold – Orla looks like the cat that got the cream with her very own lap to rest on all afternoon. The bathroom is spotless, and Fanny follows me around tidying up as I make dinner for Saoirse.

Although we have been coping really well, the house is constantly dirty and untidy, and we need someone to help us if we are not to become a pair of worn-out drudges. If I can just look at a clean sink in the morning, I know that at least one part of my life is in order. All hail Fanny.

I take all three babies to the doctor as they are all coughing like miners. We sit in the waiting room and the babies get fussed over by the elderly people there.

'You won first prize there, didn't you?' says a nice old bloke. Thady smiles at him. Orla screams. Frank dribbles. An old lady gets out a picture of her twin grandsons and hands it around. Someone passes round a bag of boiled sweets. The triplets have turned a crowded waiting room into a nice little social event.

'What seems to be the problem?' asks the doctor.

'Well, it's really the girl I'm worried about, but I thought I might as well bring them all in, because if one's got it, the other two probably have as well!' I've read a lot about how triplet mums manage doctor's appointments. One lady just takes one baby and says, 'The other two have got what this one's got,' thus avoiding the hassle of getting three sick babies to the surgery, and the near impossibility of getting a triple appointment at short notice.

The doctor listens to their chests and says they are fine, but Orla is quite congested. I'm to steam her and give her Calpol, but she's not really ill. Right. So she's just got a rather unfortunate personality at the moment.

Tuesday 15 November

I'm booked in for the baby massage course at the local clinic. Eva, our health visitor, has suggested I take Orla for some one-on-one time. Orla, however, has other ideas, and screams herself through the first nap of the day, only to finally drop off just when we should be heading out the door. I let her sleep, unfit for the struggle of getting her there and undressing her when she is too tired to get any benefit from it. Instead, Rich and I enjoy an hour of chatting on the sofa. Saoirse is at pre-school and all the babies are asleep. Tomorrow I have gained a twenty-four hour pass to Dublin to see my friend Deidre in a new play about motherhood. Deidre's daughter Holly is nine months old, but because of the triplets I haven't met her yet so we have a lot to chat about.

'Will you be OK with all the babies by yourself, Rich?' I ask, feigning a guilty conscience.

'Why? You're not going to cancel if I say no, are you?' he says, smelling a rat.

'No.'

'Well then. You go and enjoy yourself, love. Don't worry about me, sat at home looking after *your* kids and *your* dog.'

'OK. And you can drop me off at the airport.'

Wednesday 16 November

Hurray! Rich drops me at Stansted at 10.30 a.m. He won't be picking me up until 3 p.m. tomorrow. A precious day away. I want to go shopping, have a few drinks, enjoy hanging out with Deirdre in Dublin. I go to check in, but cannot see my flight listed. I am directed to the sales desk.

'The 12.05 flight has been cancelled. The next one is at 15.30, OK?' says the bored young Ryanair man.

'What? What do you mean cancelled? When was it cancelled?'

'About five minutes ago.'

'Why?'

'Something wrong with the plane,' he says, absentmindedly plucking a thread from his nylon tie.

'Bugger it!' I shout.

'Shall I book you on the 15.30?' he says, nodding towards the sign warning customers not to be abusive when they are left high and dry and no one shows a flicker of concern.

'Well, I don't have any choice do I? What compensation do I get?'

He raises an eyebrow in amusement. 'This is a low-cost airline, so we don't do that.'

'What do you mean – because the fares are cheaper we have no rights? No comeback at all? You can just leave us all here and we have no right to complain?'

He doesn't answer me. Heard it all before. Blah, blah, blah. Angry premenopausal woman ranting about her rights. I feel like collapsing on the concourse and shouting, 'Don't you know I have triplets and this time is very precious?'

But I do that great British thing of tutting in fury and move away from the desk. If I call Rich now, he's probably not out of the airport yet. He can come and get me and we can spend a few hours at my parents' house until the next flight. It's only twenty minutes away.

His phone rings and rings. He doesn't answer. Shit. He's bloody left it at home. I leave a semi-abusive message on his voicemail – something along the lines of 'What's the point in having an effing mobile if you leave it at home all the time, you effing clown?' – and resign myself to almost five hours of hanging about. I can't even go through to the heady shopping village of departures until the next flight checks in, which is three hours away. Bastards.

Eventually, I arrive and the play, *Dandelions* by Fiona Looney, is great. It's about women's friendships and motherhood, and most of the scenes take place in a suburban kitchen just after the school run. It's very accurately drawn, the 'slightly bored treading water until it's time to collect the kids' atmosphere, and it moves me to tears. It makes me realize how sustaining these relationships are. Lou, Linda, Anoushka. Women hanging around in each other's houses, taking each other's kids in, if one needs a break. It's how we all get through the monotony, the emotionally draining aspects of rearing children. It's not at all sentimental and 'yummy mummy' though. My favourite exchange comes when a new mum moves in next door and the two main characters are discussing how many children she seems to have:

'I only saw one car seat in the car.'
'They might have older children. Did it have a baby sunscreen on the window?'
'Yes, I think so.'
'They've just got the one then. They still care.'

When the new mum comes to visit with her (adopted) daughter, our heroines suggest sticking the baby in the front room 'so we won't hear her'. The look of horror on the new mum's face prompts gails of laughter from all the second-time-arounders in the auditorium. It's a lovely moment, and I'm reminded of the healing power of laughter. We all need to hear this stuff, to know that it's not just us who struggle with the crying and the constant demands. To know that it's actually quite normal to hate the howling and the noise levels. To know that every time we shut the door or push the pram to the bottom of the garden and leave it there, we are in good company.

'Let's have another drink!' I say in the bar afterwards.

'Steady now,' says Deidre. 'You don't want to make yourself ill.'

Thursday 17 November

I wake next morning with a hangover after two vodkas. I'm so out of practice. I call Rich to see how the babies are.

A woman answers the phone.

'Oh,' I say, stupidly. 'Who's that?'

'It's Lou, Jackie – sorry!'

What's Lou doing there? It's only 8.30, and it's not a nursery day. So all those jokes about rearranging their clothes when I come back into the room have been an elaborate double bluff, have they?

Rich takes the phone from Lou.

'Hello, love,' he wheezes.

'Hello. What's wrong?'

'Me back's gone,' he says, clearly in pain. 'I've just had to get the babies out of bed on my hands and knees. I can't straighten up. Lou's going to mind them, while I go to the chiropractor.'

'Oh shit!'

I'm powerless. I have a terrible image of Rich prowling around on all fours like a wounded cat, three babies dangling from his jaws. Why can't things just be OK? Now I feel really anxious to get home – but not so anxious that I don't enjoy an impromptu spree in the children's section of Dunne's Stores on the way to the airport. I buy three tiny Ireland rugby shirts for the triplets and a big one for Saoirse purely so that I can see my dad break into one of his rare huge smiles.

Back home, Rich is doubled up and in a lot of pain.

'You did it just to spite me, didn't you?' I ask, trying to make him laugh.

'Ooh, it 'urts, ducky,' he says. He looks grey with pain.

I busy myself tidying the kitchen, which is a disaster area. He has managed to feed and change the babies, but the detritus – dirty nappies, bottles, spoons, cups, clothes and bibs – defeated him. It's my penance for going away.

We sit and watch the transmission of 'Who Rules the Roost'. We haven't been shown any of it, so we are watching it for the first time as it goes out on air. It's not bad at all. I was half suspecting a hatchet job on Rich, but in fact he looks like a bit of a hero. If anything, I come across as an old bag, telling him to 'Shut the fuck up' for singing loudly when I'm tired. Couple stuff, caught on camera. But mostly it's OK. And, of course, the fact that it was filmed in the summer, when the babies were just a few months old, makes the film a lovely reminder of the early days. Apart from one thing. Every time I look at myself on screen, instead of thinking how well I am coping, how articulate I am or how amusing I can be, all I can think is, 'LOOK AT MY HUGE ARSE!' I hate being such a typical woman, but I can't help feeling really pleased that I have lost almost two and a half stones since then. Phew. I feel like I am sprinting away from all that 'baby fat'. Except you and I both know it wasn't baby fat.

It was cake fat.

Saturday 19 November

I am at the Tamba AGM in Milton Keynes. As a 'celebrity' mum of triplets, I have been asked to draw the raffle – oh, the glamour – but I am mostly here to get involved and see what I can do to contribute to the world of multiple motherhood.

The morning is mostly housekeeping business, but there's a great bit where they show a film they have made called *Parenting with Multiples in Mind*. It's about how to foster individuality and close family relationships when there is more than one baby at a time. Mostly it's common sense stuff – think twice about dressing them the same, make individual time for each child, make sure they have their own friends, etc. – but just the sight of another set of triplets makes me cry with joy. It's so nice to see people in our situation. I'm astonished by how alienated I have been feeling watching baby programmes and childcare advice shows – the families on those shows just don't face the same issues we multiple mums have to deal with. How do you put three on the 'naughty stair'? They'd have a ball.

During the lunch break, I flash pictures of my triplets around. People are polite but there is nowhere near as much oohing and aahing. I feel a bit miffed – What's wrong with my babies? – then I realize why. Most of these women have got twins. Some have even got triplets. They've got their very own matching set of babies at home. Seen it. Been there. Had the epidural. Triplets? Big news. I come face-to-face with Sue Plenty, Tamba's supertwins coordinator. I tell her that her name gave me the only laugh of the day when I first found out I was expecting triplets.

'Yes, we had a similar set-up as you,' she says. 'Our first child was only about eighteen months old when our triplets arrived.'

'It's like having quads really, isn't it?' I say.

'I think it might well be harder, actually. At least with quads they are all the same age, and they need roughly the same things at the same stage of development.'

Only someone who has been through it would know this. It's great talking to other parents of triplets. This is why groups like Tamba are so important. I ask what role lobbying has to play in their aims, money often being a major concern for new parents of multiples. Surely the government could fund home helps for parents of twins or triplets who are in need?

'We've lobbied before, but even when MPs have twins, we find that they just can't see what the problems might be because they don't have the same hardships,' says the Tamba chairperson.

'It's about awareness, isn't it?' I say. 'We need Jamie Oliver to have twins. He could do for multiples what he did for school dinners.'

Thursday 23 November

The builders are cracking on. By this time next week, we will have a three-storey house. Despite our excitement at getting a room back for ourselves – at present, our bedroom contains two cots, a wardrobe stuffed to the gills with baby clothes, a change station, several boxes of nappies and random discarded toys – we already know that it still won't be big enough. I look at our tiny patch of garden and try to imagine four pre-school children kicking a ball around. No wonder Linda says she has to take Finn to the park every day or he'll explode. Kids just have so much energy. It's not fair, especially as more and more of us are leaving it until we are old and knackered. Our local park on a Saturday morning is full of balding dads in Gap jeans puffing along after little bruisers on tricycles. Thank God for my bath.

My bath.

It arrives while I am out with Saoirse and when I get back it is sitting, magnificent, in the front garden. I played around with acrylic, I toyed with resin, but in the end I decided there was no substitute for a cast-iron roll top. All my life I have made do with fake goods, second best, cheap imitations. Now, more than ever, when I can least afford it, I want the best, for those moments when it all gets too much and the only thing that will fix it is a nice long soak in a hot tub brimming with expensive product.

It's called a Brunel, after the bridge-building engineer, and its solid shell is encased in sheets of gun-metal grey cast iron, riveted together with ship-sized bolts. It is a thing of great beauty and it is going to sit just under the dormer window, where I will soak and take in the view of Christchurch spire. This isn't just a bath, it's a massive indulgence. It's not just a lifestyle but a lifesaver. As Sylvia Plath said, 'There's not much that can't be fixed by a good long soak in a hot bath.'

On second thoughts, maybe she's not such a great role model on the mental-health front.

I watch with glee as Gary, Terry and Rich haul it up through a hole in the roof. It is 175 kilograms of heaven, even though it causes them untold hell to get it up there. Tough. It's the closest they'll get to suffering a triplet pregnancy.

Friday 25 November

The boys have got a gig. I get a call from the twin agency they are signed up with.

'Hello, is that Mrs Clune?' says a nervous assistant.

'Miss Clune, yes,' I say, once again aware of how unusual it is to be unmarried with four kids.

'We've had a call from someone at the BBC because they're doing a reconstruction of, well, you know a few years ago there was that nurse that killed all them babies? She murdered them. I think she poisoned them or something.'

'Erm, yes—'

'Well, they want to use your babies.'

Lovely. So they want to bump my little baby boys off in their first acting job. The thought of them even representing such vile and unthinkable acts is really creepy. My first instinct is to say no. I couldn't bear to see anything horrible happen to them, even if it is only acting. The fact that these things did actually happen to some dreadfully tragic children makes it even worse. But then I think about it for a bit. Maybe this is an important programme, one that will give an insight into a disturbing modern pathology. Maybe people need to see this, to help them to understand some of the extremes of human behaviour. Maybe our boys will be taking part in a noble docudrama that will help medical professionals spot dangerous stuff in the future.

Plus, of course, we'll be paid. Sorry, but we're actors ourselves. It's a gig.

So now we have to rush around trying to get medical letters, photos and copies of birth certificates so that the local council can grant a licence. The boys will need this in order to be able to 'work' as they are minors. It's very exciting. The only problem is we can't get an appointment at the clinic as they are all booked up. What's wrong with these people? Don't they know that showbiz is at stake here?

And the boys aren't the only ones in the spotlight. Rich and I both have castings at the same time today, so we have to take them all into town and juggle them between us. Rich is up for a chocolate commercial and I have a second meeting for the international tour of *Mamma Mia*, the Abba musical. I only went up for it for a laugh – I'm so out of practice I thought they'd laugh me out of the room – but when I started singing my voice just came flying out from nowhere. I felt really bad because I'd spent the whole time in the waiting room telling all the assembled West End Wendys how useless I was going to be.

International touring with four kids under the age of three?

Hmmm. Interesting. I ask for the details of the tour and it turns out that it's only four cities, with what they call extended 'sit downs' – Belfast for a month, Edinburgh for two, and Cape Town and Pretoria in South Africa for three.

'We could do that,' I say to Rich, giving in to the temptation to jinx the whole thing before I've even been cast.

'I wouldn't come with you,' he says. 'I'd stay here with the kids.'

I'm stunned.

'What do you mean – you wouldn't come? I couldn't go on my own and leave them all for that long!' What is he thinking?

'Well, I suppose we could all go to South Africa, but I wouldn't want to go to Belfast and Edinburgh.'

'Why not?'

'I just wouldn't. It'd be better for the babies to stay at home. We'd come and visit you for weekends—'

'Oh, thanks!' I am really hurt. I see us as a unit now. What one does, we all do. When Saoirse was little I took her on tour twice, but I often left her at home if the journey was too difficult or too long. Sometimes I didn't see her for five or six days. It was hard but it meant she built up a great relationship with Rich and with his mum Celia, which was lovely for all of them. But leaving four kids behind? Somehow that is just unthinkable. Normally in disagreements like this I am logical, I try to listen and I think about his point of view, but this time I throw a tantrum.

'Fine, well if that's the way you feel, if it's really not that important to you that we're all together, I'll hire a nanny and take them all with me and you can be at home doing whatever the fuck it is you want to do here,' I say, before flouncing upstairs to bed.

Once I've calmed down, I think about it some more. Would I follow Rich on tour with all the kids? Probably not. The logistics of all the stuff we need, the beds, the space, the chairs, the toys, is just too exhausting. Our house looks like a showroom for Babies 'R' Us. How can we transport all that? We try to downsize whenever we go up north to see the girls and Celia, but it makes life more difficult if we don't have their bouncy chairs, high chairs, swings, mobiles, change tables, etc. They get fed up being propped up on pillows during the day. They need their stuff.

I console myself the pessimist's way by telling myself that it's all academic anyway because I won't get the part. I try to be positive about life as much as possible, but in this profession it just leads to heartbreak, so these days I think the worst in order not to suffer the massive, crashing disappointment that often ensues. 'The losing is OK, it's the hope that kills you,' as some football pundit once said.

Monday 28 November

No call from my agent. The phone aggressively doesn't ring, but sits on the kitchen unit taunting me with its smug muteness.

We are at my parents' house while the stairs up to the loft are going in, and Rich is out today erecting a greenhouse. The triplets have a terrible cold, and they scream every time we lie them down because their noses are thick with snot. The boys' chests sound very bad, and I worry about them in particular because they were intubated. I ring NHS Direct and they advise me to take them to see a doctor 'just to be on the safe side'. How will I get two babies to the doctor three miles away with only my dad's old car and no car seats? The boys are so ill I really don't want to take them out at all. It's cold and foggy. TB weather. I call the local surgery. I'll get an emergency doctor to come out. A frosty receptionist answers and I tell her my situation.

'Are you registered with us?' she says.

'No, we live in London.'

'Is it urgent?' she says tetchily, like I might just be ringing for a laugh.

'Well, I've got three coughing, very unhappy babies and two of them have had RDS, so yes,' I say, 'it is. Can a doctor come to the house?'

She sighs heavily, like I am asking her to come and give us a piggyback to the surgery herself.

'No,' she says.

'No?' I can't believe it. What does she mean 'No'? This is the NHS.

'I don't think he will. They don't do it usually. You'll have to come in. In ten minutes. We close soon,'

What am I supposed to do?

There are no car seats in my dad's car, so, weighing up the pros and cons of risking their safety on the short journey to the doctor's or their lives with an unchecked chest infection, my mum climbs into the back (with her arthritic knee) and I shove Thady and Frank at her. She holds onto them like her life depends on it.

In the waiting room the boys are all smiles. Maybe they're

just glad to get out of the house. They rarely go out. It's just too much hassle when it's cold and wet.

'Typical,' I say. 'They'll probably grin at the doctor, and he'll think I was making it all up.'

'I'll pinch them as we go in,' says Mum.

The doctor is brisk and impatient at first until I start hitting him with some medical jargon and he realizes I am not the patronizing stereotype of a mum of four he probably holds dear. He listens to their chests and says that they are clear. I'm relieved. Calpol cocktails all round. We get them home, dose them up and put them to bed, where they scream for a good two hours.

Finally they fall asleep, but I lie half awake all night to make sure they are breathing properly. Miraculously, they sleep solidly until 7 a.m., and I give praise to the god of Junior Paracetamol Suspension once more.

Tuesday 29 November

Jesus. They've only gone and given me the part in *Mamma Mia*.

What are we going to do now?

I accept, on the proviso that they know I will have quite a lot of baby-shaped baggage.

Rich is out Christmas shopping, so I call him and give him the news. It's as much a huge deal for him as it is for me.

'Bloody hell,' he says. 'I need the loo.'

The production company want to send me to a personal trainer and a voice coach to get me 'match fit'. Bring it on. It means we'll be able to pay for the loft, even if my soak in the bath will have to wait for a while.

It's a very daunting prospect, though, launching myself back into the familiar world of dressing rooms, rehearsals and first nights. I have spent the last year either pregnant or tied to three babies. I feel scared. Most women find the return to work after babies a bit of a daunting prospect. Imagine having to do it by standing in front of three thousand strangers singing 'Dancing Queen' in a white satin catsuit. I'm worried about how we will cope, but I have no alternative but to take the job and resolve to make it work for us. People think I'm mad even considering taking triplets and a toddler on tour with me, but then they think I'm mad anyway, so we might as well take our little circus on the road. It'll be a laugh. I'm sure there will be times when it will be tough, as they won't be with me all the time, and if they walk for the first time while I'm belting out 'The Winner Takes It All' in Belfast I'll be heartbroken, but it will also be a great adventure – especially the South Africa bit. I can't wait to see Saoirse's face when she sees her first real live zebra.

I mentally plan out the next year. June, July and August will be spent in Cape Town and Pretoria.

'We'll miss summer in Wanstead. Ice-creams in the park. Pushing the buggies to the swings,' I say to Linda.

'You can have summer in Wanstead any old year,' she says. 'This is a once-in-a-lifetime opportunity, and it's great that it's happened before the kids are in school. You wouldn't be able to do it then.'

She's right, of course, but I can't help feeling a twinge of sadness that I will be – temporarily – leaving this suburban, cosy backwater with all its yummy mummies, its Tumbletots and its church-hall playgroups. There is a pleasing rhythm to the week, dominated largely by the children's social diaries. Much as I have grumbled and complained about not fitting in, I have been warmly welcomed by the local community here, and have made a few good friends. Now I am about to rip it all up and bugger off for six months. Oh, well. I was a fraud anyway. I was only playing at being a provincial mum, as we all probably do. You make the best of it because you have to, and actually it's been pretty good. But I always knew deep down that the roar of the greasepaint and the smell of the crowd is where my heart lies. Back to my old life – but with four kids in tow.

I hope I can still do it. Going onstage in front of thousands of people requires balls and I have a terrible fear that, along with the four kids, I've given birth to my nerves as well.

Wednesday 30 November

I am booked to sing at a posh private party in front of lots of rich and famous people. I dig out an old sparkly evening dress and pour myself into it. It fits. I have lost almost three stone and am now lighter than I was when I got pregnant with the triplets. I am an inspiration. I should be featured in *Woman's Own*, standing proudly with my entire body in one leg of my maternity trousers. The gig goes very well, and I find it surprisingly easy to slip back into public mode. Afterwards, I stay for a drink and get chatting to human-rights barrister Geoffrey Robertson. He is fascinated by the triplets, and we get talking about nannies.

'We have Fanny the Nanny three afternoons a week,' I say. 'She's from Bolivia.'

'Very brutal regime,' he says. 'She probably suffered a lot.' It's nice to have a conversation about nannies that doesn't involve their shortcomings and how little you can get away with paying them.

'You haven't got a German nanny then?' asks Geoffrey.

'No,' I say. 'Why?' Is there some cultural advantage, I wonder?

'Well, they used to masturbate boys to sleep,' he says matter-of-factly.

'YOU ARE JOKING!' I shout, choking on my champagne.

'Yes. Not now, of course. But years ago.'

Later, in bed, I tell Rich.

'Good God,' he says. There's a brief ruminative pause.

'Ducky,' he says.

'Yes?' I say, half asleep.

'Can *I* have a German nanny?'

Sunday 4 December

At a first birthday party for the daughter of an Indian couple we know. They have hired an entire Indian restaurant and the place is full of families eating amazing food and enjoying a children's entertainer. We pitch up with all four kids and place the triplets on top of a table in their car seats. We are instantly mobbed by well-wishers. One young woman gazes at the babies for ages, then takes a heap of photographs.

'I hope you don't mind,' she says. 'I want to put a picture of your babies on my altar, then I am going to pray for triplets.'

Monday 5 December

My first session with Bella, the personal trainer. We have agreed to meet early in the morning, ostensibly because I have four children to tend to during the day, but mostly because I know if I don't do it first thing I will run away and hide. The stairs up to the gym are bad enough, and I have to stop near the top for a breather. I don't want to turn up at reception looking like I'm about to have cardiac arrest. She makes me do half an hour on the treadmill and fifteen minutes on the cross-trainer. It is hellish. I am so unfit. I try to explain that from about the middle of the pregnancy I could barely walk, so it's not surprising that I am so weak and wobbly. I don't tell her about the Belgian buns.

She nods understandingly, then increases the incline on the treadmill. Bitch.

Thursday 8 December

The boys have their first acting job. We have no one at home to help us, so we take all four kids along and sit for most of the day waiting to be 'used'. I entertain Saoirse by wheeling the two of us up and down the small hospital corridor in an old wheelchair. Thady is first on set, and he is required to lie in a small cot and look sleepy. The dialogue is based around two nurses discussing how sleepy and ill he looks despite the fact that he is due to be discharged. Little do they know that the evil nurse has been drugging the babies. We wait until Thady falls asleep and I wheel him into place on the mocked-up ward.

'Quiet on set, please,' says the director. 'We don't want him to wake up.'

But Thady is able to turn now and has fallen asleep on his tummy.

'This is 1991,' says the director. 'I don't think they would allow that, so you'd better turn him over.'

I oblige, but a combination of being moved and being in a much colder room makes him wake instantly. He spots the boom microphone hovering over his head and watches it, fascinated.

'What will happen if we offer him this bottle? They need to try to feed him but fail,' says the director.

'If you show him the bottle, he'll want it,' I say.

'I thought you'd just fed him?'

'Yes, I have – but have you seen the size of his cheeks? He didn't get that fat by watching his calorie intake.'

'OK. So just put the bottle near his mouth and we'll cut away in case he goes for it. And . . . action!'

The cameras are rolling.

Nurse 1: Come on, wake up, sleepy!

Nurse 2: I'll go and get his feed.

Thady is craning his neck and cooing delightedly, mugging at the camera and generally looking like the most awake and delighted baby you've ever seen.

Nurse 1: Funny . . . he doesn't seem to want his feed.

Thady virtually rips the offered bottle from the actress's hands.

Nurse 2: Maybe he's gone hypo . . .
Thady grins, coos even louder and dribbles happily all over the bottle, now firmly clasped between his bonny fat little fists.

Director: CUT! What about the other one – is he asleep?

Frank is wheeled in and put in his brother's place, but he too wakes up when he senses he is in a different room. He takes one look at the boom and breaks into an identical grin. He thinks it's the best laugh ever. He starts making really loud cooing noises that echo around the empty ward. The cameraman stifles a giggle and the sound man looks defeated.

'I'm picking all this up,' he says. 'I'm sorry, but they don't sound like they've been drip-fed morphine to me.'

Frank is wheeled out again and the director has a quick pow-wow with the crew.

'Thank you, Jackie. That's all we need you for today!' she says. 'We're going to use the dummy for this bit.'

And with that, they wheel in a horrible rubber doll dressed in an identical Babygro.

My boys have been replaced by a dummy. They have failed. They were just too darn happy.

Welcome to showbiz, kids.

Saturday 10 December

Carey and Georgia from across the road have offered to babysit so Rich and I head into town for the evening. We go to see a very good play that is an hour and a half long with no interval – perfect – and find ourselves in the West End at 9.30.

'Let's go and have a drink,' he says.

'OK. Let's go to that nice bar we went to the day before I was due with Saoirse.'

On our way to West Street we pass the Arts Theatre, scene of our first meeting four years ago.

'It's our anniversary!' I realize with a start.

'Is it?' says Rich. He'd been the fire officer there and I was performing. He had tried to tell me off for having my – heavily pregnant – dog in the building, claiming she was a fire hazard. I'd told him to piss off, and the rest, as they say, is history.

'Look – the theatre's shut down!' he says. The front of the building is dark. We peer through the glass doors. The bar, scene of much flirting four years ago, is dark and dusty. A pile of junk mail lies on the door mat.

'Weird,' says Rich.

We walk on and find West Street, but the bar is nowhere to be seen. We walk up and down for a bit, thinking we might have got the wrong street. Finally, we find a boarded-up building.

'This is where it used to be,' I say.

'Blimey, everything's closed since we got together!' says Rich.

'Oh well. Let's go to that hotel near the BBC. They've got this bar that sells forty different vodkas!' I say, trying to keep the mood light.

'It'll probably have burnt down,' says Rich, who does not adapt quickly when plans change. The fact is that in our four years together we only really went out for the first twelve months. After that it was babies all the way, and while we were eyes down for a full nappy a lot has changed. Businesses have folded, theatres have gone dark, bars have ceased to be the place to be. London has moved on – but not for us. In our minds it is still 2001, and we are still cool.

We stroll along Oxford Street, admiring the Christmas lights and thinking about this time last year. On 10 December 2004 we were still in blissful triplet ignorance. It would be a full twelve days before our world would be changed forever.

We get to the hotel and follow the signs for the bar, but end up in a fancy dining room where loads of suits are having dinner.

'I'm looking for the Tsar's Bar,' I say to a waitress.

'Oh, it's closed down – this was it,' she says, indicating the room behind her.

'You're joking!' I say.

'Come on, ducky, let's go home,' says Rich, defeated.

Tuesday 13 December

My fortieth birthday. All day people ask me how it feels to have hit the big Four-Oh, and I have to stop and think for a minute. I have no idea how it feels. I am too busy to have feelings about an abstract marker in my hectic life. I struggle to find something to say (for it seems one must say something on one's fortieth) that doesn't sound either cheesy or dismissive. In the end, I settle on saying that I'm fine about it, that I really haven't given it a lot of thought. Thirty-five friends gather for dinner at the Soho Hotel, and I am delighted to have squeezed myself into my pre-pregnancy black satin pencil skirt. True, I have to wear reinforced underwear and I can only sit down for short bursts, but I am in it nonetheless. By the end of the evening I have worked out how I feel about being forty.

'All I know is that I am the happiest I have ever been,' I tell Carol, an old friend and fellow lesbian turncoat. Carol hit forty in June, and recently started a relationship with a man called Keith who is sixty-five. On the face of it, our lives probably look quite absurd, me with my four babies and she with her pensioner boyfriend, but if my forty years have taught me anything it's that happiness is not only elusive but also has a habit of popping up in the least expected places, like flowers on a bomb site. If we always knew what would make us happy, then (poverty and illness aside) there would only be happy people (or deliberately unhappy people) in the world. The truth is we can often be surprised at how seemingly shattering life events can turn out for the good. This is what makes life so extraordinarily terrifying and exhilarating in equal measure. If someone had told me on my thirtieth birthday – spent dressed as Jackie Kennedy at a themed party in the Hackney flat I shared with my girlfriend Phil – that in a short decade's time I would be the mother of four children and living with my boyfriend in suburbia, I would probably have turned the music off, shooed everyone out and gone to have a good cry under the duvet. Little would I have guessed that I would be the most contented and fulfilled I have ever been.

Makes you puke, doesn't it?

I try hard to get behind the philosophical soft pedalling to analyse why I feel happy. Am I living proof of the anti-feminist mantra that the most rewarding role for a woman is

motherhood? I don't think so. It's not the babies per se that
have made me happy, although I do admit to a certain increased
sense of connectedness to the world that parenthood brings.
Has having triplets meant that I have unconsciously lowered
my expectations of life and therefore increased my sense of
perceived well-being? On the contrary, my expectations are
now far higher – I am busy and demanded upon, therefore I
expect fast service, higher pay for my precious time and more
professional respect. No one messes with Triplet Mum. Still,
the precise nature of my happiness, and its origins, eludes me. I
feel driven to give an account of it. People don't like it if you
say you're happy and you can't tell them why. They don't like
it almost as much as if you tell them you are unhappy and
spend the next three hours detailing your misery.

'Do you feel wise?' asks Carol.

'Not wise exactly,' I falter.

'Wise people never think they have the answers,' says Keith
(somewhat wisely). 'They just admit that there probably aren't
any.'

And it's true. I'd like to be able to say that there is a
prescription for waking up with a smile in your heart but there
isn't. I'd like to say that all you need is love, support, enough
money (but not too much), good health and a sense of humour,
but many people have all of these things and still feel hard done
by. I try to examine what the past year has given me, apart
from the obvious physical evidence.

I feel stronger for having got through almost thirty-five
weeks of a very tough pregnancy. There is an element of 'if
you can do that then you can do anything' in my make-up
these days. I don't feel frightened of very much any more, and

the absence of neurotic fear is very liberating. I have little patience with people who moan about their lot in life. If it didn't make me sound like Norman Tebbit, I would say, 'Get your head down and get on with it. Things aren't as hard as they might at first appear.' These babies have made me tougher. And softer. I can't read about children dying now without crying big fat tears.

I feel very proud that I have achieved several milestones professionally this year, despite the fact that I have had three babies and a toddler to take care of.

I am delighted that Rich and I have made such a good team, and that he has been so incredibly good-humoured when I have left him in sole charge on the days when I have run off to work. Now I know what people mean when they use the phrase, 'He is my rock.'

I feel very fortunate that, despite my intense misgivings about this year, we have managed to get through it with very few low points. I could never have anticipated it being so oddly enjoyable.

I have managed to lose four stone in weight despite the stress and the work involved in bringing up four babies. I feel pretty bloody smug about that, and in truth, being quite a superficial person at heart, this is probably what is pleasing me the most tonight. There is no one so pleased with herself as a recently thin person.

All in all, I feel a deep sense of achievement, both professionally and personally, and I'm not ashamed to say that for me achievement equals happiness. I know I'm not perfect. There have been times when I have been less than kind, when I have neglected the kids in favour of my own pleasure, when I have relied too heavily on Rich's good nature, when I have been short-tempered and demanding. But I can live with that. I'm forty. And I think I'm doing pretty great, actually.

Saturday 17 December

Orla has started to speak.

'Da da da da da!' she says, very pleased with herself. This new development has improved her relationship with Rich no end. He grins with pride every time she says it – about every three minutes at the moment – as if she is specifically addressing him and not just practising the easiest and therefore the first syllable most babies utter. I'm just jealous. The boys continue to be avid thumb suckers. If they are close together for a nap, they're not fussy whose thumb they suck. They'll grab any nearby digit and latch on. It's very sweet, but does make them look a bit dumb, bless them. Orla will grab at anything within her reach, pulling at my earrings, my hair, a nearby light cord. She is desperate to get out and at it. Meanwhile, the boys' idea of fantastic entertainment is to lie on their backs while I wiggle my fingers in the air about a foot above their heads. They go berserk, kicking their legs and spasmodically twitching like hillbillies witnessing a UFO. It's hard not to get drawn into stereotyping them as the bright girls and the simple boys, but both Saoirse and Orla are so much more aware of what's going on than the boys, who are happy with a bit of oral gratification. *Plus ça change*, as the French say.

★

I am very tired. As this year draws to a close, I feel as though I am staggering towards some imaginary finishing line, even though I know January will be a very busy month, and 2006 an even busier year than this one. At the gym today, I try an 'Abs' class – a series of excruciating crunches and abdominal exercises. Ten minutes in, I give up and am happily lying on my mat watching as Those With Abs crunch away.

'Want a pillow and a nice book?' barks the instructor sarcastically, as she walks past.

'That would be nice,' I say politely, when what I really want to say is, 'You try having four babies in two years and let's see how many sit-ups you can handle, Ms Washboard.'

I actually don't feel as though I *have* any abdominals any more. If I ever did. Although I have now lost almost four stone since June, putting me at my lowest weight since this baby lark began, my stomach still hangs down like an elephant's scrotum. I feel self-conscious about it in the changing rooms, catching sight of it in the communal mirrors, the C-section double scar still red and angry. My body tells the story, even if I never mention the triplet word here at the gym.

Thursday 22 December

Four Christmas stockings hang over the fireplace. Four parcels sit under the tree. The Christmas cards we receive this year have a long list of names at the top. Some people don't bother to write them all out, just addressing the card to 'Jackie, Richard and the brood/clan/Addams Family'.

It is exactly a year since we found out we were expecting triplets. As I change them all this morning, I am full of tears. When I think back to this time last year I can't believe how my life has jack-knifed. It has been very hard at times, but in general I am amazed to say that Dad was right – having these babies has been the best thing that has ever happened to me. A truly extraordinary event.

I know how cheesy, rose-tinted and irritating this probably sounds, but I don't care because it's the truth, and it feels necessary to acknowledge the good things about having three at once in the face of so much perceived misfortune. The triplets are incredible, and Saoirse is the most delightful child we know. I don't know what the next few years hold. I'm sure there will be a lot of tears, a lot of fighting and a few trips to casualty, but I wouldn't change it for the world. All I know is that when the babies are out of the house – when Rich takes them up north or to the park – it is spookily quiet and, far from finding it the peaceful haven one would expect, I don't like it at all. I hear babies crying wherever I am, and I instinctively get up to attend to them, even though mine are a couple of hundred miles away. Sometimes I have to switch the radio off because a certain music frequency sounds like babies crying and I'm up and down like a yo-yo. I can't wait until they get home again so I can squidge their big fat faces. What did I do before triplets? I have no idea. I read a post on a triplet website by a woman who is going through a grieving process. Despite having three children already, she yearns for more and can't accept that for her the baby days are over. Oddly, I know how she feels. I am so jealous of my pregnant friends, despite

374

all the times people say, 'You're not going to have any more, are you?', despite the hardship ahead of them, despite the fact that my own family is already stretched to the limits. Although I have four children, I only had two pregnancies, and I missed out on something. I doubt very much that this feeling will manifest itself in an actual pregnancy, but it is quite powerful. Creating life can be addictive.

This morning, I put the two boys side by side. They are becoming harder to tell apart every day. The only thing that differentiates them at the moment is Frank's easier smile and the small skin tag he has on his right ear. It's incredible how alike they are.

'How do you know it's Frank that has the skin tag?' asked my dad worryingly the other day.

We don't. Oh well.

'Look, Saoirse,' I say. 'They're twins!'

'No – they're tricklets,' she corrects, but the way she says it sounds a bit like 'chocolates'. And everyone knows chocolate is a good thing. I am amazed that we have done so well. We are often told we are 'brave', 'inspiring' and 'so cool'. I don't think we are any of these things. I think the key to our relative sanity despite our plethora of children is the fact that we have low standards (of cleanliness/personal hygiene/what constitutes a good night's sleep or a good social life) so we have remained quite perky. I think we *made the decision* to cope, and that has seen us through the tough times. Today, I read a study that declares that hard work is the key to happiness. This year has certainly been that. Twelve hundred nappies, a thousand feeds and goodness knows how many years lost from our lives through sheer stress, but my three chocolates have made me happier than I've ever been.

That's the biggest shock of all.